Musics of Belonging:

The Poetry of Micheal O'Siadhail

Musics of Belonging:

The Poetry of Micheal O'Siadhail

Edited by

Marc Caball and David F. Ford

Carysfort Press

A Carysfort Press Book

Musics of Belonging: The Poetry of Micheal O'Siadhail
Editors: Marc Caball and David F. Ford

First published in Ireland in 2007 by Carysfort Press Ltd
58 Woodfield, Scholarstown Road, Dublin 16, Ireland

Typeset by Carysfort Press

Cover design by Alan Bennis

Printed and bound by eprint limited
Unit 35, Coolmine Industrial Estate, Dublin 15, Ireland

This book is published with the financial assistance of
The Arts Council (An Chomhairle Ealaíon), Dublin, Ireland

the arts
council
an chomhairle
ealaíon

Contents

Preface

Micheal O'Siadhail's achievement of a large body of poetry has been the subject of many articles and reviews and of some academic theses, but there has not yet been a book solely devoted to him and his work. In order to achieve this, the richness and scope of his work has required gathering a diverse team of authors, several of whom have already written critical assessments of his poetry elsewhere. The largest single group of contributors are literary critics, but others come from poetry, musical composition and musicology, painting, translation, history, theology and religious studies, and philosophy.

The title 'Musics of Belonging', which is taken from the poem 'Crying Out' in *Globe*, partly acknowledges the recurrence of music in O'Siadhail's poetry, which is explored by many of the essays. It also indicates the pervasiveness of belonging - above all in love to wife and friends, but also to a range of communities and places (Dublin, the Aran Islands, Ireland, Norway, Europe, Japan, school and university, diverse literary traditions and languages) and to humanity around the globe. And the plural 'musics' suggests the polyphonous quality of his poetry, its interweaving of so many influences, themes, forms, and dimensions.

Our hope for this book is that it will stimulate fuller appreciation of a poet who already has an extensive and devoted following in several countries, reads to large audiences, and is also known as a broadcaster and prominent figure in Irish cultural life. We trust that it will serve the needs both of those who are professionally involved with poetry in literary, cultural, and academic life and of a wider body of general readers. It seems timely to bring together a volume of new essays by this distinguished and varied team of authors, while as editors also being well aware that there is still a great deal more to be done to do full justice to O'Siadhail's work.

Marc Caball
David F. Ford
July 2006

Acknowledgements

The production of this book has been very much a collaborative enterprise, and the editors thank all those who have had a hand in it. First, our gratitude to the many readers of O'Siadhail's poetry who have insisted on the need for the book and encouraged us in conceiving it. Then there are the contributors who have sent in their essays (and song) on time and patiently responded to often numerous editorial suggestions. We have found what they have written illuminating and often moving. Dan Farrelly and the Carysfort Press have been a model of professionalism, and it has been a privilege to be part of their successful endeavour to add a lively new dimension to Irish publishing on literature and the arts. Generous permission has been given by Bloodaxe Books for the extensive quotation of O'Siadhail's poems, and by the Crawford Gallery to use the portrait of Micheal O'Siadhail by Mick O'Dea on the cover. In Cambridge, Beatrice Bertram has helped enormously with the bibliography and Paul Nimmo has been invaluable in his proofreading and putting together of the whole book into publishable form.

Further thanks are due to a wider circle of enablers, including Marie Rooney, Audrey Conlon, and David McConnell (whose hospitality in the Department of Genetics, Trinity College Dublin, has been most welcome for planning meetings), and also to Oliver Conlon, Dermod Dwyer, Judith Sheppard, and Noel Sweeney for helping to ensure that the conception of this book could be realized.

Notes on Contributors

Seóirse Bodley: Born Dublin 1933. Studies in Ireland and Germany led to an appointment in the Music Department of University College Dublin, of which he is an Emeritus Professor. Influences on his compositions include a range of musical styles from the European avant-garde to Irish traditional music. Works include five symphonies, two chamber symphonies, and numerous orchestral, choral, vocal, and chamber pieces. His music has been performed and broadcast in Ireland, North America, Europe, and China. He is a founder-member of *Aosdána*, Ireland's academy of creative artists.

Kim Bridgford directs the writing program at Fairfield University, where she is a professor of English and editor of *Dogwood* and *Mezzo Cammin*. She is the author of three books of poetry: *Undone* (Cincinnati [OH], 2003), nominated for the Pulitzer Prize; *Instead of Maps* (Cincinnati [OH], 2005), and *In the Extreme: Sonnets About World Records*, winner of the Donald Justice Poetry Award (West Chester University Poetry Center, 2007).

Lorraine Byrne Bodley is Lecturer of Music at the National University of Ireland, Maynooth. She is the author of two books: *Schubert's Goethe Settings* (Aldershot, 2003) and *Goethe and Zelter: Musical Dialogues* (Aldershot, 2007). She has co-edited two books with Dan Farrelly: a piano reduction and German translation of *Claudine von Villa Goethe's Singspiel set by Franz Schubert* (Dublin, 2002) and a series of musicological essays: *Goethe and Schubert: Across the Divide* (Dublin, 2003). She is editor of *Goethe: Musical Poet, Musical Catalyst* (Dublin, 2004) and the apograph: *Seóirse Bodley: Three Congregational Masses* (Dublin, 2005).

Marc Caball is Director of the Humanities Institute of Ireland and the Graduate School in Arts and Celtic Studies at University College, Dublin (UCD). He served as first Director of Ireland Literature Exchange (ILE) between 1994-2000. During that time, he worked closely with ILE's founder chairman, Micheal O'Siadhail.

David Cain is a minister in the United Church of Christ and Distinguished Professor of Religion in the Department of Classics, Philosophy, and Religion at University of Mary Washington, Fredericksburg, Virginia. He is author of *An Evocation of Kierkegaard / En Fremkaldelse af Kierkegaard* and many essays on Kierkegaard. Professor Cain came to religious studies by way of a love of theatre, literature, and poetry, and teaches a course called 'Studies in Faith and Literature'. He is a member of the Board of Directors, Center for Faith & the Arts, Salisbury, North Carolina, where Micheal O'Siadhail has read.

David F. Ford studied Classics at Trinity College Dublin, and later Theology in Cambridge, Yale, and Tübingen. He is currently Regius Professor of Divinity at the University of Cambridge. He is the author of numerous books, including *Christian Wisdom. Desiring God and Learning in Love* (Cambridge, 2007), *Theology: A Very Short Introduction* (Oxford, 2000), *The Shape of Living* (London, 2002), and *Self and Salvation: Being Transformed* (Cambridge, 1999). He is the Director of the Cambridge Inter-Faith Programme and is a member of the editorial board of a number of major journals.

Daniel W. Hardy is a Senior Member of the Faculty of Divinity at Cambridge whose life's work has been in the constructive response of theology to contemporary life and thought since the 18th century. Alongside continuing ministry in Anglican churches, he has held posts in Britain and the USA, at the University of Birmingham, as Professor of Divinity at the University of Durham and as Director of the Center of Theological Inquiry in Princeton, New Jersey.

Maurice Harmon is Emeritus Professor at University College Dublin. He has published studies of many writers. His translation of *Acallam na Senórach* (The Colloquy of the Old Men) appeared in 2001. He edited *No Author better Served. The Correspondence between Samuel Beckett and Alan Schneider* (2001) and wrote *Sean O'Faoláin. A Life* (1998). His poetry collections include *The Last Regatta* (2000) and *The Doll with Two Backs* (2004). His *Selected Essays* were published in 2006.

Sarah Kafatou is American by birth and Greek by marriage. She earned her BA and MA at Harvard University and an MFA from the Program for Writers at Warren Wilson. She is the author of a history of Latin America in Greek, and her poems and essays have appeared in various periodicals, particularly the *Harvard Review*. She is also a painter, with two one-person exhibitions to her credit so far. At present she lives in London.

David C. Mahan holds his master's degree in religion and literature from Yale Divinity School (MAR 1995) and his PhD from Cambridge (2005) for his dissertation *Poetry as Public Theology: Poetic Witness in the Work of Charles Williams, Micheal O'Siadhail, and Geoffrey Hill.* He currently serves as Director of the Rivendell Institute at Yale University, an interdenominational Christian study center and campus ministry. He and his wife Karen reside with their three children in Hamden, CT.

Margaret Masson has an MA in English and Religious Studies from Aberdeen University and took her doctorate in English Literature at the University of Durham. She has been a lecturer in English in the USA and UK and has taught postcolonial literature, Shakespeare, the biblical background to literature and D. H. Lawrence at the University of Durham. From 1992 – 1999, she was Senior Tutor at St John's College, Durham, and since 2004 has been Senior Tutor at St Chad's College. She is a Trustee of Traidcraft, and is married with two young children.

Rory Miller is a Senior Lecturer in Mediterranean Studies at King's College, University of London, where he teaches courses on EU and US involvement in the Middle East and on the history of Zionism, anti-Zionism and anti-Semitism. He is the author of two books: *Ireland and the Palestine Question, 1945-2004* (Dublin and Portland [OR], 2005) and *Divided Against Zion: Anti-Zionist opposition to a Jewish State in Palestine, 1945-1948* (London, 2000). He is also associate editor of the academic journal *Israel Affairs.*

Mick O'Dea was born in Ennis, County Clare, and studied at the National College of Art and Design and the University of Massachusetts. He taught in the National College of Art and Design from 1981 until 1999, and was awarded an MA in European Fine Art from the Winchester School of Art in 1997. He is an RHA and a member of Aosdána. He has won many awards, and has exhibited widely in Ireland, Latvia, the UK, the USA, and Spain. His ongoing profession as a portrait painter has brought him many commissions, including commissions from Hong Kong, Europe, and the USA.

Mary O'Donnell lives near Straffan, County Kildare. Her first three poetry collections were published by Salmon Poetry (*Reading the Sunflowers in September; Spiderwoman's Third Avenue Rhapsody; Unlegendary Heroes*), and have been followed by *September Elegies* (Belfast, 2003) and her selected poems, *The Place of Miracles* (Dublin, 2006). Her fiction includes *Strong Pagans, The Light-Makers, Virgin and the Boy,* and *The Elysium Testament.* Formerly *The Sunday Tribune*'s Drama Critic, she is a regular contributor to RTE Radio and has presented many programmes on literature, including the European poetry translation series 'Crossing the Lines'. She is a member of the Irish academy, *Aosdána.*

Audrey Pfeil (née O'Toole): Born in Dublin in 1938. Graduated from University College, Dublin with an M.A. and Higher Diploma in Education. Taught at Secondary Schools in Ireland, USA and Germany where she is married and resides. Poems and short stories published in 'The Salmon', 'Passages', and 'Image', and broadcast on RTE (Irish Radio). German poems published in 'Das Gedicht', 'Lieb Vaterland', and 'Der Wald steht schwarz und schweiget' (Edition L).

Richard Dilworth Rust is Professor Emeritus of English (University of North Carolina at Chapel Hill in the United States). With a specialty in American literature, he has published on the American Civil War, Southern literature, and authors such as James Fenimore Cooper, Washington Irving, Henry Wadsworth Longfellow, Edgar Allan Poe, Nathaniel Hawthorne, Herman Melville, Mark Twain, Henry James, and Eugene O'Neill. He was the General Editor of *The Complete Works of Washington Irving* (30 volumes). His essay on 'Micheal O'Siadhail, Irish Poet for the World' appeared in the *Irish Literary Supplement* (Fall 2006).

Maurya Simon has published seven poetry volumes, including *Ghost Orchid,* which was nominated for a 2004 National Book Award. Her book of ekphrastic poems, *WEAVERS,* was published in 2006, and *The Mapmaker's Art* will be issued in 2007. Simon has received an NEA Fellowship, a residency at the American Academy in Rome, and an Indo-American Fulbright Fellowship. She is a Professor at the University of California, Riverside and lives in the Angeles National Forest in Southern California.

Cover Note

Painting the Poet

Mick O'Dea

At a function in the Merrion Hotel, Dublin, sometime during the spring of 2003, the director of the Crawford Gallery, Peter Murray, invited me to paint a portrait of Micheal O'Siadhail. I immediately accepted.

The day came three months later when Micheal arrived at my apartment in Mountjoy Square. I had decided that I was going to make this a large portrait by my standards and in addition I wanted to use the interior of the apartment as the setting for the portrait with O'Siadhail's head reflected in the over mantel mirror.

I placed him on a chair that I had just fitted within the contours of my coffee table. This ensured that I had level eye contact with my subject, who was sitting even though I was standing. Thus we embarked together on a voyage that was to last nearly three weeks.

Initially there were things to be dealt with before we really got going. Two days after painting him wearing a wine-coloured jacket and brown trousers he came in with the red waistcoat that his wife Bríd had ordered for him some years before. With black trousers, black shoes and white shirt our colours were firmly nailed to the mast.

I knew from the beginning that my encounter with Micheal was going to produce a painting of some significance. Both of us were up for the project and from the start it was a collaboration. My challenge was to catch a big personality and presence.

His eyes were fixed firmly at my gaze. He was searching as much as I was, and in between moments of intense observation the subjects covered ranged far and wide. I was struck by his profound insight, and his illuminations on the creative life put substance on many things that were fugitive for me.

Three weeks after the painting commenced, it was more or less finished. By then Micheal, Bríd, Paula Nolan, and I had become firm friends. The painting and its progress had become part of our lives as we ate, talked, and laughed together. It documents a series of moments in a privileged time. I hope it will give pleasure to generations of people to come in the same way that I know the work of Micheal O'Siadhail will.

1 | Life, Work, and Reception

David F. Ford

Micheal O'Siadhail's work as a poet has made frequent reference to his life. He can hardly be called a confessional poet, yet his poetry and other writings have had varying autobiographical content, from sustained portrayal of his formative years in *The Chosen Garden* to the complete absence of the first person pronoun both in *The Gossamer Wall: Poems in Witness to the Holocaust* and in *Globe*. Yet, as will emerge, even the Holocaust poetry is deeply rooted in his life, and some light is thrown on this and other books by placing them in the context of his biography. In his case, as in that of most artists, it is difficult to say just what that light shows, and the primary emphasis must, as throughout the essays in this book, be on his published work; but I have certainly found the study of the life and of the work mutually illuminating, and offer this chapter as evidence.[1]

It has been fascinating to attempt to trace the reception of his work, culminating in the responses given by contributors to the present volume. Most of the other published responses are scattered in a wide variety of literary journals, newspaper reviews, academic dissertations, and books, but the labour of seeking them out has been rewarding, and has enriched my own critical appreciation of O'Siadhail's poetry. It is to be hoped that in due course the history of the reception of his poetry will be told more thoroughly. In cases where the limitations of space have not allowed for discussion of significant responses, I have given references as pointers for future researchers.

Early Life and Clongowes

Micheal O'Siadhail[2] was born into a middle class Dublin family on 12 January 1947. His father, a chartered accountant, had been born in Co. Monaghan and worked most of his life in Dublin, and his mother was a Dubliner (she is commemorated in 'Memoir', *Poems 1975-1995*; 'Merging', *A Fragile City*; 'Promise', *Our Double Time*). There was also an older sister and a younger brother.

His first school was St Michael's (1952-59). The trauma of his childhood was poliomyelitis, a serious disease of the spinal cord, which he contracted when he was nine. Treatment and recovery took several months, and there were no permanent physical effects. But the time of withdrawal made a long term impression, allowing him to return to normal childhood with a new perspective and also with a deeper relationship to his mother. A more extended trial was that she suffered continual ill-health through his childhood and beyond. Primary school was also the place where he first met poetry. In the preface to *Poems 1975-1995* (perhaps the most revealing of his brief excursions into autobiography) he says:

> I still have tucked away from my primary school four pages of *Poets and Poetry for Irish Schools (Senior Book)* … . Looking at these tattered pages now, I notice the wistful mood of the anthologist. I remember as a schoolboy how they filled me with peculiar tears, half delight and half a strange boundless desire. A moment becomes a touchstone and a life is shaped. (15)

There were also some deep experiences from these early years that he later saw as seminal (see 'A Short Biography' in the same collection).

When he was twelve he persuaded his parents to send him to boarding school at the Jesuit-run Clongowes Wood College,[3] where a friend from St. Michael's was being sent to join his brother. At Clongowes successive school magazines show him as an all-rounder. He was academically successful, won debating medals, captained the Junior Cup Team in Rugby, took lead roles in drama, produced the school play, was president of the Academy, and edited the school literary magazine, where he published his first poems. These were years when the grip of poetry tightened on him and many of those who knew him at school were not surprised that he became a poet. There was also the influence of Tom McIntyre, who was his English teacher as well as a writer.

Ten poems in *The Chosen Garden* give his own account, from the perspective of early middle age, of Clongowes as a world of its own that distanced him from home: routines and rituals, initiations ('the fittest thrive'), influential teachers, rugby, a humiliating fall from grace, and a flash forward to a school reunion. He has said that in many respects he never returned home and that his friends brought him up. Friendship has been a recurring motif in his life and work.

From Clongowes he went to Trinity College Dublin to study Celtic languages. The roots of this choice lay in a profound experience some years earlier.

The Aran Islands and Irish

In 1961 he visited the Aran Islands off the coast of Galway in the west of Ireland. The nine poems under the heading 'Fists of Stone' in *The Chosen Garden* are his testimony to this transformative encounter. He lived for several weeks in a completely Irish-speaking community that had changed little in a thousand years, and had no electricity, no police, and no priest. He returned on many occasions and Máirtín Ó Cadhain later said that O'Siadhail's Irish was as good as any native speaker of his generation in Connemara. He went on to study Irish at university and became the leading authority on modern Irish dialects, and he wrote the first three of his books of poetry (about ten per cent of his total output) in Irish. Since *Springnight* (1983), all his writings have been in English, and it is worth reflecting on this development.

The 'Fists of Stone' sequence reveals the volatile mixture that inspired his turn to Irish. There is youthful idealism, and willingness to take on the world, coming up against the historic tragedy of a rich traditional life engulfed in dispossession, humiliation, shame, and loss. 'Visionary' is the poem that best sums this up, but there are also nuanced evocations in 'Stranger', 'Folksong', 'Leavetaking', and 'Timepiece'. The intensity of immersion in this culture, as he takes on 'my second nature, a grafted skin' ('Stranger'), goes with a meditation on the 'losers' of history, who recur through his works – here in 'Folksong' he mentions 'Picts, Mayas, tribes of the Suquamish ...'. Later there will be others, together with Hitler's many victims. There is also, however, a recognition that the Aran islanders themselves are not simply victims but are finding ways of coping, in one decade, with 'a few centuries of Europe's change' ('Timepiece'). There is not in their response, or in O'Siadhail's mature reflections, any hint that nostalgic, quixotic (literally so – 'Leavetaking' has an islandman as Sancho Panza rejecting Don Quixote's tilting at windmills) resistance and attempts to turn the clock back will work. That is a line associated in Ireland with some language 'revivalists', but O'Siadhail never identified with them.

Rather he, like the Aran islanders, came through to a new 'settlement'. This includes continuing to speak Irish, and also to speak and value other small or threatened languages in which at different times in his life he has become fluent – Welsh, Icelandic, Norwegian, Catalan (I have heard from native speakers how good his grasp of their languages is). His poet's way has been to give testimony in English from within and between various linguistic and cultural worlds, to draw on their literature, folklife, music, and history, and so in practice to treasure diversity while trying to enrich and renew the global language of English with his own particular contribution. This means that he is not a bilingual poet – he has only ever written poetry in one language at a time (and during his time in Norway he wrote poetry in Norwegian good enough to be broadcast). But the English in which ninety per cent of his work to date has been written is the product of a practice and awareness distilled from many linguistic roots. The significance of this for languages and cultures in the twenty-first century is worth further consideration, and there are signs in his latest work (especially *Globe*) that O'Siadhail himself is heading for a more explicit engagement with such themes.

Trinity College Dublin

O'Siadhail arrived in university in 1964 at a time of upheaval. *The Chosen Garden* names the elements and evokes the moods, especially in the two sequences 'A Blurred Music' and 'Turns and Returns'. His autobiographical account describes Dublin in the 1960s:

> There was a raucous prosperity, the television replaced the piano, a huge surge of freedom as we broke the taboos and, socialists all, lived our Bohemian student life. At Trinity College where I was a student, it was fashionable to talk of existentialism, the philosophies of Sartre and Camus. The ideas of Marx, Nietzsche and Freud, postponed by the wars, were now generally in the air. Beckett's *Waiting for Godot* seemed to have caught the mood. We were all angry young men and women and read those paperbacks about sociology and psychology, and we felt we knew what lay hidden behind everything. ('Preface' to *Poems 1975-1995*, 13)

O'Siadhail joined the College Historical Society, a 1000-member debating club, won its maiden speaker's prize, won the Scottish-Irish Debating competition in his first term, and was briefly an officer of the society. But he left that world, and his time was mainly divided between study (he became a Foundation Scholar in his second year and went on to a first class degree), writing poetry for the literary magazine *Icarus*, drama (he was an active member of College Players), participating in a number of English-language and Irish-language circles within Trinity (he headed the Irish-language society An Cumann Gaelach for a year), and a hectic social life that took place mostly elsewhere in Dublin, including some intensive relationships with women. As he wrote in his first book of poetry, women especially have shaped who he is:

A wonderful cloth, my shirt of linen,
My chequered gift, a self they've woven,
This shirt that's closer than the bone,
The bright women of my world have given.
    ('Compliment', *The Leap Year*)

His later major academic work, *Modern Irish. Grammatical structure and dialectal variations* (Cambridge University Press, 1989), is dedicated 'to the memory of three teachers, friends and colleagues: David Greene (1915-1981), Máirtín Ó Cadhain (1906-1970) and E. Gordon Quin (1910-1986)'. These were the key formative figures in his Trinity years.

Gordon Quin was a distinguished comparative philologist and lexicographer who specialized in the Indo-European languages. He was a model of rigorous scholarship and of long range patience and persistence in work – a sort of academic alpine gardener.

Ó Cadhain was one of the most gifted twentieth-century writers in Irish and also a lecturer in Celtic Languages in Trinity College. He was both a creative author deeply rooted in Ireland, who devoted much of his life to writing, and a European intellectual at home in the literature of several languages as well as the classic works of psychoanalysis, psychology, and sociology. O'Siadhail was very close to him during his final years.

Of these three older mentors it was David Greene who was most influential. He was Professor of Celtic Languages in Trinity College and then Senior Professor at the Dublin Institute for Advanced Studies. He was larger than life, a man of huge intellect, polymathic interests, and a large circle of diverse friends from around the world. He once said to Máire Cruise O'Brien about O'Siadhail: 'Now I have found my student!' A tribute to Greene written by O'Siadhail in 1994 is entitled *Athair de mo chuid* (*A Father of Mine*).[4] He was the main father figure of the first half of O'Siadhail's life (see 'Revenant', *Our Double Time*), and the relationship grew into deep friendship.

If one were to choose just one effect of the relationship with Greene on O'Siadhail as a poet, it would probably be his linguistic cosmopolitanism. Greene knew languages from several branches of Indo-European as well as modern Hebrew. He revelled in their diversity and interrelationships, both as a scholar and as a deeply civilized citizen of the world. O'Siadhail entered enthusiastically into this heritage, helped by his exceptional feel for language, and it may be that no other contemporary has been able to distil poetry from such rich linguistic knowledge and appreciation. His recent attainment of fluency in speaking and writing Japanese has taken him beyond even Greene's range.

Norway

Towards the end of his time in Trinity College O'Siadhail had a choice between a scholarship to Cambridge University to learn Chinese and a year in Oslo University studying Scandinavian folklore on a Norwegian Government state scholarship. Both Quin and Greene had studied in Norway, and O'Siadhail decided to follow them for the academic year 1968-69. The coursework was in Norwegian, Danish, Swedish, and German, and in addition he lived with a group of Icelanders and learnt Icelandic. He emerged with *Laudabilis* in the Grundfag (basic degree) and a diploma as teacher of Norwegian language.

Norway became O'Siadhail's second homeland. Most years since then he has returned for periods of up to six weeks, and some of his closest friends are there. Scandinavian literature has also been a constant (and usually unrecognized) inspiration for his poetry. Key influences include Sigrid Undset (on whom there is a poem in *Globe*), Gunnar Reiss-Andersen, Herman Wildenvey, Einar Skjaeraasen, Halldis Moren Vesaas, Karin Boye, and Dan Andersson, together with the Eddas and the Sagas.

Academic posts, Marriage, and Poetry: the Leap Year and Beyond

O'Siadhail returned to Ireland in 1969 as a lecturer in Celtic Languages in his *alma mater*, Trinity College Dublin. His teaching received rave reviews from students, but as he wrote later: 'I enjoyed it but knew it would exhaust me.' ('Preface' to *Poems 1975-1995*, 14). Ó Cadhain died in 1970 and O'Siadhail took over the classes in Irish that had been Ó Cadhain's passion. These were the genesis of *Learning Irish* (Yale University Press), a book accompanied by cassettes or compact disc, that has been the leading basic language course in Irish for the past 17 years.

The major event of these years was his marriage to Bríd Ní Chearbhaill. She was born in Gweedore, a Gaeltacht (Irish-speaking) area in Co. Donegal in north-west Ireland, and came to Dublin to train as a primary teacher. They met when O'Siadhail moved into a flat above her, and were married on 2 July 1970. In a life of many friendships, this has undoubtedly been the central relationship. He has frequently written of her, often in sonnets (see especially the sequence in the section 'Rerooting' in *The Chosen Garden* in *Poems 1975-1995*) and above all in *Love Life* (2005), which moves from falling in love into marriage and the years of life together. For most of those years Bríd was a teacher (see 'Mistress' in *Love Life*) and later headmistress in an inner city Dublin primary school. She also worked closely with Micheal on editing and on a range of other things associated with an active literary life (he has never had a literary agent), in particular hospitality. She had to take early retirement due to Parkinson's disease in 1995 (see 'Parkinson's' in *Love Life*, and the final part of Margaret Masson's chapter in this volume).

Despite much teaching and academic research (he was awarded the MLitt degree in 1971 for his thesis 'The Responsive System in Irish'), he was increasingly drawn to writing poetry and realized there would be too little time and energy for it in Trinity College. So in 1973 he resigned his lectureship and had what he later called, in the title of his first collection of poems, his 'leap year' (*An Bhliain Bhisigh*, 1978 – this collection is explored further in the essay by Marc Caball in this volume). He saw this as a decisive transition. Even though much of the work he did during 1973-74 was academic, there was a shift in priority towards poetry. This went with another vital shift: he discovered something beyond 'the abyss' and despair that had haunted his years as a student and lecturer. In his own words:

> Many glimpsed the abyss and peered over its edge. I recall in those years I often walked and sat in St Stephen's Green in Dublin, a stone's throw from where I was born. For all the terror of our century, for all our angst and knowingness, just wandering there watching ducks in a pond and listening to the gossip and laughter of people as they passed, the world seemed sweet and new. There were tiny glances of infinity. And slowly I gave in to the wonder of the world. All I needed to do was to dare, to tauten towards the light like a sunflower. I was 26 and this would be my 'leap year'. ('Preface' to *Poems 1975-1995*, 13-14)

David Greene offered a way forward by inviting him to apply for a post in the Dublin Institute for Advanced Studies. This was a research institute set up by the Irish leader Éamon de Valera in 1940, in order to specialize in the disciplines in which he himself was most interested: Celtic languages and three branches of physics. O'Siadhail was a research assistant and later (1980) a professor there for thirteen years, producing a stream of academic publications as well as five volumes of poetry. Greene, a colleague in the Institute until his death in 1981, appreciated and encouraged both the scholarship and the poetry.

O'Siadhail established himself as a leading authority on modern Irish and its dialects and introduced into this field an array of approaches, especially that of Chomsky, from contemporary linguistics. In 1977 he returned to the Aran Islands to research what became a book on building and domestic terms in the dialect. He was invited to deliver named lectures in Dublin, Yale, and Harvard, and in 1982 was a visiting professor in the University of Iceland. He was also exploring new fields. From 1976 till 1983 he took regular music lessons and became a competent pianist, and he completed extramural courses in chemistry in University College Dublin. He and his wife also began their collection of contemporary Irish art and sculpture, and in 1985 were able to house it when they moved into their present home in Booterstown on Dublin Bay (see 'A Circle' in *The Chosen Garden* and several poems in *Love Life*).

As a poet, these were years of apprenticeship, as he explored, first in Irish and then in English, a range of forms, subjects, and perspectives. Yet at the same time there is a maturity from the start – he was 31 when the first collection was published and had gone far beyond juvenilia. In my judgement, any selection of his best work would have to include many poems from this period's five volumes, and they are all included in *Poems 1975-1995*. If compelled to choose just half a dozen I would certainly include 'Loss', on the death of Bríd's father. I would be tempted to add 'Roofing' from the first collection, a love poem that can be set alongside any from later volumes, and has the added interest that it is his own translation from an Irish original that arose from his close study of building terms in the Aran islands (the importance of this linguistic study for O'Siadhail's early Irish poetry is explored further by Caball in his essay in this volume – the way in which O'Siadhail translates his own earlier work into English is deserving of still further study). Characteristic themes emerge from the start: despair, women, love, friendship, language, school, vocation, music, city life, science, Irish and other cultures and histories. There is a wrestle for meaning, with no easy resolutions – both the form and the content are hard-won.

In 1982 the Irish Government set up *Aosdána*, the Academy of Distinguished Irish Artists. It has a limited number of members, elected by their peers in the Academy, and election is a key sign of having 'arrived' as a writer, visual artist, or composer. O'Siadhail became a Founding and Life Member of *Aosdána*, and in 1986 was elected to its governing committee. Other forms of recognition came during these years, such as receiving the award of the Irish American Cultural Institute Prize for Poetry in 1982 and representing Ireland at the European Poetry Festival. When *Springnight*, his first collection in English, was published in 1983, it was for a time on the Irish bestseller list, and his popularity with Irish readers has been sustained since then. It has been helped by appearances at poetry readings, arts festivals, on television and radio, in interviews, and in newspapers, by being a judge in national literature, poetry, and drama competitions, having his poetry set to music by composers such as Seóirse Bodley, Colman Pearce, and James Wilson, and having his portrait painted by leading artists, Michael Kane, Brian Bourke, and Mick O'Dea (the latter is on the cover of the present volume).

Poetry Alone

In 1987 he took the decision to resign his professorship in order to write poetry full-time. The insecurity was compensated by a liberation of energy for writing, and the effects were visible in the next book, *The Chosen Garden*. His own description of the difference between before and after this momentous decision was:

> The quality of concentration I could then afford made me move from collections united by an angle of vision to books with an architecture, an overriding focus. It took me five years to complete *The Chosen Garden*. It was an effort to face my own journey, to comprehend and trace one's own tiny epic: setting out, challenging the world, ordeal and failure, the underworld, achievement, the delight of return and re-rooting to open to the world in a new way. A journey from the garden chosen for me by my parents, through boarding school, youthful excesses, ideologies, despair, learning to love and reconnect with society, to the garden I'd chosen for myself. ('Preface' to *Poems 1975-1995*, 14)

As O'Siadhail says, the architectonics of the books published since he went full-time have added a dimension to his work. They have blended the character of a symphony's movements with something of a novel's plot. The quotation above traces the autobiographical sequence of *The Chosen Garden*.

The movements of *A Fragile City* (1995, included in *Poems 1975-1995*) are less straightforward. The Rilke epigraph[5] of the opening section, 'A Filtered Light', suggests key themes of light, face to face, and compassion, which are then developed in interplay with the book's embracing concern with trust, betrayal, and boundaries in the cosmopolitan 'fragile city'. The whole book can be read as a meditation on the face, partly inspired (as Mary O'Donnell's chapter in this volume notes) by the philosopher Emmanuel Levinas, on whom there is a substantial poem in the most recent collection, *Globe*. The second section, 'Veils and Masks', faces questions of exclusion, global injustice, gender issues, shame, scapegoating, and whatever 'intrusive face' interrupts the private bliss of lovers:

> *... between our gazes*
> *shadows of the stricken fall.* ('Intrusion')

That lead poem in the section, opening with two lovers in their 'sweetest hour', concludes with what might stand as a summary of O'Siadhail's moral vision, simultaneously exploring the depths of intimacy in love, friendship, and marriage while passionately concerned with public responsibility and the common good:

> *Is love a threadbare blindfold?*
> *'Yes', say our shadows, 'unless*
> *you turn to face the faceless.'*
> *Who'll re-envisage the world?*

'Boundaries', the third section of *A Fragile City*, takes up a pervasive issue in a time of rapid change and global horizons:

That need of lines. That leap's desire. ('Hopscotch')

names and quarrels of a shared place,
frail rootedness, complicities of ease,
womb of overlaps and shifting boundaries. ('Gull')

Again the personal and the public are spliced together, Irish divisions alongside personal tragedies, and cosmic perspectives ('Meditations' on Niels Bohr, Alain Aspect, and Werner Heisenberg strikes a scientific note that recurs throughout O'Siadhail's *oeuvre*) with ordinary acts of caring for the sick.

The final section, 'Feast', is a *tour de force* of celebratory poetry. It is that rare thing in any literature: a realism that, doing justice to misery, tragedy, fallibility, and fragility, yet can overflow in delight and joy in life and still somehow ring true. Some of the titles set the tone – 'Abundance', 'Leisure', 'Celebration', 'Delight', 'Courtesy', and 'Dance'. The epigraph from George Herbert's 'Love' gives the secret. It is O'Siadhail's final emergence, made possible by fragile trust and love, from the compulsory gloom, cynicism, knowingness, and despair that had overshadowed his student years. The fragility and contingency of it intensify the urgency of celebration, and there is an anticipation of the later volume on the Holocaust (especially its final section 'Prisoners of Hope') in the testimony even from a death camp to a 'desire to feast':

At Auschwitz Wolf hums Brahms' rhapsody by heart
As Eddy, thief turned juggler, rehearses his art ...

Abundance of joy bubbling some underground jazz.
A voice whispers: Be with me tonight in paradise. ('Invitation')

Besides the new architectonics, since the move to full-time writing there has also been an alternation between more personal and more public themes. *The Chosen Garden*'s autobiography is followed by the urban and cosmopolitan *A Fragile City*; then comes *Our Double Time* with its friendships, families, and bereavements, followed by *The Gossamer Wall: Poems in Witness to the Holocaust*, immersed in a whole people's trauma and its aftermath; and recently *Love Life*, containing his most intimate and daring personal poetry to date, has been succeeded by the historical and spatial reach of *Globe*. This means that it often makes more sense to think of the 'odd' and 'even' books together rather than in sequence, and that is what the next two sections will do.

Our Double Time and *Love Life*, Form and Content

If *Our Double Time* (1998) is set alongside *The Chosen Garden* (1990), it is clear that there has been significant development, both in the more formal aspects of the poet's craft and also in engagement with common themes.

O'Siadhail's poetic techniques and forms are paid considerable attention in other essays in this volume. Better than any generalization is the close reading that Maurya Simon and David Mahan apply to a few poems. Richard Rust's magisterial, pioneering analysis describes some of what he calls O'Siadhail's '*tour de force* of forms found throughout the globe and through time'. He traces the range of borrowings and adaptations, the *terza rima*, sestina, sonnets, haiku, slanted or near rhymes, syncopated rhythms and creation of new forms. He focuses on the match of form and content, how verse forms are themselves metaphors, and how musical forms (motet, fugue, polyphony) pervade O'Siadhail's poetry. He also captures something of the thrill of well-wrought forms and of the virtuoso precision of O'Siadhail's language, and outlines the 'larger forms' of whole collections (what I have called the architectonics) in *The Chosen Garden*, *Our Double Time*, *The Gossamer Wall: Poems in Witness to the Holocaust*, *Love Life*, and *Globe*. Rust's broad coverage is complemented by Margaret Masson, Mary O'Donnell, Lorraine Byrne, and Maurice Harmon on other aspects of his poetic craft, and especially by Kim Bridgford's concentration on just one form, the sonnet, of which O'Siadhail has published over a hundred.[6] Bridgford calls him 'one of the world's greatest living practitioners of the sonnet'.

From these analyses the formal discipline and creativity of *Our Double Time* is clear. The rationale of its movement through five substantial parts (one of which is further divided in two – *Our Double Time* is his longest collection to this point) is less obvious than in the previous two collections, and the new complexity of form corresponds to a richness, density, and sense of multiple tensions both on and beneath the surface. In terms of his development there are clues in the one new collection that was not published as a separate book. The twenty-three poems of 'The Middle Voice' were the 'new' in *Hail! Madam Jazz. New and Selected Poems* (1992) and they anticipate the stance and mood of *Our Double Time*. They have death (though not too intensively) and birth, voices, genes, married love, the influence of others on him and him on others (see 'Tradition', 'Rondo', 'Largesse', 'Feedback'), jazz ('Cosmos'), and celebration ('Summerfest'). But the title is perhaps the vital clue: between active and passive voices there is the middle voice (found in Greek and Icelandic), and with that the sense of middle age, looking backwards as much as forwards, yet somehow freer from compulsions of past or future:

> How will it all happen? That strange
> floating openness. A trust. A patience. ('Three Rock')

There is no doubt what is the dominant theme in *Our Double Time*: death. O'Siadhail was 51 when it was published, there are references to having been in intensive care (his hospital thoughts echo those of Patrick Kavanagh, who may well be the Irish twentieth-century poet with whom O'Siadhail has the deepest affinities), and the shift from *The Chosen Garden* is from the autobiography of a young man with most of life ahead of him through the early middle age of 'The Middle Voice' to a later middle-aged looking backwards and forwards in vivid awareness of mortality. 'Ageing' reflects on this new stage in three sonnets: the 'new inwardness', the richer recollection, 'some ease of live and let live', both sadness and joy, memory and hope, and running through it all a new, matured desire:

> Things tipped in a scale of yearning and understood.
>
> ...
>
> Yearning light shines through my broken being.

The pervasive mood is the optative of desire (see especially 'Knowing', 'Nocturne', 'Quartet', 'Oak', and 'Cadenza') and the embracing image is of a return to Eden. There is more about the passivities of existence, from the genes we inherit to a death we do not control, and the ways in which his own life has been shaped by those who have died. The sequence in 'Namings' includes his grandmother, David Greene, Caitlín Maude (the singer-lover before his marriage who made the deepest impact), Etty Hillesum (the Dutch Jewish Holocaust victim who reappears in *The Gossamer Wall*), Heloïse, George Herbert, Rilke, and others. They are often complex tributes, not without tension, anguish, and ambivalence. They culminate in 'Apprentice', a dense recapitulation, distilling the essence of how he has been shaped by the dead and how the learning goes on. Compared with *The Chosen Garden* there is in this section a sense of his own formation that is richer and more complexly conflictual.

The double section, 'Crosslight', offers a fresh but seasoned simplicity, and a quicker tempo. Its climax is a remarkable series of jazz poems (see the essays by Lorraine Byrne and Richard Rust in this volume). The book might have ended there – the mood is similar to that of the final poems in *A Fragile City*. Instead there is 'Voices', twelve poems striking in their formal innovations and perhaps best seen as a concentrated autobiography through gratitude for his deepest relationships:

> All praise my lovers, and listen how I grow,
> My voice welling in your voices' overflow.
> Completing a completion, abundance overspilt;
> As if I keep on filling what's already fulfilled.
> O voices within shaping everything I do,
> Even in my soliloquies I collogue with you. ('Overflow')

I see these twelve as perhaps the most accomplished and profound sequence of his *oeuvre* so far. The poem for his wife, 'Matins for You', may be his best single love poem, anticipating the themes that *Love Life* explores for a whole book. Its line of Irish is later included in 'Tongues' together with other lines in other languages (Italian, Icelandic, Norwegian, and German) from other poems in the sequence, suggesting the uniting of these people and their languages in his own life. 'Secrets of Assisi' is one of his most mysterious poems, in line with its title, evoking St Francis through the eyes of St Clare (they were the subject of a letter from Francis in an earlier poem, 'Letters from Assisi' in *The Image Wheel*, which is explored in the essay by Maurya Simon in this volume). The sequence has poems about realities that have been at the core of his life: close friends, a lover, music, language, and Dublin, represented by St Stephen's Green. The final set of four sonnets, 'Our Double Time', recapitulates the whole book. It begins with leaving hospital, a reminder of death:

> To have been to the edge, just to be allowed return
> To moments of utter in-loveness, utter unconcern.

It goes on to celebrate 'time doubled', the intensification of perceiving and living that can happen when death is faced; then finally death itself is reimagined in terms of the 'point of no return' in love-making, giving birth, D-day, and Dante approaching heaven in his *Paradiso,* glimpsing the 'distant face of Beatrice'.

Love Life (2005) is the most recent of the more personal collections, and other chapters in this volume, especially those by Margaret Masson, Richard Rust, and Mary O'Donnell, have dealt with it from diverse angles. It seems more peaceful than *Our Double Time*, though its evocation of young love is also freer than anything in earlier books. It is also more about ordinary life – a marriage stretching over thirty-five years. I would add a few remarks to what the other chapters say about it.

First, there is its utter realism about the agonies, the ecstasies, and the everydayness, avoiding many pitfalls of rosy- or dark-tinted love poetry. The soberness of this (which does not rule out playfulness and humour) is in line with the fact of Bríd having Parkinson's disease. It is also a personal dimension of the more public realism in the book it followed, *The Gossamer Wall: Poems in Witness to the Holocaust* (2002), whose subject matter had, as will be discussed below, elicited from O'Siadhail a narrative style of extreme concision and self-discipline.

In addition there is also *Love Life*'s intertextuality, its resonances with so much other literature on love and other matters. The most obvious is the Bible's *Song of Songs* (or *Song of Solomon*), knowledge of which greatly enriches the reading. But also woven in are Genesis and other parts of the Bible, Greek mythology, Petrarch, Shakespeare, Dante, Rilke, Ibsen, Heloïse, Herrick, George Herbert, Oscar Wilde, Homer, an array of Irish, Japanese, and Scandinavian poets, Brian Friel, Pindar, Rumi, and many more. There is also in this collection an array of resonances with his own poetry, both with previous poems and with the poems in this collection.

Finally, there is its uniqueness: it is hard to think with what to compare this poetic testimony to a long marriage in all its seasons.

The Gossamer Wall and Globe

O'Siadhail's sounding of some of the darker personal depths in *Our Double Time* prepared him to face mass death and historical trauma in *The Gossamer Wall: Poems in Witness to the Holocaust* (2002). There could be few more formidable challenges to a poet, including the denial that it should even be attempted. Why did O'Siadhail take it on? The poems themselves give several answers.

First, there is the unique window of history within which it is written:

> Still the stamped forearms of first witnesses.
> Indelible warnings: this might happen again.
> Still a moment when testimony and story meet
> Before the last attesting faces will retreat
> To echo chambers of second-hand remembrance. ('Numbers')

He is acutely aware that soon there will no longer be living eyewitnesses. There has been time for a vast mass of literary, visual, and other responses to accumulate and for some historical perspective to be gained. Yet still, for a few more years, any account can still be tested against the judgements of survivors. Indeed he has said in interviews that for him the most encouraging responses to *The Gossamer Wall* have come from survivors who have told him the book rings true.[7] This window, before all is 'second-hand remembrance', is arguably the time when classic testimonies to epochal events are best written, whether the Gospels of the New Testament or Tolstoy's *War and Peace*.

A deeper reason for taking up the challenge is the significance of the event itself. Writing at the time of millennium celebrations around 2000 he suggests that

> ... it may well be
> That on the shaft of its middle decade

(And not its end) the twentieth century
Turns … . ('Numbers')

He probes into history for the origins of this cataclysm, seeking it in Christian hatred, prejudice and scapegoating of Jews ('Forebodings', 'Wilderness'), in the Thirty Years War and subsequent German history, in the Enlightenment's narrowing, cutting back the multiple flourishings of the Renaissance ('Hankerings'), in the secularizing French Revolution and the making of modern Europe ('Reverberations'), in the First World War and its aftermath ('Lull'), and in the individual people, including Hitler ('Entrance'), whose decisions helped to shape history.

But its meaning is not just in its origins and causes, or in the pathologies – religious, political, racial, cultural, individual – that it revealed. There are also its further implications: O'Siadhail risks searching out its meaning for the present and for hope in the human future. This is the thrust of the final section, 'Prisoners of Hope'. There is never any playing down of the scale of the horror, but it is not allowed to have the last word: *Out of this eruption, can we prepare another climate?* ('Dust-veil')

The fourteen poems are shot through with interrogatives, subjunctive maybe's, qualifications, and allusive quotations from victims, survivors, Hebrew poetry, and especially the Hebrew scriptures. Yet there is a persistent note of hope, trust, and even celebration. The 'why?' of the writing of this poetry is summed up in 'Never', O'Siadhail's response to Adorno's challenge about the possibility of poetry after the Shoah:

> That any poem after Auschwitz is obscene?
> Covenants of silence so broken between us
> Can we still promise or trust that we mean? ('Never')

It goes on to set the emptiness, coldness, negativity, and narrowness of evil ('A black sun only shines out of a vacuum') over against evocations of 'fullness of being': rich conversation, 'the restless subversive ragtime of what thrives' and

> Endless dialogues. The criss-cross of flourishings.
> Again and over again our complex yes.
> A raucous glory and the whole jazz of things.
>
> The sudden riffs of surprise beyond our ken;
> Out of control, a music's brimming let-go.
> We feast to keep our promise of never again. ('Never')

The last line suggests a key element in the philosophy: the most adequate response to the reality of evil is the goodness, life, and trust that can be realized in community that can celebrate together and refuse to allow evil to define it. The practical implications of this, besides feasting, include refusal to give up on the search for meaning and the sustaining of hope against hope, the cultivation of wise remembering and constant alertness –

> Can how we remember shape what we become?
> …
> *Memory a frequent waking out of forgetfulness* ('Waking')

– (cf. 'Babel' and 'Imagine' on possible contemporary seeds of future shoahs), and especially commitment to the core Jewish practice of repair of the world:

> White noise and quivers. Shifts of geology.
> What might be salvaged? Hesitance
> Of first mendings. Delicate *perhaps* or *maybe*
> Tracing detours of repaired advance. ('Repair')

> Our promise to mend the earth? A healing trust? ('Soon')

Such themes clearly open up some of the most fundamental issues of human existence, and O'Siadhail's concern with what he has called a 'ministry of meaning' is the most embracing reason for tackling this topic. He is not only concerned with the Shoah; other genocides and traumas figure in the poems too, and there is no point in any quantifying comparison:

> And yet there's no Richter scale of tragedy.
> How to measure suffering? A calculus of pain?
> Behind each agony a name, a voice, a face. ('Signatures')

Perhaps the most complex issue dictated by this subject matter is that of human freedom and responsibility in the context of massive historical forces. This recurs again and again in different guises, and is most explicit in the first section of his poem on Hitler:

> Convulsions in mother earth, the trembling rock;
> Blind forces, a chronology of fault segments.

> Ground swell of history, compulsions of an epoch;
> Part of, tied into, caught up in grand events.

> Marionettes? And yet decisions made, the ties,
> The hitches, the twists which ravel us into a plot

> Too intricate to comprehend. The eye tries
> To follow its loops but strays in baffles of a knot.

> Implications of grand doings and small choices.
> Both bound up and binding. A complex ligature

> Shaping this history that's also shaping us.
> Could there be a Desolation without *der Führer*? ('Entrance')

That question is sustained throughout the book. The imagery of earthquake and volcanic eruption is interwoven with that of human initiative and responsibility, and it is clear that neither the force nor the freedom can be denied.

Yet such abstract generalities as 'force' and 'freedom' are utterly inadequate to do justice to the density of this history. Only narrative close up to people and events can do that. I have so far concentrated on the opening and closing sections of *The Gossamer Wall*, where there is more reflection and probing of ideas, and more effort to make sense of long stretches of history and large issues in human existence. But these are not at the heart of the book's 'witness to the Holocaust'. That comes in the other three sections, whose core genre is narrative, and whose dead centre is 'Figures', the section on the extermination camps.

The strict structure of the five sections reinforces the centrality of narrative testimony. The five form a chiasmus. The first, 'Landscapes', and the last, 'Prisoners of Hope', correspond to each other by dealing with the pre-history and aftermath of the event respectively. The second, 'Descent', and the fourth, 'Refusals' have two parts each, and these correspond as follows. 'Northeim' (first part of the second section) on how a German town became Nazi matches 'Le Chambon' (second part of the fourth section) on how a French town risked saving hundreds of Jews. 'Battalion 101' (second part of the second section) on the individuals in a special execution squad operating in Poland in the wake of the German army is parallel to 'Spoors' (first part of the fourth section) on acts of individual resistance to the genocide. And at the centre, as the pivot of the book, is 'Figures'.

This structure is uniquely symmetrical and precise among the architectonics of O'Siadhail's books. It has a rigour and discipline that imply an extreme need for form in order not to be overwhelmed by the content. This is reinforced by the most striking formal feature of 'Figures': all fourteen poems are sonnets. Again, precision and rigour discipline the expression of something that threatens to escape and even to render meaningless all expression. As in Wilfred Owen's use of sonnets for the horror of the First World War, O'Siadhail uses his favourite form, which is so often used for love, to distil, from the standpoint of the victims, the enactment of gratuitous evil.

Others in this volume comment on this extraordinary sequence (see Richard Rust, Mary O'Donnell, David Cain, Rory Miller). My one further remark applies more generally to all three narrative sections. They are something new in O'Siadhail. They sustain an intense realism into which the poet does not intrude but which is utterly based on testimony from victims, survivors, and historians – unusually for poetry, the sources on which it is based are given at the end of the book. It is as if the subject matter gives rise to such powerful feeling that the form needs to embody restraint, gaining its effects more by bare statement and reserve, or even by understatement. Yet this low-key realism has a cumulatively devastating impact. Readers are drawn into the story step by step until by the end of 'Figures' they are totally immersed. With immersion comes a groping after some sort of meaning, some orientation that might make historical and moral sense. That is what is slowly and tentatively opened up by the individual stories of resistance and the communal courage of Le Chambon, concluding with contemporary reflections in 'Prisoners of Hope'.

If I were choosing one core lode of meaning to abstract from the narrative testimony of *The Gossamer Wall*, it would be the deep confrontation between gratuitous evil and gratuitous feasting.[8] These might be seen as the poles of 'dark mystery' and 'bright mystery' between which the participants and the readers are pulled. There is the vacuum or abyss of evil, a constant threat as much today as in the Nazi period, and there is the superabundant fullness of life, which is perhaps even harder to credit today. The daring claim of the book is that only wholehearted, vulnerable participation in the second can really meet the first.

> Risks. Fugues of detours. Spirals of reprise.
> *A feast of rich food and well-aged wine.*
>
> A light too broad for any black sun to shine.
> Scope of conversations, brilliance of what is;

To love the range and fullness yet to recall.
Your golden hair, Margarete, your ashen hair ...

Next year in Jerusalem! Parting toast and prayer.
And still they breathe behind a gossamer wall. ('Reprise')

The most recent book, *Globe*, carries further some key themes of *The Gossamer Wall*. The relationship between the two is analogous in certain ways to that described above between *The Chosen Garden* and *Our Double Time*. *Globe* takes further the exploration of the darker sides of human existence, and it gives a fuller, more complex, and more nuanced account of the dynamics of history; there is a wider range of characters introduced, with developed portraits of a sort only approached occasionally in *The Gossamer Wall*; and the sense of deep tension, dialectic, and ambiguity that *Our Double Time* evoked largely in the personal realm is in *Globe* traced on a larger, more public canvas. It is also the book where O'Siadhail's blend of intellectual and imaginative power is seen engaged on the most comprehensive scale so far. The present volume therefore chose this as the one collection to be discussed in a full chapter. Daniel Hardy's analysis engages with O'Siadhail's conceptual and poetic sophistication and especially asks how a fresh vision and understanding of our world is being articulated here. The leading maxim is 'see better and you will see farther', and Hardy shows how O'Siadhail offers readers ways to help them do this for themselves.

I would add two further comments. First, *Globe* is the collection in which there is most resonance with previous collections. It is as if O'Siadhail has recapitulated (though with variations and innovations) his decades of thoughtfully representing and addressing the state of our world, and has offered a further realistic yet fundamentally hopeful 're-envisaging' of it as

Made, broken and remade in love,
Lived-in boneshaking pizzazz
Of interwoven polyphony above
An understated theme.
The only end of jazz is jazz. ('Only End')

Second, that final line, suggesting 'jazz for jazz's sake', is perhaps the deepest continuity with his earliest poetry, especially evident in *A Fragile City*, *Our Double Time*, *The Gossamer Wall*, and *Love Life*. In *A Fragile City*, it is there in the contemplation of 'Leisure' and in the four-part 'Dance' that concludes:

Blouses. Men with cummerbunds. The gleam
and sizzle of dresses. To glorify what is.

No matter what this dance will be here.
Blessed be its weavings and its intricacies.

O fragile city of my trust and desire!
Our glancings. No longer any need to possess. ('Dance')

In *Our Double Time* it is life for life's sake:

A morning leaving hospital, suddenly the height,
The breadth, the depth. ...
      ...
Everything vibrates. A voice. A scent. A colour.
Charged and marvellous ... . ('Our Double Time')

The Gossamer Wall finds it in its most radical and even scandalous theological form, 'for God's sake', at the heart of some Jewish responses to the Holocaust:

So it's the way of Hallow-His-Name.
Kiddush Ha-Shem. Humble acceptance.
For many just the sign of their silence. ('Hallowing')

In *Love Life* it is there between the lovers as signs of infinity:

Bird flight at sundown.
Afterwards the aftershine.
Infinite moment. ('Ceremony')

Yet what soars between us!
You and me
Flickering delight
In infinity,
Daily flight
In the sun. ('Gaze')

Life 1987-2006

Going full-time allowed for a fuller role in the wider culture too. In 1988 O'Siadhail was selected as a member of the Arts Council of Ireland, the body that distributes government funding, and he soon became chairman of its Literature Committee. In 1989 he was appointed to the Cultural Relations Committee of the Department of Foreign Affairs and represented Ireland at various international events. In the years following he was guest editor for *Poetry Ireland Review*, a judge for several literary and drama prizes, and in 1998 he himself received the Marten Toonder Prize for Literature, which is awarded every three years for a distinguished career in literature. One prize that he could not win is significant: in 2003 he received a special recommendation from the judges for the Wingate Jewish Quarterly Literary Prize in the 'fiction' section, since there was no provision for poetry – a sign of recognition by the Jewish community of his achievement in *The Gossamer Wall: Poems in Witness to the Holocaust*.

O'Siadhail's first commission for music came in 1987 (*The Naked Flame* to music by Seóirse Bodley), and others followed with composers Colman Pearce, Bodley again, and James Wilson. These were years of many public readings, often accompanied by appearances in the media, with tours, some for up to two months, in Ireland, Britain, North America, Germany, and Japan. The latter tour coincided with the publication of his work in Japanese, and he himself had by then learnt enough to lecture and introduce his readings in Japanese.

The major public achievement apart from his poetry has perhaps been his founding of Ireland Literature Exchange (ILE), set up in order to promote Ireland's literature in translation abroad. This was funded by both Arts Councils in Ireland, the Cultural Relations Committee of the Department of Foreign Affairs, and Bord na Leabhar Gaeilge, a diversity of sources which testifies to Micheal's powers of persuasion and many contacts. In 1993 he became its first chairman and served till 2000. By that time it had established itself as a valuable sponsor of translations of works from both Irish and English: under his chairmanship, 254 Irish literary works were translated into 27 different languages with the support of ILE.

These were years of domestic stability in Booterstown after a period of much moving from house to house. The house overlooks Dublin Bay, and during the five years of immersion in Holocaust literature before completing *The Gossamer Wall*, O'Siadhail took up sailing there. After graduating from sailing school he bought a second-hand Ruffian-class yacht, and the sailing imagery of many poems in *Love Life* shows how deep the new sport went.

Reception

A list of those reviews, articles, and academic works on O'Siadhail's poetry that I have been able to trace is given in the bibliography at the end of this volume. It is not appropriate to try to summarize them here, but I will select for comment a few landmark examples of the reception of his work in chronological order, with a view to my attempt in the final section to set it in relation to other poetry.

The first three collections were met by a range of perceptive reviews in Irish and English, of which two are especially worth noting. Brendan Kennelly, a poet and Professor of English in Trinity College Dublin, with whom O'Siadhail was much later to do many joint poetry readings, was the first to recognize the quality and the promise. His review of *An Bhliain Bhisigh* (*Leap Year*, 1978) spoke of O'Siadhail's 'genuine lyric gift', his poems being 'musically convincing ... the product of a probing intelligence and a capacity for delicate brooding on a variety of subjects', and showing 'his power of compression, his talent for concentration, his crafted and crafty resolution to let each poem speak for itself'. Kennelly concludes:

> Finally, it is clear that O'Siadhail is a dedicated writer. Like most truly dedicated people, he has a deep awareness of leisure, indeed of idleness ... . In idleness, it is possible to allow God's creation to be seen in a little of its infinite variety.[9]

The second is a review of *Runga* (*Rungs of Time*, 1980) by Máire Mhac an tSaoi (Cruise O'Brien). She revels in the richness of the language and the penetration of the mind:

> Micheal O'Siadhail does something that has not been done in Irish for perhaps some hundreds of years. He brings home to us the scholar's passion for his work, that 'curiosity' which Dr Johnson identified as the noblest and longest-lived of all human passions ... . [T]his book has made one reader at least, the reviewer, feel that in reading them she has made that rare and touch-minded thing, a friend. This is a superbly unboring book.

Yet she also reflects prophetically on the fact that she is writing the review in English because of her longing to introduce O'Siadhail to more people as a 'rivetingly interesting acquaintance', and on the tragedy that 'there are, incredibly, still living some young people who can write this kind of Irish, but to what extent do they have a public?' She admits that almost every reader would need a good dictionary to comprehend this Irish, which is 'a superb literary language with all the spontaneity and colour of a living vernacular allied to a contemporary and scholarly sophistication'.[10]

Springnight (1983), O'Siadhail's first collection in English, made an immediate impact. Frank Delaney, looking back sixteen months after it was launched, wrote:

> What is most exciting about O'Siadhail is that no subject seems too strange or mystic for him ... . He is more international, less local, less parochial than many of his contemporaries, which is why *Springnight* was so refreshing and, one presumes, so successful.

Delaney noted the critics had compared *Springnight* with the poetry of the young Seamus Heaney, but he himself saw O'Siadhail as very difficult to place:

> It is hard to describe what tradition O'Siadhail writes in – it may be that he has done something rare, that he has created his own tradition, is unlike any or all of the assembled troops of his predecessors.[11]

That daring suggestion will be reconsidered in my closing section.

One of the critics who conjured up the young Heaney was Augustine Martin, Professor of Anglo-Irish Literature at University College Dublin:

> Apart from the technical finesse and the quiet originality of its style, this collection of poems has the bonus attraction of a mature and subtle intelligence at work in all its parts. We feel the presence of a poet who has learned not only how to write but how to live. The last time I had this feeling – and wrote of it – was when I read some early poems of Seamus Heaney in *Irish Writing* almost twenty years ago.

Martin also faced an aspect of O'Siadhail that over the years has repeatedly provoked the critics, his ability to appreciate life exuberantly yet perceptively: 'Too often we associate affirmation with naivety, *angst* with sophistication. O'Siadhail gives us the lie in a volume which is a shrewd and varied celebration of the life force.'[12]

Martin reflects further on this in his review of O'Siadhail's next collection, *The Image Wheel* (1985):

> His finest effects are when the emotion – always close to the surface, eager to affirm and celebrate – is caught and controlled within an equally determined impersonality of technique.[13]

Martin and several other reviewers single out 'Loss', on the death of his father-in-law, as 'exquisite', 'superb'.

There was a gap of five years, covering O'Siadhail's transition into full-time writing, before *The Chosen Garden* appeared in 1990, and Brendan Kennelly observed this:

> Micheal O'Siadhail's *The Chosen Garden* is a deeply impressive collection, the sort of book which takes years to write, is worked and re-worked, carefully structured to show the poet's changing experience and presented finally in an elegant and shapely way to the reader.[14]

Ciaran Carty notes how 'O'Siadhail reaches for the universal while being honest to his own experience', but also that he refuses to 'conform to any of the neat categorisations by which

Irish writers tend to be regarded'[15] – raising again the problem of how to place him which I will address in the final section below.

'These poems neither fit nor defy the accustomed categories for Irish poetry' is the opening of the review by Victor Luftig (Yale University) of *Hail! Madam Jazz: New and Selected Poems* (1992).[16] This selection covered his published work to 1992 and gave critics the opportunity to view the *oeuvre* to that date as a whole – Luftig sees it as marking 'a decisive stage in both Micheal O'Siadhail's poetic career and his life'. He, like others (including some mentioned above), puzzles over O'Siadhail's relation to earlier and contemporary poets. He is not satisfied with O'Siadhail's ways of echoing other Irish poets (Eavan Boland, John Montague, Rita Ann Higgins – the faintness of some of the echoes makes one wonder whether they should be identified as such), and he worries about a certain directness, explicitness, and absence of irony, while recognizing that 'to get the most pleasure out of Micheal O'Siadhail's poems means to set aside such awareness and to embrace instead his expressed enthusiasms – for music, nature and language ...'. He also begins to explore O'Siadhail's use of classic forms and traditional metres, his attraction to the sonnet, and his achievement in poems such as 'Loss'.

Among other reviewers' attempts to relate O'Siadhail to the tradition of poetry, suggestions include Shelley (Fred Johnston), Wordsworth, and Donne:

> There is something in his poetry that recalls both the directness of, say, Wordsworth at this best, and, at the same time, a penetrating intelligence that challenges the reader with a complex imagery that is like that found in John Donne. [17] (Jeff O'Connell)

Donne recurs alongside George Herbert in critical responses to the next collection, *A Fragile City* (1995), and the book aroused press comment when it was launched by the Taoiseach (Prime Minister) of Ireland, John Bruton. The writer Ulick O'Connor wrote:

> Micheal O'Siadhail grows with every book he publishes. His craft increases to accommodate new depths of his perceptions. There are poems in *A Fragile City* which have not been surpassed by an Irish poet in the last thirty years.[18]

There was criticism of the book too, especially of its repetition of themes, such as that of the face. Fellow poet Brian Lynch wrote a mostly negative double review of the book alongside one by Brendan Kennelly. Kennelly came off worse, but O'Siadhail is charged with 'niceness', 'unevenness of tone and image', 'metaphorical disconnections', and even 'an almost total disregard for metre'.[19]

Our Double Time (1998) saw a quantum leap in the number of reviews, in Ireland and elsewhere.[20] Their number also allows for fuller comparison, the results of which are somewhat depressing regarding the variability of critical judgements. Rilke and Yeats are the main poets to whom he is compared, sometimes to his advantage, sometimes not. His formal rigour is both affirmed and criticized, as is the focus on personal themes – he is praised for being 'bravely uninterested in guardedness',[21] but other reviewers show why such courage is needed. Sometimes the clashes between critical verdicts are striking in their straight negation of each other, even on the same poem. The *pièce de résistance* is an especially vitriolic series of put-downs by Catriona O'Reilly. Each of her brief dismissals – of the treatment of Rilke, of the quality of the title poem, of the success of his forms, of the personal content, and of his response to a Beethoven quartet – is contradicted by other reviewers.

Compare, for example, her view that his treatment of music is 'spoiled by a wholly unnecessary attempt to describe what a Beethoven quartet is *like* to listen to'[22] with Kevan Johnson in the *Times Literary Supplement*:

> O'Siadhail has a marvellous sense of group and orchestral dynamics, perceiving the 'paternal, ever-present rumble' of the double bass, the 'riffs of light and dark', hearing a 'ballet of voices' and, gloriously, 'the violin's long struggle to joy'. 'Quartet' – on one of Beethoven's late string quartets – is exceptionally good.[23]

O'Reilly's crude hatchet job is very much the exception, however, and for the first time there is a solid set of serious reviews. The relation between his poetry and his performance in live readings is described (*New Hibernia Review*) and the Scandinavian affinities and Europeanness are perceived (Eibhlís Ní Dhuibhne Almqvist). Yet very few critics engage perceptively with the thought of the collection, only one has the technical vocabulary to do justice to the forms, and none discusses its architectonic.

It was impossible for critics to ignore the substantive content of *The Gossamer Wall: Poems in Witness to the Holocaust* (2002). In 2005, Shalom Goldman, writing in *Jewish Currents*, looked back on its reception:

> While a vast literature on the Shoah has entered Western literature in the past decades, O'Siadhail's contribution was unique in a number of ways, not the least of which is its Irish cultural orientation. Within Ireland, the response of book critics and other cultural pundits to *The Gossamer Wall* was very enthusiastic. *Irish Times* critic Patsy McGarry called the book 'an exceptional achievement, evidence of the poet's wounded fascination before such human evil and testifying to a painstaking labour of something akin to outraged love for all those who suffered'. The reading public in Ireland, England, and Scotland responded with similar enthusiasm and O'Siadhail's poetry readings were very well attended. There has been an equally sympathetic response in the U.S. to O'Siadhail's work.[24]

The theme evoked a set of thoughtful reviews, though by no means all agreed with his approach to either form or content, and a couple implied that the whole enterprise had grave problems. Yet the sense throughout was of deep matters being treated with appropriate seriousness and of differences that were rooted in the intractability of the subject matter – Michael Kinsella's review is an example of critical probing into anguished, irresolvable issues.[25] Strikingly, there was almost a consensus that what appeared the most daring move of all, the central sequence of sonnets on the death camps, had been worth the risk. The poet David McLoughlin summed up the sense that here poetry was doing something that only it could and yet had to innovate in order to do it:

> If poetry is to succeed in its deepest function, that of spiritual seismograph, then it must provide the images that allow new ways of interpreting, and facing, reality. This ... I believe, is what O'Siadhail achieves.[26]

One of the most complete reviews, which in its brief compass touches upon the poet's development, the match of form to content, the imagery, the narration, the rhymes, and the resonances with other poetry, concluding with a succinct summary of its achievement, is that of Sarah Kafatou in *Harvard Review*:

> What distinguishes this book is the great skill and sensitivity with which these events are selected and told. O'Siadhail calls upon an array of traditional verse forms, these being among

the most serviceable vessels we have for carrying the overwhelmingly difficult emotional content (think of Wilfred Owen's sonnets on the agonies of trench warfare when reading O'Siadhail's sonnets set in the camps) ... . Think of other poem sequences dealing with such material, for example Ruth Whitman's *The Testing of Hannah Senesh*. In the best of them, as in that book and here, an infinitely-long story, untellable in its entirety, is condensed into a few intense images, a sequence of clear and resonant notes. These, long after the cataclysm and far from it, continue to tremble in the air. As O'Siadhail puts it, 'Those years Ireland's oaks had narrowest rings.'[27]

The last collection for which there has been time for reception is *Love Life* (2005). The media took considerable interest in it around its launch and there were many interviews with O'Siadhail. The reviews were generally good, the fullest being Eugene O'Brien's in *The Irish Book Review*, one of whose concerns is again to relate O'Siadhail to the tradition: '[T]his is one of the most beautiful books of poetry that I have read. There is a fusion of the physical and the cerebral aspects of love here that is reminiscent of John Donne.'[28] By the time of writing, few reviews have had time to appear so far in journals outside Ireland, and the most substantial responses to the book are in the present volume.

A further dimension to the reception of O'Siadhail is that of academic studies, of which the most significant are those by Schricker and Mahan (see bibliography). A major aim of the essays in this volume is to take such studies further. Overall, O'Siadhail has been quite well served by his reception in the literary press and journals and by the wider public (especially in Ireland, Britain, North America, and Japan). Academics are only now beginning to grapple with the rich complexity of the work, as witnessed in the present book. Part of the purpose of the final section is to take the measure of this challenge.

Conclusion: The Challenge of O'Siadhail

As has emerged in the previous section's survey of its reception, O'Siadhail's poetry is difficult to categorize, and reviewers do not know quite how to place it. It is easier to deal with accepted schools, styles, and influences. O'Siadhail poses a multiple challenge: he is more widely and deeply read in more languages than most of those who comment on him, and the influences on him are commensurably diverse; his appreciation of language itself is likewise hard to match (see the academic works in the bibliography); adequate critique of his artistry in form, rhyme, metre, genre, and vocabulary requires both considerable technical knowledge and reference to poetry in many languages and periods; but more important than all these factors is the challenge of the content.

O'Siadhail tackles major issues, both personal and public, and there is also a constant interanimation between his life and his work. It is not only that the poetry is grounded in intensive study of relevant fields – literature, language, science, history, music, art, sailing, philosophy, hermeneutics, religion – but that he has immersed himself in relevant practices: thirty-five years of marriage; long-term friendships; learning to play the piano in mid-life; becoming fluent in several languages, culminating in learning to write as well as speak Japanese; collecting art works; going to sailing school; founding and chairing Ireland Literature Exchange; public reading of his poetry in many countries; and much else.

Faced with all that, one obvious conclusion is that it requires a response of comparable complexity, sophistication, and intensity. It demands literary critics of a distinctive kind, some of whom are contributors to this volume. It also needs those from other fields who refuse to accept the marginalization of poetry in our culture, and who see that it can be a primary way to go deeper and more broadly into questions of meaning, truth, goodness, beauty, and wisdom, and into how these are involved in the shaping of our lives and our world. They can then take his poetry with full seriousness in its integration of form and content, head and heart, personal and public, past, present, and future. The present volume therefore complements the literary critics with others from the fields of history, musicology, philosophy, theology and religious studies, painting, musical composition, and translation. Yet the complexity is paradoxically combined with accessibility: his books have consistently sold well, and his readings are popular. This is partly a case of 'art concealing art' – most of the stylistic sophistication does not draw attention to itself – but it is also because the content faces issues at the heart of life and society that most people do not expect to be simple and are thus willing to accept a certain amount of difficulty. But with the difficulty and the multiple resonances and levels of meaning he also often says certain things with memorable directness and immediate impact.

The primary focus throughout must be on the poetry, and appraising it is greatly assisted by connecting the challenge of O'Siadhail with that of other poets with whom he has affinities. The essays in later chapters make their own suggestions about his poetic genealogy and influences, and I have already noted an array of names that arise from O'Siadhail's poetry and prose and from the reviews of his works. In what remains of this essay I want to add my own thoughts on this, without any sense that there is only one right set of conclusions. Indeed, the very variety of O'Siadhail's influences and resonances means that there are likely to be diverse ways of placing him and that many of these might complement each other. I want briefly to draw attention to just a few key figures from different traditions who, in my judgement, best illuminate his conception and practice of poetry.

I begin with the Irish poetic tradition up to the present. O'Siadhail has studied closely the early monastic poetry, with its fresh bursting out of nature, and also appreciates folk poetry such as Connemara love songs. The more immediate influences and parallels, however, are contemporary, and he is a close reader of Irish poetry of the twentieth and twenty-first centuries. If I were choosing to trace the influence of just one key figure it would be Patrick Kavanagh (1904-67).[29] There are in fact many echoes of Kavanagh in O'Siadhail's poetry, but there is also a set of deeper affinities. Each has an unguardedness, a directness prepared to risk exposure, and is not afraid to rejoice as well as lament. This may be connected with the ways they keep open channels to the premodern – Kavanagh's rural Monaghan, O'Siadhail's Aran Islands – and are not hemmed in by modernism or too mesmerized by irony.[30] They minister a meaning that is open to the transcendent (Kavanagh once wrote: 'The poet is a theologian') and is simultaneously personal and public – Kavanagh's 'The Great Hunger' and 'Lough Derg' parallel O'Siadhail's more public collections. Then there are the sonnets. Much of Kavanagh's greatest poetry is in this form – 'Dear Folks', 'The Hospital', 'October', 'One',[31] 'Come Dance with Kitty Stobling', 'Miss Universe' (echoes of Madam Jazz?), 'Yellow Vestments', and above all 'Canal Bank Walk'.[32] These combine mastery of a disciplined form with intense love of a superabundant life that opens beyond itself. To read them alongside O'Siadhail's sonnets (especially those in *Our Double Time*, which has more sonnets than any other collection and also more resonances with Kavanagh) is to taste the same spirit. At its root is the 'life for life's sake' attitude that I identified above in O'Siadhail through commenting on his line 'The only end of jazz is jazz.' Kavanagh in his autobiography wrote:

> It took me many years to learn or relearn not to care. The heart of a song singing it, or a poem writing it, is not caring ... . In the beginning of my versing career I had hit on the no-caring jag

but there was nobody to tell me I was on the right track ... . In the final simplicity we don't care whether we appear foolish or not. We talk of things that earlier would embarrass. We are satisfied with being ourselves, however small.[33]

Within English poetry, a name that has occurred frequently among the reviewers is John Donne. He brings to mind a further set of O'Siadhail characteristics. The most obvious is the exquisite love poetry, physical, passionate, and intellectual at the same time, shaped in highly disciplined forms, with a delight in language that plays with multiple meanings and can develop a metaphor through a whole poem. Donne also took a strong interest in the world of his time as it underwent massive changes and opened up to great discoveries in geography and science. O'Siadhail's poetry of science, cities, and (especially in *Globe*) a world in transformation has a similar Renaissance sensibility. And, as in Kavanagh, there is a transcendent dimension inseparable from earthiness. Donne's playfulness is also there in both Kavanagh and O'Siadhail – Kavanagh spoke of the main feature of a poet being his 'humourosity. Any touch of boringness and you are in the wrong shop.'[34]

Besides Donne, however, I would draw in the less obvious John Milton. Like Donne, Milton honed his verse through writing it in another language, Latin, and in addition he mastered several other languages and many branches of knowledge. He too unites the personal, the public, the intellectual, and the transcendent. But the further dimension, seen above all in the epics *Paradise Lost* and *Paradise Regained*, is that of engagement with the whole worldview of his time, attempting to articulate a vision of reality for an age of upheaval. His poetic response to the trauma of civil war (which for political reasons often had to be done indirectly) relates to the darker side of O'Siadhail's poetry, especially in *Our Double Time*, *The Gossamer Wall*, and *Globe*.

It is interesting to speculate where O'Siadhail's Miltonic side might ultimately lead him. He is deeply concerned with the future and with the flourishing of the world. There are enough signs, especially in *A Fragile City*, *The Gossamer Wall*, and *Globe*, that O'Siadhail's vision continues to grow. In the wake of a century of ideologies largely dissipated in wars, genocides, failed utopias, and environmental disaster, and facing a fast-changing and complex world still riven by conflict, his own conception of the poetic vocation as involving a 'ministry of meaning' may yet bring him to an even larger work wrestling with the crisis of ultimate meaning.

Another key influence is Dante. Dante's achievement in envisaging a cosmos in which love is central and ultimate, where despair and evil are realistically faced but do not have the last word, resonates with that of O'Siadhail. Dante's epic vision is lit by the smile of Beatrice without ignoring either the vicious politics or the dazzling intellectual achievements of his day. It also weaves in the poet's own life and that of his great model, Virgil. O'Siadhail's autobiographical poetry has at its best the Dantean quality of recognizing one's tiny place in the cosmos combined with overwhelming awareness of the dignity and responsibility of the poet's vocation.

If space permitted I would reflect on others, especially the French poet Paul Valéry and the Swede Karin Boye. But I conclude with one who is mentioned by reviewers, and on whom O'Siadhail has written, Rainer-Maria Rilke. Again, one finds the love interest, alertness to the transcendent, and elaborate attention to form. But it is appropriate to end this study of O'Siadhail's life and work with reference to the way he unites them. Rilke is a model of dedication to his calling as a poet, embodying an intensification of vocational identity that dominated his life and which often found its deepest expression in a sense of wonder:

To praise is the whole thing! A man who can praise
comes towards us like ore out of the silences
Of rock. His heart, that dies, presses out
For others a wine that is fresh forever.[35]

Put that together with Kavanagh's 'humourosity' to set the intensity in relief, and one senses the tone and mood in which O'Siadhail's life and work come together.

2 | A New Voice in the City

Marc Caball

In 1978 Micheal O'Siadhail published his first poetry collection consisting of thirty-four poems in Irish in a volume titled *An Bhliain Bhisigh* ('The Leap Year').[1] The present essay seeks to explore aspects of the thematic range of this collection that may be said to prefigure several of O'Siadhail's later concerns. Broadly speaking, the notion of seasonal nature in an urban setting, specifically in central Dublin, depicted against the backdrop of daily life, looms large in terms of theme and imagery in these pithy and often provocative short lyrics. In his thematic focus on the evolving aspects of nature within the city, O'Siadhail combines a deep-rooted Gaelic consciousness of the natural world with an assured and acute urban awareness. Indeed, it is a combination of innovation and tradition that makes *An Bhliain Bhisigh* such an interesting case study in the delineation of O'Siadhail's poetic and intellectual evolution. This essay will primarily explore and assess these poems in the context of their own internal coherence and vitality. However, it will also be argued that his first collection is both counter-pointed and to some extent situated by another work published by O'Siadhail in 1978, a socio-linguistic study of household terminology in the Irish of Inis Meáin, Co. Galway.[2] Intellectually and emotionally, it is evident that O'Siadhail's poetry draws on a rich and complex amalgam of influences – *An Bhliain Bhisigh* is notable in its own right as a remarkably assured poetic debut but more crucially, perhaps, it also represents a point of embarkation for an artistic, intellectual, and linguistic journey which is surely unmatched in contemporary Irish poetry.

In his intimate and loosely biographical introduction to *Poems 1975-1995*, O'Siadhail speaks of his genesis as a poet and provides a fascinating if admittedly allusive account of the background which foregrounds his emergence as the author of *An Bhliain Bhisigh*. A self-confessed late poetic starter, he alludes to his youthful confusion and to his belief that he has lived his life 'at a watershed'.[3] The product of the comfortable securities of 1950s middle-class suburban Dublin and a conservative Irish Catholic, albeit Jesuit, secondary education, he evokes a world where 'the piano was in the sitting-room and it seemed Chopin was still sounding a hundred years after his death in Paris'.[4] Clearly relishing the sense of liberation, excitement, and new possibilities engendered by the sixties, he speaks of his Bohemian student life at Trinity College Dublin and describes his generation with characteristic insight:

'We were all angry young men and women and read those paperbacks about sociology and psychology, and we felt we knew what lay hidden behind everything.'[5]

The promise of the 1960s yielded to the global political and economic uncertainty and disillusionment of the 1970s. The creative intellectual and social ferment of the previous decade had been supplanted by disappointment and alienation: 'For many of us there was a tristesse about the 1970s, a let-down as life settled into its ordinariness. Many glimpsed the abyss and peered over its edge.'[6] Following post-graduate study in folklore and Scandinavian languages at the university of Oslo during the academic year 1968/69, O'Siadhail returned to Dublin to take up a position as a lecturer in Irish at Trinity College.

It may have seemed that a long and productive career in university teaching and Celtic scholarship lay before him – yet life as a lecturer was not for O'Siadhail and he feared that the inevitable emotional and intellectual commitment, which he would be required to make to a university career, would seriously vitiate his artistic capacity. Leaving Trinity, O'Siadhail secured an academic research appointment at the School of Celtic Studies in the Dublin Institute for Advanced Studies:

> There I'd stay for 13 years until I left to devote my life entirely to poetry. The mixture of writing and linguistic research was more congenial. But in the end, I didn't want to divide my energies any more. The quality of concentration I could then afford made me move from collections united by an angle of vision to books with architecture, an overriding focus.[7]

Published early in O'Siadhail's career as an emerging scholar of international distinction in Celtic linguistics at the Dublin Institute for Advanced Studies, *An Bhliain Bhisigh* was conceived within a very rich angle of vision indeed – an angle formed within the Gaelic literary and oral tradition blended with the richness of European modernism.

If St Stephen's Green in central Dublin defines the locus of *An Bhliain Bhisigh* spatially, its linguistic and intellectual parameters are considerably broader. David Ford, in his essay in this collection, provides an account of O'Siadhail's exposure to the Gaelic culture of western Ireland as a young boy and his subsequent deep immersion in Irish language and literature. As a student of Irish at Trinity College, O'Siadhail was greatly influenced in particular by the scholarship and wider cultivation of three Trinity academics: Máirtín Ó Cadhain (1906-1970), radical activist and a towering figure in modern Irish prose; David Greene (1915-1981), Celtic scholar, polymath and *bon viveur;* Ernest Gordon Quin (1910-1986), a scholar of Old Irish and noted alpine gardener.[8] The profoundly humane and sophisticated learning of these men made a lasting impression on O'Siadhail. His marriage in 1970 to Bríd Ní Chearbhaill, a native-speaker of Irish from Donegal, further deepened his sense of connection with the Irish-speaking culture of the *Gaeltachtaí*. The academic fruits of this deep knowledge of contemporary Irish are evident initially in a study of regional dialects published in 1975, which he co-authored with the German scholar Arndt Wigger.[9] A late starter in poetry perhaps, nonetheless, O'Siadhail's first collection is the product of an 'angle of vision' which is mosaic-like in its intense combination of scholarship and life experience.

As a starting point for closer consideration of the poems in *An Bhliain Bhisigh*, it is necessary to return to O'Siadhail's understated biographical foreword to *Poems 1975-1995*. Recalling the sense of disappointment which accompanied his transition from student to adult working life in the deflated atmosphere of the early seventies, he describes how he gradually rediscovered a sense of wonder and renewal in St Stephen's Green:

I recall in those years I often walked and sat in St Stephen's Green in Dublin, a stone's throw from where I was born. For all the terror of our century, for all our angst and knowingness, just wandering there watching ducks in a pond and the listening to the gossip and laughter of people as they passed, the world seemed sweet and new. There were tiny glances of infinity. And slowly I gave into the wonder of the world. All I needed to do was to dare, to tauten towards the light like a sunflower. I was 26 and this would be my 'leap year'.[10]

The 'leap year' poems mark a rite of passage in the poet's life – they represent a conscious abandonment of alienation and ennui and they mark O'Siadhail's henceforth characteristic engagement with the diversity of human experience, often quietly quotidian, yet not infrequently mysterious when presented through the focus of his lens. Moreover, in his use of Irish as a means of expression, O'Siadhail was also surely demonstrating his sense of affinity with smaller cultures and languages and with the road less travelled. Perhaps also, he was animated by a sense of nostalgia for an ancient culture whose romance and aesthetic he had first encountered as a boy. Tellingly, in his elegy on Máirtín Ó Cadhain he alludes to the tensions inherent in blending an imperilled ancient culture with modernity:

> Those closing years, probing and embattled,
> he sought somehow to wed
> the avant garde with the vanishing, straddled
> a destiny – a watershed,
> new and old flirting and parting in that head.[11]

Mirroring the audacious literary example of his late Trinity mentor, O'Siadhail's 'leap year' poems are a similarly daring exercise in blending the language of scattered rural communities in the west of Ireland with a self-consciously urban and European frame of thought and reference.

A sense of wonder and delight in the everyday infuses the 'leap year' poems. The collection is prefaced by a verse of thanks which records the author's heart-felt gratitude to the 'beautiful and delightful woman who presented Mícheál with a year's stipend to enable him sit on a bench in Stephen's Green' and which goes on to reflect on the benefits to art of idleness.[12] This poetic note of acknowledgement introduces two important themes in the collection: the author's joy in the manifestations of nature in the city and the significance of women in his life. All these poems are informed by the type of *joie de vivre* which O'Siadhail has spoken of rediscovering during his visits to St Stephen's Green. In a concise and playful four-lined lyric *Altú roimh ól* ('Grace before alcohol'), the poet humbly seeks the favour of the almighty to allow him submit dutifully to dissipation:

> Cuidigh liom a Athair chóir
> Géilleadh go humhal don drabhlás

so that he may return again to the presence of the almighty to secure forgiveness:

> Le ghoil athuair i do láthair
> Ag iarraidh maithiúnas.[13]

This piece is at once reverential in its prayer-like form and disconcerting in its frank celebration of bacchanalian revelry. A similar endorsement of life and vitality is undertaken in *Lá Croídhílis* ('Red-letter day') when the poet argues that life must be fully embraced and lived to the maximum:

> Tá fhios ag síol Adhaimh is cait an bhaile
> Nach bhfuil nóiméad féin le cur amú.[14]

In the preface to *Poems 1975-1995* it has been seen that O'Siadhail spoke of the revelation to him of 'tiny glances of infinity' during his visits to St Stephen's Green and how slowly he 'gave into the wonder of the world':

> And it seemed as if life began to expand. I wanted to seize just one of those glances of infinity. I wanted to tell the world. Strangely, the wonder keeps eluding me and yet I always believe the next poem will refract a little more. So a universe which might have narrowed became now an endless jazz improvisation.[15]

In the poem *An Droichead* which O'Siadhail has himself translated into English with the title 'The Bridge', he elaborates on 'the abyss' which preceded his reawakening and his self-conscious engagement with life and poetry.[16] He admits to his puzzlement over the years as to the story ascribed to the Curé d'Ars about a Frenchman who prepares his soul in the moments between leaping from a bridge and hitting the water:

> B'fhada gur thuig tú an cúram gan cion
> Nó gur shiúil tú féin ag ceann an droichid
> Ansiúd ní léar aon tsolas nó go dtugtar spléach
> Thrí shúil an droichid.[17]

> For years I couldn't understand his strange pilgrimage
> Until I too had walked to the edge of that bridge
> And there staring into the dark had caught a glimpse
> Of light in the bridge's eye.[18]

Eschewing a literal translation of his own words, O'Siadhail opts for a rendition that privileges elegance and clarity above precise adherence to his original. Most notably, in the original Irish version the poet addresses himself in the second person singular form while in the English text he speaks in the first person singular. The 'strange pilgrimage' of the English is more starkly a 'loveless task' (*an cúram gan cion)* in the Irish original. Pondering the import of the story in his own case, he reflects on his own personal sense of transcendence in the face of an abyss of despair:

> Idir an áirse agus cúr na habhann
> A slánaíodh muid féin.[19]

> In that space between the arch and the river's foam
> Am I made whole?[20]

Here again the original Irish is leaner and more intense in impact than its English offspring. Interestingly, the Irish word *áirse* or arch occurs in the list of building terms collected by O'Siadhail on Inis Meáin. In the relevant entry in his *Téarmaí tógála agus tís as Inis Meáin*, he gives the term *áirse an tsimléir* ('chimney arch') and, noting its derivation from the French *arche*, he provides an example of its usage in a sentence recorded from an islander,

Dara Beag Ó Fatharta.[21] Likewise, the English rendition 'Am I made whole?' is preceded more definitively without a question mark by the Irish verb *slánaigh* which Niall Ó Dónaill's *Foclóir Gaeilge-Béarla* (1977) translates as 'make whole, redeem, save'. The redemptive implications of his experience are confidently articulated in the Irish while in English O'Siadhail is more circumspect and almost diffident in his articulation of a transformative moment. Had the youthful self-confident embrace of life been tempered by a more cautious attitude by the time O'Siadhail published his translation in 1999, or is this an instinctive reaction to a different community of readers?

O'Siadhail's delight in the seasonal workings of nature during the course of a year in St Stephen's Green looms large in these lyrical celebrations of immediate, often apparently unremarkable, pleasures which so enhance human experience. However, these works are not classic nature poems *per se*. More often than not, nature is the medium through which pathways to transcendence are signalled. O'Siadhail makes no attempt, however, to delineate an authoritative template for life in these lyrics. In drawing back from the abyss, he offers his readers pointers, sometimes insights, from his experience by way of guidance and unobtrusive example. In the poem *Lus na gréine* ('Sunflower'), he comments indirectly, through the painterly image of a sunflower responding to the nurturing warmth of the sun's rays, on his own self-conscious positive reversal of fortune:

> Seans é díriú ar an solas
> Is má chailltear, feanntar,
> Má lúbaim le domhantharraingt
> Má chúbaim, brisim.
>
> Abair liom a dhuine gur fiú é
> An t-ogach beag is lú
> Is cuirfear billiún bláth amach,
> Bláthannaí mór is fiú.[22]
>
> The danger of tautening towards the sun:
> To lose is to lose all.
> Too much gravity and I'm undone;
> If I bend, I fall.
>
> Tell me it's all worth this venture,
> Just the slightest reassurance,
> And I'll open a bloom, I'll flower
> At every chance.[23]

O'Siadhail's ability to paint a picture in words of the 'tautening' sunflower reaching towards the sun attests not only to his technical virtuosity in moulding and shaping language, in this case in both Irish and English, but it also draws attention to his deep and informed interest in contemporary art.[24] The poet's avowed commitment to exploiting life's potential is confirmed deliberately and almost boisterously in the third and final verse of this exhilarating composition:

> Mol anois go haer mé
> Mol a chroí go solas mé
> Mol mé, mol mé, mol mé

Is mairim go deo.[25]

Then praise me all the way to the sky,
Praise me with light, lover,
Oh, praise me, praise me, praise me
And I live forever.[26]

These lines resound with evangelical fervour with their almost feverish demand for praise
from his beloved. Once again, there are subtle differences in the texture and timbre of the
author's translation, which hint at the impact of the passage of the years and a certain
concomitant reconfiguration of emphasis. In the original version, the poet speaks directly in
the vocative case to an individual as 'my dear or beloved one' (*a chroí*). It is arguable that
'lover' is much more specific and a great deal more sexually charged than the essentially
generic Gaelic invocation. Yet the exquisite benefit of alliteration in the triad of imperatives
'Mol mé, mol mé, mol mé' is superbly effective and a great deal more resounding than the
comparatively restrained 'Oh, praise me, praise me, praise me'. However, the final line of
affirmation is effectively a word for word translation with an equivalent resonance in both
languages. The 'Sunflower' is at one level a charming piece on nature's fecundity yet at
another more profound level it is a clarion call to arms. It illustrates graphically O'Siadhail's
mastery in deploying the everyday to mediate the extraordinary. In 'Port an éin' ('The bird's
tune') the poet presents a similar paean to nature, in this case focusing on the freedom of
birds flying high over the landscape. Charming in its apparent naivety, it is also a meditation
on freedom and the potential for constraint, both physically and spiritually, in the world of
men.[27] The short but condensed 'Grianstad' ('Sun stop') exemplifies O'Siadhail's Stephen's
Green project in its affirmation of growth and vitality over winter and decay.[28]

In these poems the weather looms large thematically and consequently in terms of
imagery. Not surprisingly, there is a heightened awareness of the changing seasons from the
poet's park bench vantage point. It is as if O'Siadhail discerns a particular microclimate
within Dublin's centre that approximates metaphorically to the changing rhythms and
fortunes of the individual's life. In these works, the weather, ironically a staple of Irish
conversation, assumes the outline of a broader meditation on life and its varied course. The
relentless adumbration of the seasons provides a salutary template for the individual's
course. The imagery in 'Séasúr' ('Season') is playful yet concrete in its portrayal of change
and complementary sustainability. O'Siadhail describes how in the previous season the trees
had shed a covering of leaves which resembled a library-full of yellow leaflets ('leabharlann
iomlán billeogaí buí'). This act, had been undertaken, in the apparent hope that dancing
naked together they might tickle the sun's feet.[29] In a modern era obsessed with the transient,
fixated by the latest news story, the advent and departure of winter are immutable and
certain:

Seo é an geimhreadh. Seo í an fichiú aois.
Níl aonbharr nuaíocht a dhéanfadh cúis.[30]

And still it's winter. Still this twentieth century.
What news item will we run today? What's the story to break?[31]

Of course, the most startling news is also at first glance the most mundane and perhaps
undervalued in an age obsessed with the trivial and transient. The trees and the birds

continue in their ageless cycle of growth and decay. The earth now speaks of its potent life-giving energy:

> 'Mair a dhuine, tabharfaidh mise an féar'
> Sin a dúirt an talamh thrína chodladh aréir.[32]

> The hard-crusted soil turns in its sleep and cries:
> 'Just live, man, I'm busy pushing up the daisies.'[33]

In an ingenious invocation of burial six feet under following death, O'Siadhail daringly deploys the colloquial 'pushing up the daisies' in his English reworking of the poem to affirm its opposite – life rather than death. In the original, the earth sustains 'grass' ('féar') – at once more ubiquitous and more pastoral than the daisy – the quintessential denizen of countless suburban gardens. Winter is fading and renewal is imminent in the changing of the seasonal guard. 'Resurrection' ('aiséirí') is at hand. The image of a sacred ecology sustaining the life cycle invests this poem with a latent sense of the spiritual and its message is emblematic more generally of the commitment of the 'leap year' poems to engagement, joy and wonder.

Affirmation of life is also at the centre of another of the 'leap year' weather poems. 'Graffiti' is to some extent a young man's composition in its palpable sense of opportunity and potential. However, it is also about entering a new phase of experience and consciousness. The summer has been the hottest in a hundred years, the work has been the hardest and the wine has been the sweetest and the women, as ever, were beautiful:

> An samhradh is teocha le céad bliain;
> An obair is cruaidhe agus an fíon is blasta.
> Mar is iondúil, tá na mná níos breácha
> Ná ariamh.[34]

> The warmest summer in a hundred years;
> The toughest work, the sweetest wine;
> As usual the women were even finer
> Than ever before.[35]

Yet the summer has also been a turning point in the poet's life. During this summer, the poet had arrived at an acceptance of unresolved questions and unfulfilled desires – he wonders aloud if this frame of mind is consequent on age or perhaps it comes about as a result of spiritual enlightenment:

> Seo é an séasúr nuair a hamhdaíodh ar deireadh
> Na ceisteannaí gan réiteach, an pléisiúr gan santú.
> Ar aois é seo nó léargas eile ar na flaithis
> Thrí chró na snáthad?[36]

> This was the summer I at last conceded
> The unfathomables, even pleasures I'd miss.
> Was this ageing or a glimpse of paradise
> Through the needle's eye?[37]

The poem's final verse is masterly in its evocation of a monk in early Christian Ireland who chronicles the onslaught of Viking raiders in a fearful note on the margins of a manuscript.[38] O'Siadhail also has an entry for his own personal annals: he had one good season, a fruitful summer of insight.

The influence of early Irish poetry on O'Siadhail, especially in regard to the treatment of nature in Old Irish lyrics, seems beyond doubt.[39] In a poem entitled simply 'Early Irish Lyric' in *Springnight*, O'Siadhail explicitly acknowledges his debt to his monastic literary predecessors in the Irish language:

> Once again picture him near St. Gall,
> A monk in exile. Cinctured, diligent,
> He is glossing, paving a Latin grammar.

The monk, significantly an Irishman of European learning and discernment, finishing his work ('To-day's Lesson prepared'), begins to daydream and thinks of spring and records his delight on the margins of a manuscript:

> 'A hedge of trees overlooks me; for me
> A blackbird sings – news I won't conceal ...'
> Febrile, meticulous, he chronicled the astoundment.
>
> A thousand years ago on the lower edge
> Of a vellum folio. This is another spring
> And we are brothers conjugate in ecstasy.[40]

O'Siadhail's use of inverted commas alerts readers with typical understatement to his immersion in Gaelic literature. For the monk's exclamation of joy in the trees surrounding him and the blackbird's song derive directly from verses written on the lower margins of the St Gall manuscript 904 – the latter contains a copy of Priscian's treatise on Latin grammar compiled by Irish scribes during the first half of the ninth century.[41] It is arguable, however, that the influence of Irish poetry is most marked in the 'leap year' poems with their taut and concise articulation of essential verities. Indeed, O'Siadhail's metaphorical year of internal exile in Stephen's Green is counter-pointed neatly by the image of the early Irish scholar monk in his continental exile contemplating divine creation within the learned ambience of the scriptorium.

O'Siadhail's delight in women's company and their influence on his life recurs throughout his work over the years. In a range of 'leap year' poems – *Thusa* ('You'), *Graffiti*, *An Binse* ('The Bench'), *Comaoin* ('Compliment'), and *Máthair* ('Mother') – he reflects on his debt to women who had intersected with his life and who had coloured his experience in so many different ways. The deep attachment of a child to his mother and the maternal primal influence on her offspring is explored in a touching though wholly unsentimental fashion in *Máthair*. Alluding to the nativity story's depiction of the star guiding the wise men to Bethlehem, he speaks of his mother as a 'réalt eolais' ('star of knowledge').[42] The effect of her demise is profound and not a little violent: his guiding star has fallen from the sky ('an réalt as an spéir') and his life has been torn from its supporting hinges ('Gur thit an saol as na lúdrachaí'). In another revealing example of how O'Siadhail's work as a scholar at this period informs his artistry, it is worth drawing attention to the fact that 'lúdrach' whose meaning is defined by Ó Dónaill's dictionary as 'pivot' or 'hinge' was among the domestic terms collected by him on Inis Meáin with a somewhat different meaning to the standard definition.[43] O'Siadhail's gives the meaning of the word in its plural usage on the island as the general composition of a piece of furniture such as a bed or a chair.[44] The latter meaning when applied to its usage in *Máthair* is even more cataclysmic than its standard dictionary definition as it evokes comprehensive disintegration.

In the poem 'Comaoin', which O'Siadhail has translated to English under the title 'Compliment', he speaks movingly about how a number of women have shaped and formed his consciousness. The piece begins with what surely is a subtle affirmation of the poet's feminist beliefs:

> Bhí na mná ariamh uiríseal
> A chuir an cogar úd i gcluais an fhir
> Gur fireannach gaisciúil é Rí na nDúl
> Ach tá fhios againne níos fearr.[45]

> Were those women meek and humble
> Who once whispered in a man's ear
> That a god was a dominant male?
> Then tell me that we know better.[46]

It seems in fact that the poet would have his readers understand that such women were far from 'meek and humble' and it is implied that their intellectual agility seriously vitiated any claims to an exclusively masculine divinity. Curiously, in his original version the divinity is incontrovertibly the Christian God ('Rí na nDúl', which Pádraig Ua Duinnín renders as 'King of the Elements', i.e., God) while the English version of the poem has the generically classical 'a god'. Likewise, the English version is less certain in sentiment as a result of a question mark where the Irish original implies irony more than ambiguity. In a masterful retort to the implication of godly ascendancy in the opening verse, O'Siadhail observes how goddesses have transformed his existential trajectory:

> I measc mhná na cruinne gile
> Casadh corrbhandia i mo bhealach
> Aníos thríd an scafall sealadach
> A tóigeadh idir am is spás.[47]

> Among the bright women of the world
> There have always been those goddesses,
> As we crossed our makeshift scaffold,
> A universe built in time and space.[48]

The use of 'makeshift scaffold' to describe life's trajectory is at once poignant and powerful in the way it underlines transitoriness and impermanence. Moreover, scaffold's secondary meaning as a platform for execution by hanging or beheading hovers menacingly in the verbal undergrowth. In this case also, it is intriguing to note that O'Siadhail recorded its Irish form *scafall* under the rubric of building terms on Inis Meáin.[49] A handful of women have marked the poet's character and personality indelibly – indeed he muses if they can possibly have appreciated the extent to which they would leave their imprint on him:

Mo léine álainn, mo léine féin,
Mo phearsantacht phíosáilte, mo dhán breac,
An léine is gaire ná an craiceann
A bhronn mná na cruinne orm.[50]

A wonderful cloth, my shirt of linen,
My chequered gift, a self they've woven,
This shirt that's closer than the bone,
The bright women of my world have given.[51]

The influence of these women has enveloped him like a shirt worn close to the skin. In the Irish original, he is explicit in linking this shirt to 'my patched personality' ('Mo phearsantacht phíosáilte') and to 'my variegated gift' ('Mo dhán breac' – *dán* variously meaning 'gift' and/or 'poem'). Although neither Ua Duinnín nor Ó Dónaill list *píosáilte* ('patched') in their respective dictionaries, O'Siadhail recorded a colourful example of its usage from Bean Uí Fhatharta on Inis Meáin.[52] If the author of the 'leap year' poems has been moulded by strong women, it is clear also from these poems that his commitment to scholarship influenced his artistry in ways that are latent but nonetheless significant.

By way of conclusion to the foregoing review of aspects of the 'leap year' poems, it is proposed to review briefly O'Siadhail's other publication in 1978 – his academic monograph on the building and domestic terminology of Inis Meáin in the Aran Islands. It has been demonstrated that this work intersects with the language of his poetry in ways that are quite unique and reflective of the author's immersion in Gaelic island life in the period 1975-76. This glossary is as much anthropological in focus as linguistic. Divided into five sections, the listing of terms and words, frequently further illuminated by examples of usage in the speech of identified islanders, centres on terminology related to house construction, furniture and other domestic equipment, clothes and personal accessories, provisions/food, and cooking/domestic work. O'Siadhail recorded this material intermittently during 1975-76 from 24 Irish-speakers on Inis Meáin. The majority of these islanders were aged over 50 years while the remainder largely fell within the age bracket 30-50 years. A small minority, 4 respondents, were aged between 20 and 30 years.[53] These entries, apparently of largely dialectal and philological interest, are also a rich source for the social history of Inis Meáin. For example, in his preface O'Siadhail remarks on the influence of American English on certain aspects of island life, especially in regard to personal dress, in contrast to the stability evident in a domain less immediately subject to contemporary external trends as mediated through emigration, house building.[54] The material he gathered on Inis Meáin both exercised direct influence on his choice of vocabulary as evidenced above but it also exemplifies O'Siadhail's interest in everyday objects and practices. A few examples suffice to demonstrate the extent to which he mastered the islanders' rich vocabulary and the world view enshrined in these markers of economic, social, and cultural values. Words and phrases such as *lián* (trowel), *lota* (loft), *aghaidh an scátháin* (front of a mirror), *billeog an bhoird* (table top), *bosca an tsiúcra* (sugar container), *cabhar an pheiliúir* (pillowcase), and *crúiscín cré* (a clay vessel, holding water for instance), randomly chosen here, reveal O'Siadhail as anthropologist. It is arguable that the 'leap year' poems are anthropological in their concern to discern the universal in the quotidian – consequently, the poet's deployment of language and scholarship informed by his urban identity serves to create a body of work that is simultaneously contemporary and traditional.

In a review of *An Bhliain Bhisigh* that he published in 1979, Máirtín Ó Direáin (1910-88), now recognized as one of the leading poets writing in Irish in the twentieth century, remarked on O'Siadhail's mastery of the Irish language and his ability to manipulate the language to communicate depth and complexity.[55] Ó Direáin marvelled at O'Siadhail's apparent artistic maturity and noted the essentially metaphysical nature of the poems. Praising the thematic continuity and logic he discerned in his work, he encapsulates the essence of the 'leap year' poems as reflecting O'Siadhail's disinclination to accept a definitive existential paradigm and a consequent commitment to life and its rich potential.[56] The 'leap year' poems constitute an impressive poetic debut – their clarity, simplicity, and depth a testament to their author's technical skills and self-assurance. The quiet confidence of these poems and their delight in nature and humanity signal a new and remarkable beginning in Irish poetry.

3 | A Life of Love, a Love of Life: O'Siadhail's Love Poetry

Margaret Masson

Introduction

Micheal O'Siadhail's love poetry, like all his poetry, defies conventional categories: it is counter-cultural and cross-cultural, transcendent and intensely of this world, a tribute to one particular woman loved through more than three decades and a homage to the love of all women through all time. Its roots and context are Irish, but its scope traverses the globe. Its voice is intimately lyrical, yet it is structured upon a rich series of experiments with poetic form ranging from the sonnet to haiku.

The love poetry is an important strand throughout O'Siadhail's oeuvre. We see its most sustained exploration in *Love Life* (2005), a remarkable collection of poems which chronicle the poet's love affair with his wife. From the first overwhelming erotic intensity of desire, the changing moods and faces of love are followed through the weathering of maturing love to the anticipated desolation of bereavement which shadows the book's final section: 'who will be lonely for whom?' ('At Sea', 108).[1]

Countless poets through the centuries have written cycles of love poems and O'Siadhail's indebtedness to some of them – Shakespeare, Herrick, and Donne to name but three – is alluded to in his poems. Most love poetry focuses on the intensity of the initial passion and the pain of the ending.[2] Its dominant assumption is that romantic rather than married love is the stuff of poetry, a sentiment perhaps most famously articulated by Byron's Don Juan:

> There's doubtless something in domestic doings
> Which forms, in fact, true love's antithesis;
> Romances paint at full length people's wooings,
> But only give a bust of marriages;
> For no one cares for matrimonial cooings,
> There's nothing wrong in a connubial kiss:
> Think you, if Laura had been Petrarch's wife,
> He would have written sonnets all his life? (*Don Juan*, iii.8)

Even Seamus Heaney – despite the fact that a number of his own poems celebrate married love – has this to say in an interview in 1981: 'I think home life kills ... I mean home life, at its best, obliterates the necessity for any kind of poetry. Well, unless it's an unhappy home!'[3]

O'Siadhail, through his poetry, could not disagree more profoundly. His love poetry embraces romance but is not Romantic. It is utterly earthed in the realities of a flesh and blood woman who is intimately known – 'No courtly sighs. No amorous unattainable' ('Rhyme', 19). Yet it maintains its sense of the wonder, discovery, and joy in exploring a love that has grown familiar and is involved in the daily round of 'domestic doings'. What may be unique in O'Siadhail's love poetry (with the possible exception of the Brownings) is that it explores one love – the love of one's spouse – over a lifetime, and is written during that lifetime while both lover and beloved are still alive.[4] His 'love life' is the life of love, much more comprehensive than the limited – if intense – range of experience usually associated with the phrase. O'Siadhail takes the very seasoning process – the mystery of how a love grows, ages, mellows, and yet retains the possibility of self-transcending ecstasy – as one of his key themes. In so doing, he celebrates a richness and range of love that may be unparalleled in modern poetry. O'Siadhail's work expands the category of love poetry.

In challenging this traditional opposition between romantic and married love, O'Siadhail's sees the differences between the two unified in the deep truth of paradox, and it is through a series of these paradoxes that I would like to explore his love poetry in this chapter. Much of his poetry, both in theme and language, is structured on a conception of love as both grace and destiny, freedom and discipline, ecstatic and everyday, total fluke and yet inevitable as bedrock. In love, the lover loses him or herself in order to be found – transformed – and the fluid boundaries between self and other are, for O'Siadhail, a source of recurring fascination. In love, one is taken beyond the boundaries of oneself, as the lover moulds and is moulded by the beloved. And whilst O'Siadhail's articulation of love is earthed and rooted in the everyday, the physical, the ordinary rhythms of life, here and there it offers glimpses of the transcendent Other. This sense of paradox is a motif which runs through all the love poetry. It is also at the heart of his poetic language. A lyrical poet unafraid of intense emotion, O'Siadhail is also an accomplished technician: in his craft as poet, we see the perfect blend of gift and discipline. His poems model the unobtrusive but rigorous constraints of an imaginative structure that allows the voice to soar.

1) Grace and Destiny

The poems which chart the beginnings of love ponder what is perhaps O'Siadhail's most striking cluster of paradoxes: the way in which love is both gift and pledge, covenant as well as desire, an unexpected, unearned grace which is predicated on the sense that one's love is a destiny. The poems about falling in love are suffused with a sense of amazement, of wonder at the grace of finding and being found by love. 'Out of the Blue', a poem from an earlier collection, captures O'Siadhail's sense of the sheer blind luck of it all – 'the quirk of fortune' which steers lovers together –

> I am still after many years
> baffled that the needle's gift dipped in my favour.
> Should I dare to be so lucky?'[5]

Threaded through this and other poems is the shadow side of this overwhelming sense of good fortune – the shiver of the unthinkable missing:

> Think that I might never have happened on you ...
> Supposing ...
> I'd faltered or somehow failed to recognise
> My counter-face .... ('Healing', 16).

And yet for all the sense of gratuity, the arbitrary good luck involved in falling in love O'Siadhail is also very aware of individual agency – the choosing, the receiving, the consenting to 'foolish love'. And it is a real choice which it is possible to imagine going a different way.

In 'Out of the Blue', this kind of alternative possibility – the dread imagined missing which heightens the sense of giftedness – is expressed in the image of the compass needle wavering then fixing on its pole: the hesitation, then the resolution. Articulated is both the sense of the arbitrary, precarious giftedness of love and the individual's responsibility to choose, to respond, to take hold of love and allow it to take root.

For all this sense of the huge luck involved in finding one's match in love, there is, in O'Siadhail's poetry, an equally strong sense of the inevitability of it all, the feeling that one has simply met one's destiny, come home. The opening poem in the collection *Love Life* is structured on the metaphor of archery, the homing of the poem's title referring both to the power and directness of an arrow aimed straight at its target and to the unswerving straightforwardness of the lover's desire. It captures both in theme and in sound the 'longbow years of longing', the long, aching vowel sounds of this opening line echoing the heaviness, the yearning of the waiting. Tension gathers into the more focused rhythms of the rest of the first section of the poem, the 'tenser stretch, fiercer shoot' which culminates in the simplicity and candour of the final line's brief vowels, 'My life takes aim for you' ('Homing', 11).

In 'For Real' (14), O'Siadhail follows in theme, language, and form, the trajectory of a love which moves from oblique, reflective wonder to the directness, simplicity, and certainty of reciprocal passion. The poem begins with an open-ended musing:

> A first gazing at you unawares.
> Wonder by wonder my body savours
>
> The conch-like detail of an ear,
> An amethyst ring on your finger.

As the poet goes on to meditate on his desire, the language, rhythm, rhyme, and imagery becomes increasingly simple and direct, slack desire gradually grows taut, focussed, more urgent, the meandering, unobserved gaze becomes the demand of the mutual gaze and its confident, closing declaration with the absolute certainty of its insistent beat carries the total certainty of a child's nursery rhyme:

> Milk and honey, spice and wine.
> I'm your lover. You are mine.

This sense of the inevitability of love is sometimes expressed in the wonder of genetic fluke. In 'Candle' (15) O'Siadhail employs a metaphysical conceit that imagines the slow evolution of genetic coding with its billions of choices and matchings over millennia conspiring to create the perfect combination of genes that constitute precisely *this* woman, so perfectly formed to be his beloved that she is for him archetypal, all that he could want in a woman:

> I think I've fallen in love again with Eve
> Who coded your genes so perfectly for me

The danger of a lover's narcissism – the whole history of genetics has been working towards making a woman just right for him – is transcended by the generosity of the tribute, the overwhelming tone of gratitude and wonder. There is humility here rather than entitlement, devotion, not self importance:

> Amazed once more I hardly dare to believe
> I fall heir to whatever you choose in me;
> Fluke and mould of planned unplanned precision.

The paradox of love is repeated through oxymoronic juxtapositions: love is both total luck and the result of decades of shaping, utterly unexpected but equally the experience of arriving home with a sense of belonging so completely experienced that it feels inevitable.

2) Ecstasy and Everyday

If tradition expects love poetry to articulate for us the intensity, excitement, and ecstasy of falling in love, O'Siadhail's love poetry certainly fulfils this brief. He is a master at conveying the delights of erotic desire and writes about sexual love in so many of its moods – the urgency of longing, the playfulness, intensity, abandon, abundance, and delirium of passion, the glaze and doze of its surfeit. 'Exposé', a poem composed in three line stanzas, is a version of *terza rima*, whose interweaving rhyme scheme creates echoes and resonances that are often apprehended subliminally. This interlocking structure reflects the erotic play between lovers and the playful overthrow of mind by body as the lure of bodily pleasure seduces the mind's habitual reign into a happy abdication. Here, metre echoes passion's rhythm in both its languorous sensuality and intent urgency. Lines of long, sonorous vowels,

> mute beguilements of attire,
> Soft options of *yes's* and *no's*

are followed by the more hurried urgency of a passion that is eager for action:

> Scatter every slither of clothes.
> Fetish trail. Pell-mell libido.

The staccato of the repeated 's' sounds, the pressure of the hard consonants, the brevity of most of the vowel sounds all contribute to an impression of building speed and pressure, which carries some of the weight of the mounting sexual tension. It is a poem containing numerous echoes – mellowing and meltdown, glazing and glisten – as if its very language is echoing the kind of lover's dialogue that is enacted here. And yet it is largely a wordless dialogue, filled with sounds that, like sweet nothings and the slipping off of clothes, are beyond the scope of articulate speech – murmurings, mute beguilements, babbles, and purrs. The mind is uncrowned, the body follows its own rhythms which climax in the 'nerve-blitz and spirit-bond' of consummation.

It is clear from his work that O'Siadhail loves the sounds of things, and no surprise, then, that another poem about sexual passion uses the conceit of a musical instrument – a concertina – to capture the delights, the dance, the game, and the abandon of sexual delight. Like Hopkins, O'Siadhail is not afraid to take risks with his metaphors, and in 'Concertina' (22), he uses both the physical movement of the 'squeeze box' and its gypsy-like gaiety to capture a more public, even raucous kind of celebration of passion.

In O'Siadhail's poetry, there is no sense of the privileging of either body or soul. The person who is spirit, mind, and memory is equally body, flesh, and bone – and gloriously so. Both physical and spiritual are celebrated, both are loved, both bring delight; the one an elucidation of the other: 'I kiss in your flesh your spirit's kiss' ('Homing', 12). This is a love poetry without dualism, an astonishingly integrated articulation of the person.

But it is in his integrated vision of love that O'Siadhail's greatest contribution to the oeuvre of love poetry may be located. Not only does he write great poetry about falling in love, he is equally interested in exploring the wonder of everyday love, of a partnership that matures and grows older, that lasts long enough to celebrate the settled middle years beyond the intensity of first passion. Byron and Heaney – and with them, the accumulated poetic tradition – clearly believed that love of the everyday variety is too prosaic to be the stuff of poetry. And indeed, in the English tradition at any rate, the novel has been the preferred medium for exploring the vicissitudes of married love. One of O'Siadhail's major achievements as a poet is his ability to celebrate the everydayness of love in poetic form, and to articulate the ecstasy, the self-transcendence possible in the ordinary rhythms of life through the constraining freedoms of poetry.

One domestic theme explored by O'Siadhail is that of building a home together, and the ways in which a couple inhabit a space and make it their own. 'Dwelling' (44) is a poem in three parts, two sonnets book-ending a series of tercets with a complex rhyme scheme. The middle poem is composed of seven brief stanzas of three lines each. Each tercet echoes the haiku form with its strong, visual image evoking much of the meaning like this:

> Season by season
> Slopes of light that home
> Our daily rondo

Or this:

> Of suns that crimson
> The sea-urchin's dome
> In our gable window.

The classical haiku is required to be self-contained and of course these individual tercets flow into each other. But each contains a striking visual image which evokes both a sense of the passage of time, the seasons of a love, and also the familiar protectiveness of a long-inhabited home. Like the lovers, each has a strong individual impact but they need each other to complete their meaning. O'Siadhail is working to a demanding pattern of rhyming here: the first and third lines of each of the seven tercets is a full rhyme; the words at the end of each middle line of each tercet rhyme according to a more complex patterning. So, for example, the first and last middle lines end with 'home' and 'dome', echoing the oyster motif of enwombed treasure that is inscribed throughout the poem. Not only do their matching rhymes situated near either end of the poem create a sense of enclosure, but their paired meaning evokes a sense of splendid domesticity, which is wonderfully echoed in the closing sonnet's final couplet:

> In the clammy ear of a mollusc oceans swell;
> Grit that sands and pearls our chosen shell.

In reminding us of the biblical parable of the man who sells everything he owns for the sake of the great pearl his heart desires, the central image structure of this poem suggests how O'Siadhail hints at the transcendent joy possible within something as domestic as making a home together.

Part of this domesticity treasured by O'Siadhail's is the joy of hospitality, celebrated in poems like 'Guests' (46). This poem's moves in three parts from an intensely private sense of home, likened as image piles upon image to a secret 'dugout, lair, fort and den' which then responds to the deeper instinct for inviting others in. This transformation reaches its peak in the middle of the middle stanza with its 'boisterous humour' and all the 'din and mischief of fun'. In the final section, the lovers are left alone once again and the poem reverts to a series of rhyming couplets: somehow the opening out has reinforced the twosome, made it richer, deeper, yet more intimate.

O'Siadhail also uses a very prosaic image of home and space to explore love's maturing in another poem. In 'Settlement' (65) it is the floorboards which offer the metaphor for seasoning love in a wonderfully allusive array of images of floorboards expanding and contracting and gradually settling down into a kind of smoothness as they lie side by side. In this homely image of the way two lovers come to fit each other – 'seasoned as cedars of Lebanon' – the reference to the Song of Songs reminding us of another love which celebrates erotic desire and the soul's longing for God.

In 'Weathering' (73) O'Siadhail puzzles over a related theme which, whilst not dominant, is threaded through the love poems over the years: how is it that two people who love and trust each other so completely are still able to inflict such hurt on each other? Like many of the poems in *Love Life*, 'Weathering' is structured on images taken from the world of sailing, an increasingly rich source of metaphor in O'Siadhail's work. How is it, he asks, that just when all seems plain sailing, a gust can get up as if from nowhere and one finds oneself battling a storm? O'Siadhail is fascinating when exploring the squalls and miscommunications of love. And in a love poetry unburdened by the demands of perfection of Romantic expectation, the wounds borne in the course of learning to love, far from signalling the end of love's idyll, serve only to make love stronger.

3) Freedom and Discipline

If one of the major distinctions of O'Siadhail's love poetry is that he charts the course of a love that endures, he also offers insights into what lies behind this kind of achievement. In

'Ceremony', for example, he writes about the kind of attentiveness brought to a Friday evening when husband and wife would dress up just for each other:

> wooers tending the smallest need
> We talked as though we rarely met
> Allowing ceremony undo the hex
> Of everydayness (81)

In the second section of this poem, O'Siadhail juxtaposes this with a series of examples of art that achieves greatness through sheer hard work and attention to detail – an actor repeating lines over and over; an acrobat who must tumble and tumble before metamorphosing into the 'smiling dancer on the rope', the pianist who must spend hours and years on finger drills before 'the encore and the low bow'. O'Siadhail is here asking us to reflect on the sheer determined and sometimes painful toil through 'hell and high water', 'thick and thin', the 'refusal to give up or in' that is known to both lover and artist. Both art and love require sustained attentiveness, and both, we are reminded, require serious discipline. From this comes the 'strange freedoms of discipline' that 'pirouette in the glory of an instant'. The apparently effortless joy, of this 'harnessed catharsis' is at the heart of one of O'Siadhail's most recurring paradoxes.

Throughout his poetry, the paradox of love's constraints and love's freedom is expressed implicitly through its use of poetic form: love (and poetry) are experienced as both artless and yet a kind of discipline, liberating and binding. The accessibility and emotional transparency of the love poetry ensures that the poet does not draw attention to its considerable technical virtuosity. Indeed, the skill of the performance – as with the concert pianist, as with the acrobat and the actor – is that it all seems so effortless, so natural. But behind this lies a sustained and highly disciplined attentiveness to language. 'Homing', for example, effectively employs a technique used regularly by O'Siadhail, that of a poem in three, sometimes four, sections, each a varied form. This allows the poem to consider a subject from a number of different perspectives, to turn the subject and contemplate it from a new angle. Throughout 'Homing', the meaning is of course carried not just through the sense of the words, but also in their sounds. The rhyme scheme – as often in O'Siadhail's poetry – repays attention. So, for example, in the second section, the delight of consummation is carried partly by a rhyme scheme that mirrors the intimacy of the coupling: the two central lines match in their final half rhymes, 'relish' and 'outlandish', the lines on either side of them also match as do the ones outside of them – the first and last lines:

> O Eros ravish and enlarge us. ...
> The arrow of our time discharges.

It is as if the rhyme scheme is forming a kind of nest with a series of layers protecting the intimate passion being expressed at its heart. This nesting pattern runs throughout the poem. In the first stanza, it divides the verse into two sections. In the third and final retrospective section of 'Homing', the rhyme scheme arches over the whole poem. In four brief stanzas comprising twelve lines altogether, the first line rhymes with the last line, the second line with the penultimate line and so on until the two lines in the heart of the poem meet – and rhyme – 'kiss' and 'Salmacis'. Dylan Thomas delighted in this kind of technical accomplishment. It is an utterly unobtrusive kind of virtuosity, often unnoticed, but it makes its own kind of statement. Not only does it add to the meaning of this poem – here perhaps conveying the coil of desire in the first stanza, the protective nesting of sexual intimacy in the second, and the spiral of memory in the third – but it also embodies an argument that is implicit throughout the love poetry: love is both gift and discipline. The lyrical voice which seems so artless is actually highly crafted, the word which seems so natural as to be 'given' may well be the product of not inconsiderable poetic labour. Likewise, the love which feels like pure gift in its luxurious expansiveness is also the result of years of choosing to live by the covenants and disciplines of love.

Sometimes this paradox of freedom and discipline is expressed through comparison with the training and formation of the religious life. O'Siadhail reflects on the way that the daily rhythm of loving – like the daily rhythm of the cloister – gathers into the habit of loving and takes root in the 'sweet discipline' of the 'contented anchorite' ('Ten to Seven', 58). The domestic images of husband and wife at home following their daily routine – 'life's canonical rhythm' – or sitting in an evening reading quietly together parallel those of the actor, the acrobat, the pianist mentioned earlier. Much less strenuous images to be sure, they nevertheless suggest the more mellow side of discipline, the formation of habit.

> Gladly I bend to the rule.
> A monk in me has grown to fit his habit.

The allusion to the cloister gestures again towards the commitment of covenant, the wholeheartedness of the one who gives up everything for what is infinitely precious, and its fruits – the 'steady passion', the 'clearheaded joy' ('Voyage', 40) are once more articulated as paradox. As art and love are paralleled in O'Siadhail's work, so are love and the spiritual quest. Far from seeing everyday love as too mundane for poetry, O'Siadhail unveils the drama of the 'infinite moment' ('Ceremony', 82), the 'all for this' which we seek in art, in love, in God.

4) Self and Other

> Gratuitous, beyond our fathom, both binding and freeing,
> This love re-invades us, shifts the boundaries of our being.

These lines capture something fundamental about O'Siadhail's view of the way love overwhelms us repeatedly and, in the course of its occupation, changes us, constantly shaping and re-shaping the very core of who we are. His poetry of love returns again and again to the way in which one loses oneself in love only to find not only one's self, but one's many selves and the seemingly inexhaustible array of personas of the beloved. To be open to love is to be open to transformation. O'Siadhail's sense of the self is at once very particular and highly fluid: there is a strong sense of the particularity of the self, both the lover's and the beloved's, but also a fascination with the way in which these boundaries blur and shift in the heat of the intense identification of erotic desire and also in the gentle decades long weathering of a shared life. However well the beloved is known, he or she always remains other, fundamentally unfathomable, still a mystery after decades of intimacy.

In his poem, 'Play', the poet invokes the beloved: 'You, my all in one, my one in all', delighting in the way that this one woman can be all women to him, that refracted through her particularity is a dizzying range of womanly roles.

> Coy, bold, knowing, insolent, outré
> Madam, goddess, nymph, vamp, flirt;
> Play each woman you know how to play. (32)

> The shock to find so many *yous* in you
> And still refind the *you* who chooses me. ('Filling in', 26)

Who one loves and is loved by deeply shapes, shifts, and defines the contours and boundaries of one's being, and in the depth of intimacy a myriad selves are discovered and revealed. Incidentally, the misogynistic reductionism often associated with the clichéd stereotyping of woman as either goddess or whore, is here subverted in the delighted celebration that one woman can be so many things and that the role play is as much for her own delight as that of her lover's. Through love, the boundaries of one's own gender are blurred and enlarged in the 'misty integration' that awakens 'my female being' ('Complementarity', 17) and in 'La Difference', the poet explores the way in which male and female may blunder through the clash of repeated misunderstandings to a 'sense of common gender', each learning to inhabit a world beyond the particularity of male and female: 'Woman me as I am manning you' ('Poems', 191). This transgendering of love comes to a humourous ecstatic ending in another poem:

> Inward and airborne,
> a soprano is gliding in my womanish heart. ('In the End', 191)

The identities one discovers in love are never separable from a wider social world. Although one often has the sense in O'Siadhail's love poetry of an intensity à deux, there is never the sense of the lovers sandbagged up against the world – or at least never for very long. Threaded throughout the love poems and their sense of the selving that is one of the great gifts of love is the assumption that sharing one's friends is all part of a web of discovery and identity. And in the presence of strangers, the lover is taken aback by

> A surprise role shift,
> A different demeanour

that reveals some new detail,

> ... sides never shown,
> Faces unseen before. ('Watch', 52)

Sneaking a 'voyeur's glance' at his wife as she teaches, unaware that he is there, he glimpses

> sides of you I rarely see ...
> you'll tot and tick off, doling out your praise ...
> steady performer, gently in charge of it all. ('Mistress', 90)

The delight in the other is not confined to how she relates to him: each and any morsel of discovery is treasured to add to the apparently inexhaustible store of knowing the beloved.

In 'Selves', a poem in three sonnets, O'Siadhail describes this kind of discovery of the self – one's own and ones beloved's – in terms of the metaphor of theatre, the 'shuffle of what we'd yet become' a kind of 'improvisation, a plot still in the making'. And again, the absolute reciprocity of the boundary shifting dimension of love is expressed:

> Long steady dialogue of gain and surrender,
> Theatre in the round, course grain of living
>
> Where both can be a borrower and a lender,
> Ourselves as much in taking as in giving.
>
> Mix of endless mongrel *you's* and *me's.*
> Cast and ragbag of our hybrid psyches. ('Selves', 83)

It is a poem that charts the surprises of a maturing marriage: the script is not what one had expected, 'the selves we thought we'd be' usurped: 'Am I the surprise for you that you're for me?' And yet through all this change and its sometimes dizzying drama, the underlying note of 'ripe delight' as the lovers slip from role to role and the fundamental acceptance of the whole range of the selves uncovered as summed up in the final imperative: 'Love my glory. Love my feet of clay.'

In the poem 'Odyssey' (104), O'Siadhail gently mocks this dimension of role play as he describes his own tendency to don yet another persona depending on where he has just been on his travels:

> Post-Japan it's tofu, rice and chopsticks.
> *Und so* suddenly I recover a German in me.

On his return home, he is aware of his wife's half amused, half perplexed response to his intense identification with each world he inhabits and his reluctance to let it go:

> I thrived a little longer in my different skin,
> Still sweet on worlds I couldn't yet let go.

In this poem, the kind of improvisation, the trying on of new selves, happens beyond the orbit of the love relationship; the beloved is the compass point that does not shift, the still point at the centre of the world: 'In all shape-shifting I return to you.'

One further variation on O'Siadhail's fascination with the questions of self and identity concern the might-have-beens: which selves might have been called forth had one ended up with a different partner. One poem that reflects on this in retrospective mood is 'Stains' (76). The poet and his wife are lying hand in hand one morning in bed; a stain on the bedroom ceiling is the catalyst for a meditation on the arbitrariness of the way life's patterns fall.

> With someone else who knows who
> We'd become: another map,
> Unlike patterns, a different stain.

Again, the implications of choosing are pondered: in choosing *this*, other choices are left behind. And yet it is in choosing the particularity of *this* woman, *this* love, that the particularity of the pattern of one's life and, more deeply, the contours of who one comes to be, are defined: identity, selfhood, is, within the world of O'Siadhail's poetry, unimaginable outside of the context of love's covenants: '*Tell me your love. I'll tell you who you are.*'

The crimson thread that runs through *Love Life* is taken from the Song of Songs and alludes beyond the Bible to a tradition of erotic love as metaphor for the love of God – the love of the mystics, of Francis and Clare. In O'Siadhail's poetry, love whether in erotic or domestic manifestation is seen as part of this same trajectory of human yearning and fulfilment in love. The self is drawn beyond itself into the beloved and once again in O'Siadhail's poetry we find the gesture towards the boundless Other:

> What infinite arousal are we made for? ...
> Native of Eden, I ache for resurrection. ('Making Up', 30)

5) The Crimson Horizon

O'Siadhail's poetry is a tribute to a lifetime's love which is gloriously unfinished. As I have argued in this chapter, it challenges and extends the genre of love poetry in the range and scope of its subject matter. Its mood is largely one of celebration and gratitude, yet it also contains piercing notes of elegy and loss. Towards the end of *Love Life*, the perspective is both retrospective and forward looking, the crimson thread of early passion is now the crimson moment of the sumac leaf's fall.

In 'Parkinson's', the poet describes how the onset of the illness in his wife brings yet another shift in the process of loving. It is a stark and beautiful poem – unflinching from this new reality, the erosion of physical confidence, the weariness with the shaking – all of which must call forth new ways to pay tribute to his love, his now 'aspen mistress'. There is ironic reversal here as well: the one who has always been the steady one now shakes, whilst he of the 'jittery hand' that spilled half her coffee when first they met is the one who must now reassure:

> What can I do? These arms enfold you.
> No matter what, I have and hold you.

It is in this final sequence of *Love Life* that we find some of its most moving poems, the poems that have to come to terms with the prospect of loss. 'At Sea' is one of the shortest poems in *Love Life*. Each of its brief stanzas is a haiku built round an image of loss, of aloneness:

> Jets whine overhead.
> Who will be lonely for whom?
> One silver gull cries.

> Yoked we throw our light.
> That one will be the first to go
> A twin star untwinned

The lonely gull crying amidst the noise and busyness of the skies, one star quietly extinguished, the other left alone in the dark expanse of the universe. Heartbreaking images and yet precise, clear-eyed evocations of what it might feel like when one's lifetime's love has died.

These questions are explored more expansively in 'Question', a poem whose gentleness and tenderness is reminiscent of D.H. Lawrence's beautiful late poems contemplating his own death. 'It's so good that we are two' becomes, in the second stanza, 'So backbreaking to walk alone' and then a kind of acceptance in the final line: 'In the shadow an angel gathers in.' The next poem in this sequence, 'If', broaches the delicate subject of what would happen if one were to go first: would the other fall in love again? It is in this kind of exchange perhaps that O'Siadhail's emotional daring as a poet is at its most obvious. His wife's reply is not without humour:

> A slow chiselling realism
> In your reply: enough
> To shape one stone.

The poet's own response is perhaps a fitting epitaph to the love poetry as a whole:

> But me ...
> I don't know how to know.
> Trusting hues of your prism,
> If I was so lucky,
> I think I'd dare.

What a wonderful tribute to a life's love: the experience of loving this one woman through a life-time has been so good, so rich that perhaps if one were lucky enough, one would dare to love again.

4 | Human Connections

Sarah Kafatou

Human connections are at the heart of the work of Micheal O'Siadhail. Personal and private to begin with, they eventually bind communities, generations, and potentially all of us in the weave of our ever-evolving history. His poetry is an ongoing celebration of these crucial, yet fragile bonds and a meditation on their meaning.

O'Siadhail writes of his own work, 'Gradually, I became fascinated by trust. It seemed to be the oil and hinge of our world.' Trust in one's own self, one's capabilities, one's life projects is the theme of 'Sunflower', the very first poem of *The Leap Year*, the first of the books in his collection of work from 1975-95. At issue for the poet is the courage to commit his life to his art:

> Tell me it's all worth this venture,
> Just the slightest reassurance,
> And I'll open a bloom, I'll flower
> At every chance.

The source of reassurance, of encouragement, as it were, of the psychological sunshine in which creativity in life and art can flourish, is what the psychoanalyst D.W. Winnicott was thinking of when he spoke of a quiet, accurate, benevolent attention as a 'holding environment'. We encounter such a source, such holding, in a poem from O'Siadhail's later book *A Fragile City*, which is centrally concerned with the tissue of community. In 'Sunlight', the poet watches a mother watching her children swim:

> An abandon and weightlessness of concern. Pure
> undergoing. Almost as if they float in the matrix
> of her being, drifting in passivities of creation. ...
> She's so full of answers before they ever call.

To notice such things, indeed to be oneself both sunlight and sunflower, to float and to be borne along in the flow of a lifetime, is the challenge taken up by this poet.

The theme of interweaving, of weaving and being woven, is also there in his work from the beginning. Like the mother watching her children, standing watch over the springs of selfhood and of creativity, other women close to him have contributed to the warp and weft of his developing personhood:

> The two or three, who somehow drew
> My threads together, wove my cloth.
>
> A wonderful cloth, my shirt of linen,
> My chequered gift, a self they've woven,
> This shirt that's closer than the bone,
> The bright women of my world have given.

Soon after these very first poems dedicated to the grounds of personal being and of creative capability comes, following the order of O'Siadhail's collected first two decades of work, a poem about love in marriage. The relationship represented here is a matter of experiential complexity, of pied beauty. Just as the rafters and beams of an old wooden house would sense the shifts as they warp and settle, so do married lovers come to know the

> strains and stresses, slow
> Givings and takings, the touch and go
> Of our attunements and compromise.

Reading, one can almost feel the supports groaning and easing into and out of place.

Importantly and appropriately, it is in this poem too that the theme of separate individuality first sounds, the linebreak underlining and emphasizing the sense:

> Somehow we're stronger
> In separateness.

A theme which is taken up in the next poem, with its telling off-rhyme of *want* with *different* as it depicts a pair of circus horses:

> They seem to want
> To veer apart as though two different
> Voices called.

The experience of joining together and pulling apart will be revisited in a later poem whose driving metaphor is that of an awakening automobile engine. In 'Setting Out', the challenge of coordination, of separate elements functioning together, is addressed on multiple levels – sexual, psychological, and social:

> The pedal gingered,
> the chassis shudders in resurrection.
>
> A flutter or two before cams and cranks
> co-operate.

The sentence following this is crucially significant:

> Pivoting on neutral, we modulate
> from gear to gear, from mood to mood.

This sentence brings the insight that unimpeded motion in a context of attunement, the freedom to move in emotional harmony from 'mood to mood', is key to a good relationship. With it comes an elated sense of freedom and access to a mutual future:

> Mention the spell of a butterfly throttle —
> the future opens.

Decades later that future, now the present, is still as fresh and alive as though just beginning:

> Come again glistening from your morning shower
> Half-coquettishly you'll throw
> Your robe at me calling out 'Hello! Hello!'
> ... Jaunty, brisk, allegro,
> Preparing improvisations of yet another day,
> As on our first morning twenty-seven years ago.

Nor will the advent of illness, later still, destroy it:

> I take whoever you are
> Or come to be
> Till one of us perish
> To love, to cherish.

After personal flourishing and love in marriage, the next theme to be addressed by O'Siadhail is work. Work, in the first place, as chosen work, the vocation and voluntary labour of the artist. Even work that is chosen may be tedious and draining:

> so cruelly you've looted
> my meagre legacy of years.

Yet such work, demanding though it may be, is willingly undertaken, indeed passionately sought:

> Rather you than your counterpart:
> a tediousness turning all to dust.

A less inspiring sort of work is wage labour. The hard work of industrial society is represented by the time clock, the conveyor belt, the paycheque, the fatigue, the danger, the comradeship, and the dignity of labour in an Oslo brewery – 'A world always hung between a hell and heaven'.

Even harder work is the subject of a poem commemorating the suffering and accomplishment of the quarriers and navvies who built the massive outstretched stone arms of Dún Laoghaire pier:

> those unnamed, who slaved with caissons, shunted
> wagonloads of boulders. The fittest survived outbreaks

> of cholera, riots, strikes; a thousand plus they reckon
> squatted on Dalkey common, bullied rocks from the quarry.
> In their embrace I consecrate a morning to their memory.

After work, the next themes to be rung are friendship – often an occasion for gratitude and celebration – and father-to-son, brother-to-brother bonds. Friendship may be an easy relationship between two people with 'nothing to prove'. The images of fostering sunshine and of buoyancy that permeate 'Sunflower' and 'Sunlight' recur in a poem about intimacy in friendship:

> we unwind, stretch in the light of
> Each other's sun. ...
> We've shot our long wedge-shaped roots
> To the water plane.
> ... No wonder a fluid runs from root
> To root, a conduit of *eau de vie*.

Sadly, some friendships do not last, as noted in 'Salute', where two former friends exchange a perfunctory greeting in the street. A broken connection can be worse than none at all:

> ... we're more than strangers,
> as if old intimacies come between us.

As long as the quarrel is unresolved one would not have things otherwise, although the broken edges grate:

> No, not regret, more a chagrin
> That a street's chance salute contains
> All of what was once affection.

In this summing-up we hear, faint but recognisable in the background, the voice of Edith Piaf singing *Non, Rien de rien, Non, Je ne regrette rien*. Discord there may be, but harmony is the stronger element in this poetry. Indeed, so strong and vital are his enduring friendships that O'Siadhail will later, looking back upon his life and contemplating his eventual death, find it in himself to write

> Valhalla's vivid and endless carouse ...
> Promises of a father's many-mansioned house.
> ... For me just my friends.

The son's bond to his father is multivalent, both because the authority relationship shifts with the years as the two become peers, 'our courses parallel, plot to converge on a horizon', and because many a mentor may step into a father's role:

> There was father after father after you.

The connection to the father undergoes metamorphosis. More troublingly, the bond between brothers is labile, jeopardized:

> Almost familiar but still vigilant,
> we zigzag. A gentle dig, a careful hint.
> ... Anxious still, we're probing one another.

Yet this is a bond that may be refreshed by mutual recognition and acknowledgement, permitting a mutation of what had been simply kinship into friendship:

> Oh, let's not waste this precious time.
> I won't mince words. You're my brother!
> ... A friendship thickens water into blood.

These poems of man-to-man connections to father and brother appear in the book called *Belonging*, from 1982. It is in this book too that the political dimension first makes its presence felt. One poem is dedicated to prisoners of conscience. The one that follows it is the manifesto 'Pacifist', in which the stresses of belonging while keeping separate are revisited in the context of watching a parade:

> I hear the drummed question.
> My pulse loves its answer;
> My mind is checking my foot.

If the poet, 'though no lover of wrongs', will not join the march, it is not simply because his head has mastery over his heart, and also not because he prefers to hold himself apart. Rather it is because his heart, less impulsive than it is empathic, has the last word:

> Grappling an enemy, I'd see
> everything through his eye,
> desire only his world. ...
> Let the drummer pass by.

This is a political poem at heart, even though the particular context – presumably Irish – has deliberately been left vague. Once the political dimension has been let in there is no excluding it. In fact the next thing to happen is that particular historical contexts begin to assert themselves, adding moral weight to the argument and extending it in space and time:

> A friend from Maryland had once described
> Seeing in his grandfather's cellar rusted irons
> That had fettered a chain-gang of black slaves.

That weight is a burden that will continue, book by book, to grow. In time, voices from the Middle Passage will swell a chorus of suffering that includes among others the Armenians being lashed toward Syria and the famine victims of Skibbereen. But not yet.

What comes next is a simple appreciation, a savouring of our common daily life. In 'Streetscene' the poet sets out to be, but cannot really be, a detached observer: 'The aim fidelity, a perfect wide-angled focus'. Despite this aim his eye is continuously drawn to one particular passer-by or another. Not only that, but he himself is drawn into the scene and becomes attuned to its emotional resonance. His word-music attests to this, the drear alliteration of d, t, and s, expressive of a shut-away existence, giving way to skipping, tripping, enlivening ch and tt sounds before subsiding to a sh:

> Hell must be dumb, a terrible dank cellar
> of wonder bottled up, shuttered from the sun,
> tight-lipped, tongue-tied, the word slips memory.

> ...a child chases
> a coin pirouetting over a gutter; touching each other
> two greying men swap hush-hush information.

It's an experience of entertained immersion that will be revisited in 'Morning on Grafton Street', where the poet feels swept up in

> the grandeur, the melancholy,
> ever-new carnival of man

and in 'Leisure', where he confesses

> I bump into an acquaintance and begin to apologise.
> 'Taking a break,
> Be hard at it tomorrow.'
> Puritan me, so afraid of paradise.

The poet as participant observer amid the casual crowd experiences a sense of flow. Not that state of concentration in 'flow', vividly described by the psychologist Mihaly Csikszentmihalyi, which characterizes highly skilled and creative people when meeting a challenge that tests the limit of their powers; rather a relaxed sense of free time, of holiday such as people may enjoy when they allow themselves to join a nondirectional stream of anonymous passers-by (no parade!) and

> stroll here infatuated, self-communing,
> lost in the lyric flow of street.

It is only natural that a poem in celebration of such leisure soon be followed by a meditation on pure play. In 'Ode to a Juggler' a street performer's 'untroubled faraway look of concentration' as she maintains her tennis balls in the air is honoured by the poet's rhyme of *motion* with *devotion*:

> Or are they stars held in motion,
> Not by gravity but by devotion
> To a great god of fun?

At stake is much more than entertainment. The point is a deep one: that not the goal, but the way is all, the playing is all. O'Siadhail as an artist is seeking that stillness within motion, that equilibrium within time that sanctifies the contingency of life and makes joy a possibility:

> I proclaim a motto theme, naming in ecstasy
> mysteries of time. Always I crave the centre—
> serenity suffused by passion, endless and complete.

It is by this measure that he would assess his life. He finds his way to it in episodes that begin in childhood, cycling through a garden gate, staring out a window on a snowy day, or climbing over a stile:

> ...startled,
> a half-dazed witness to the majesty.

Somehow, something shines out of the commonplace, something handed down flares up. The result is a refinement of the whole texture of experience, as he writes in a poem for his mother:

> Every twitch, gesture
> remembers her in me.
> All blunted whetted,
> what smouldered burns.

O'Siadhail's collected earlier work is approaching the milestone of 'Autumn Report', a summing-up of his state of soul at 36, *nel mezzo del cammin di nostra vita*, the poem which stands at the end of his first five books. Overall, the balance is positive:

> I've never felt so near the centre
> of all that is.

His next book, *The Chosen Garden* of 1990, recapitulates 'a journey from the garden chosen for me by my parents, through boarding school' – at Clongowes, setting of the first section: 'youthful excesses, ideologies, despair, learning to love and reconnect with society, to the garden I'd chosen for myself'. In it he wakes to history as a potential source of meaning within the world's contingency:

> Are our days just moments that appear
> and disappear or is every act heir
> to an act, and time that gathering river
> where histories run? Wake up sleeper!

This awakening to an ongoing story comes to rescue the poet from an apathetic depression, a feeling of purposelessness, a waste of 'nothing done':

> a thwarted will,
> a clotted mind struggling to a standstill.

And just in time, since inspired moments of oneness with the world cannot be summoned at will and the poet may feel at a loss without them, as 'dark is darker after the light'. From now on, as foretold in 'Autumn Report', the complexities of history will weave themselves through and sustain the poet's work, prompting him to speak:

> history has
> accumulated this moment, now funnels through me
> the urge to utter.

Unnumbered forerunners, he realizes more and more as he goes, have set him on his way and given him a responsibility, a mission to fulfill. 'Steady as you go, you carry someone's beacon.' The role of the poet as bearer of a tradition is reaffirmed in the first poem of his next book, *The Middle Voice*:

> A signal boosted
> onwards. Pride and humility of a medium.

For he now has a sense of himself not only as a student of history but also as a participant in it, 'a voice in the middle between a generation fading out and one coming behind and into its own'.

The middle voice in grammar is a reflexive verb, neither active nor passive but something in between. Rather than succumb to depressive paralysis, but also without presuming to know too much, the poet takes up his role of transmitter as a kind of selfless responding, a mediation on behalf of others:

> A feeling of passivity, of handing over ...

> A watch of dependence, complete exposure,

> not even trying not to try to achieve.
> This work is a waiting ...

> The middle voice fading ...

The self-effacement of the artist as servant of a tradition is celebrated explicitly in a poem for the anonymous medieval scribes and illuminators who produced such work as the Book of Kells. Their hands inscribed their texts the way a ship ploughs the sea:

> A nothingness of ego. The hand worships
> By work ...

> Tell us the voyage is all.

Although the social role of the writer is brought forward, the importance of the personal and individual remains undiminished in *The Middle Voice*. There is a poem on the beginning of life, to a godchild:

> We bow ...
> between our thanks and trust

and so re-enter, what you
Rebecca still remember:
Eden of the eternal now.

This poem is followed by one on the end of life, in which not the 'eternal now' of the womb, but the wear and tear of time, its building up and breaking down, is the theme:

Outside was spring in the east;
your brow of fever still clammy in my fist,
as I gripped the hammer's haft, began to staple
a trellis to stay March's first caress,
fresh tendrils of clematis.

Life is ephemeral, belonging to time, and this is essential to its beauty, indeed to its reality. O'Siadhail puts this so:

At last I think I know
Half of what we love is love's fragility.

If this were not true, if the world were a static one, there could be no 'pivoting on neutral', no savouring of those open moments of possibility, those intimate moments of transition in human lives and relationships when the instant

pivots possibilities, mid-points,
diminished chords poised between tonalities.

The middle voice, the voice at midpoint, is pointing forward toward *Our Double Time*, the book most directly concerned with personal mortality. But before that comes a book that meditates on the bonds and separations, the values and limits of our necessary community: *A Fragile City*, from 1995.

With this book's very first poem, set in an airport departure lounge, we are in the world of the impersonal, the public, the potentially global. But what counts, still, even here, are particular and unique personal connections, 'all the meetings and farewells'. His awareness of the irreplaceability of each individual human life helps the political O'Siadhail, first met in 'Pacifist', not to shift too quickly from the particular to the general. It also enables him to keep his head in the presence of a too imperative ideology:

Cheap Chianti, candlelight, damp sugar-bowls,
A readiness to change a world half-understood.
No, nothing could ever again be the same.
Raise a mug of wine, a hymn to the proletariat ...
That chorus and I recall how our faces would blur
Into sameness.

With maturity comes not a repudiation, but a readjustment of the youth's compassionate wish to change the world:

Maybe I've learned to fear the sweeping chorus ...
I reach across those years to re-focus a dream

> Throwing its light again as our chorus fades.
> Each life is thickening into its own fabric.
> Every face so utterly itself. Alone. Unique.

Ambition is tempered with humility, and the poet responds to contemporary events with regret and dismay. 'News of a truce broken. More shootings.' He hears the news and writes in wondering sorrow of the warring of clan against clan. In his poem *blow* rhymes with *Romeo*, *hate* with *Juliet*.

He brings to intractable social problems the notion, not of a social utopia, but of a helping hand. Sometimes more may be possible, and that will be a theme of a later book, *Globe*, but here, in a poem about a homeless vagrant, shelter and comfort can be given and that is all. Nothing much is changed:

> One evening and again he's gone
> Without trace. No mendings. No rebirth.
> Tiny alleviations, something beautiful done.
> A caress on the face of the earth.

Far from trying to change the world, at this point the poet is still striving to understand how he himself has been shaped by particular others and to acknowledge what he owes them:

> Whatever I've become – courtesy
> Of lovers, friends or friends of friends ...
> You and you and you. My fragile city.

His next book, *Our Double Time*, written in large part at 50 and concerned with mortality, records his gratitude for life and his effort to accept – no, to embrace – what cannot be changed. The little sparrow, Piaf, is still singing in the background. In the light of potential loss, the best choice is to love all we can. The worst would be a premature, defensive closing down of the spirit:

> More than anything I think I dread
> The set jawbone of grim resignation.
> Nothing to expect. Nothing to discover.
> The sullen greyness of the living dead.
>
> I go when I go. Let me go a lover.

Our predicament is like music, like the improvisations of jazz, and as difficult to put into words. The deepest truth may lie in silence, that silence in which we are all embedded:

> I grow older and it seems the silence that surrounds
> Each tone is keener, the intensity between the sounds.

The rests between the sounds are as important as the sounds themselves. Like the boy on his bicycle to whom heaven suddenly seemed to open, the grown man may sometimes experience intimations of immortality:

A majesty and awe, but even more the wonder
That something is where nothing might have been.
Even in our brokenness a beyond is breaking in.

This 'beyond' is not the afterlife; it is to be sought on earth, within the here and now, in 'ordinary down-to-earthness, so heaven-minded'. There is no expectation of another life after death, although it is true of the dead that though they are gone our relationship with them continues, as the poet testifies in another poem for his mother:

I smile your smile and know how you were right.
In your absence never before so present in me.

An exploded star still travels down its light.

Included in such ongoing relationship are those lost ones we have known and also those whose lives affect us though we never knew them,

So loomed and knotted in a history,
Textures shuttled through in me.

O'Siadhail will go on to celebrate ever more individuals whom he never knew, but whose lives have made a difference to him. One, Etty Hillesum, in appearing here foretells the subject of the book he will write after this one:

No admittance to Jews. The air I breathe is mine.
That man cycling on Beethovenstraat,
His yellow star of David a crocus in the sunshine.

All those worries about clothing, about food.
I want my life to turn into one great prayer.
So happen what may, it's bound to be good.

A fine-grained message as wagon No. 12 careers
Towards Poland. Some farmer stoops to pick up
Her final postcard from those crammed years.

Hers was an interrupted life. But each of us, even those lucky ones never touched by discrimination or violence, comes to a moment where we stand in crosslight, 'the porch light picking up where the sunlight fades'.

In crosslight now all faces of my friends.

One friend in particular, a musician living with cancer, is the subject of the beautiful sequence 'Threshold'. One exquisitely tempered rhyme after another accompanies her as she struggles to experience her terminal condition in relation to the changing seasons, the recurrent cycle of nature:

Must it be so?
The long struggle to joy of a quartet's violin

> Wonders whether she'll make it to when the sumacs show
> Crimsons a summer's lushness has hidden within.

The end of life is inevitable, the turning of the seasons inexorable, but a word that recurs in the poems of this book is 'promise'. A promise is a test of oneself, a commitment to others, a determination to keep faith, a way into the future. The notion of promising comes up in 'Flightline', a poem about jazz:

> Saxman Keith Donald told me when the solo moves
> It's loose and certain as the promise of loves.

It appears again in 'Oak', a poem about enduring friendship:

> Double openness of growing side by side ...
> That first promise we keep for one another.

And it reappears, in an incomparably darker context, in O'Siadhail's next book, *The Gossamer Wall*:

> A promise to remember, a promise of never again.
> As never before we promise never again.

'Write and record. *Schreibt un farschreibt.*' Write, record and remember. The poet does his best to follow in the footsteps of first-hand witnesses to the Holocaust. Even at several removes it cannot have been easy for him and he must often have felt, as he writes apropos of the great poet Paul Celan, the 'burden of so much ash to bless'. Celan, like Primo Levi and Jean Améry a suicide, sometimes felt so oppressed that his gift seemed to die and *sink into the bitter well of his heart.*

Relief may be sought in the contemplation of resisters and helpers. O'Siadhail retells the story of the village of Le Chambon in Nazi-occupied France. Le Chambon, which centuries before had provided refuge for a thousand French Protestants fleeing for their lives after the revocation of the Edict of Nantes, sheltered and saved the lives of thousands of Jews.

> A city of refuge. A hamlet for waif and stray.
> But where else could they go? A Chambonais' shrug
> Plays down the dangers. We had to take them in.
> I couldn't close a door against a stranger's face.

What enables such a response? O'Siadhail turns to this question in *Globe*, where in the section 'Knot-Tying' he composes biographical portraits of exemplary people. Some are moral heroes who found ways of transcending their personal idiosyncracies and particular circumstances and so created new forms of leadership, new paradigms for collective action. They exemplify what has now come to be called social entrepreneurship, though O'Siadhail does not use this term: through their innovative thinking, dedication, integrity, and competence, political and social entrepreneurs provide new, effective, and reproduceable models for social intervention and problem-solving. In Le Chambon the pastor Andre Trocmé, not an exemplary person in every regard but a thoroughly principled pacifist, provided leadership that made a difference. A neighbouring village with a similar population responded to the crisis in an opposite way: 'Against the stranger's hand, Le Mazet's shut door.'

'To the hub's eye every spoke is an avenue.' Individuals sufficiently centred in themselves can pivot in the direction of positive change. Bartolomé de Las Casas, 'boat-rocker, whistle-blower', began as a holder of enslaved indigenous Americans but became a tireless advocate of their rights and chronicler of the injustices done them. Mohandas K. Gandhi, an Anglophile dandy with marked obsessive-compulsive traits, engaged in experiments with truth and found the courage to follow up on his discoveries. Jean Vanier, Canadian graduate of the British Naval College, chose rather than command a fleet to live as a friend with two severely retarded men. His brothers' keeper, 'more listening than wanting to do things for', he founded L'Arche, a network of over 100 special communities for developmentally disabled persons in countries around the world. Nelson Mandela, 'less sprinter than long-distance runner', grew into greatness on the basis of traits acquired early and cultivated wisely over time. He enjoyed success for which he had paid the price:

> A small village boy
> he'd whiten his hair with ash in imitation
> of his beloved father. Now parent to a nation.
>
> Under a frost of grey a wise smile creases.
> Yes, to father a country, but to have lost
> my children's laughter? I've crossed famous rivers.

Micheal O'Siadhail himself has come a long way. A devotion to his craft, a keen sense of direction, and a wide-open, wide-ranging, wondering gaze have taken him this far and will undoubtedly take him farther, to questions and resolutions as yet unimagined. A compassionate heart and firm moral compass have kept him to his path. Fortunately, as he once put it, 'I was a late starter ... . We never can arrive ... . I start and start and start again.'

5 | 'Letters from Assisi'

Maurya Simon

'Letters from Assisi'

(I) Francis to His Father

Father, if only you had understood
I craved to be the man of every hour —
All your ambition slept deep in my blood.

I loved the feel of silk, the touch of power,
To gossip, joke, outshine Assisi's cavaliers;
For all the talk of bird or flower

I had your merchant's will to vie. Two years
Caught a prisoner in Perugia, I was still
Half-aware I'd fought for a town's profiteers.

A ransom – then the homecoming. 'Is Francis ill
Or in love?' people asked, wondered why
I looked so distant; I did the parties until

Something snapped. Every stricken passer-by
Now fixed his stare on me, saying 'Francis,
All turns on you; Francis, look in my eye!'

There were riches in Apulia – I had lances,
Troubadour's songs to sing. I could forget.
But haunted daily by those strangers' glances,

I sold your bale of scarlet cloth to let
Some paupers feed. Father, you whipped me,
Branded me a madman; each time we met

You cursed, so I paid a down-and-out his fee
To bless me as a father, taunt your sorrow—

For I would outdo, best the world in poverty.
I was young and life tomorrow.
Already my followers scheme for a benefice;
The road seemed short – I could beg or borrow

Rags of humility, call your care avarice.
Time unlocks compassion's garden-gate;
Father, I bid you forgive my Judas kiss.

(II) Francis to Clare

My Clare, in years to come they'll
Puzzle over us! Francesco e Chiara—
I can almost hear them chuckle.
Let them wonder! If they don't know
That love's first sight can seal
A lifetime, how will they understand?
You came to me when I already
Was sworn to mistress poverty.
Saints carry their souls in lovely
Vessels, only iron wills have made
Our rule. There's a thousand ways
To know another; we may not share
The daily flittings of the mind and yet
Each alone in prayer acclaims this love,
Still in the cell of its first perfection.

(III) Francis to His Followers

You know the joy, the stigma we prophets wear—
Bat just an eyelid and all splinter newness of another
Reborn wisdom dims. Only a while, my brothers!
Although I do not see each knot in the net of time,

As any visionary tiptoes along the fringes of his sanity
To glimpse the image-god hidden in the thoughts of man,
As every mender of history's net takes up the strands,
I tied my love-knot, hitched a thread to the work.

Though it has been twenty years since Micheal O'Siadhail's superb epistolary poem, 'Letters from Assisi', appeared in his 1985 collection, *The Image Wheel*, this sequential dramatic monologue exhibits a timeless and lasting relevance (as do the truest and most memorable poems), retaining as it does all of its original, straightforward eloquence, persuasiveness, and power. In this tri-part poem, or triptych, O'Siadhail deftly charts, chronologically, the spiritual development and emotional journey of its protagonist and speaker, the beloved twelfth-thirteenth century Catholic saint, Francis of Assisi, presenting him in Part (I) as a son addressing his father, in Part (II) as a lover addressing his beloved, and in the final section (III) as an adult saint and 'prophet' addressing his followers (and, by extension, the poem's readers). Each section dramatizes different facets of this persona's character, while subtly revealing his gradual evolution from being an 'ordinary' son and citizen of the world, to becoming an extraordinary individual possessed of great empathy, uncanny wisdom, and a visionary's depth of spirit.

The poem is self-contained and self-sufficient: it does not need nor rely upon the reader's in-depth familiarity with the story of St. Francis to create its evocative meaning and to convey effectively its personal trajectory of transformation. For instance, the first section's allusions to Francis's two year imprisonment in Perugia, and his later 'riches in Apulia' and 'ransom', serve well to expand the exposition presented in earlier and subsequent stanzas – namely, they inform the reader that Francis was born into a well-to-do family, that he enjoyed in his youth 'the feel of silk, the touch of power', and that he suffered political oppression and then a 'homecoming', until (in stanza five) 'Something snapped.' (What a marvelous line enjambment precedes this rhetorically brilliant volta!)

Francis soon thereafter reveals the outward changes that accompany his internal change of heart and mind, as he addresses his father:

> I sold your bale of scarlet [ah, the most sensual and worldly of colors] cloth to let
> Some paupers feed.

He continues,

> Father, you whipped me,
> Branded me a madman; each time we met
>
> You cursed, so I paid a down-and-out his fee
> To bless me as a father, taunt your sorrow -
> For I would outdo, best the world in poverty.

These lines wonderfully enact the implicit tensions existing between this particular cloth merchant father and his rebellious, spiritually bent son, even as they also reflect the universal antipathy felt between fathers and sons in general. This section also reveals an underlying reason for Francis to defy his worldly destiny: so he might 'best' both the secular world and his wealthy father by becoming a Christian clergyman or 'father', thereby punishing the latter with the ironic sorrow of losing his son to the 'poverty' of his spiritual calling. His father's loss is underscored by Francis's determination to become his own man, and a similar sense of loss is later repeated and re-enacted in the son's realization (made in retrospect in the penultimate and final stanzas of this first section) that his youthful scorn towards his father has become tempered with compassion and remorse, for as he matures he realizes the enduring betrayal he has visited upon his father.

Whereas Part (I) of the poem is comprised of ten tercets (with an interlocking aba rhyme scheme, thus employing Dante's *terza rima*), which make a fitting vehicle for its narrative movement, Part (II) is more succinct, appearing as a single stanza, a 15-line 'sonnet', although one employing an irregular (or nonce) rhyme scheme. In this section, Francis directly addresses 'Clare', a young heiress from Assisi who eventually becomes a novice and later a Benedictine nun, and it is interesting to note how the tenor of his voice shifts here (from an earlier seriousness) to a tone of teasing insouciance and canny awareness – thus, this new tone reflects his attentiveness both to how the world perceives the two 'lovers' and to the possibilities for spiritual love that they might enjoy separately and yet 'together' in their devotion to God. Also apparent in this section of the poem is Francis's assertive and authoritative tone, his self-assuredness apropos his spiritual calling and life-long religious commitment. He has gladly accepted and embraced his fate of being 'sworn to mistress poverty', rather than to a mistress of flesh and blood, and he is aware of the 'iron wills' that have imposed 'our rule' of chastity and abstinence for Catholic clergymen and women. His 'letter' to Clare ends touchingly with his assertion that there are

> a thousand ways
> To know another

and though he and she

> may not share
> The daily flittings of the mind[,] ...
> Each alone in prayer acclaims this love,
> Still in the cell of its first perfection.

In essence, with these final words, Francis metaphorically relates the love of Christ with his and Clare's union in spirit, equating 'this love' (their love) as mirroring the same purity and 'perfection' as God's love.

The final section (III) of this sequence is the poem's briefest. Comprised of just two quatrains, 'Francis to His Followers' completes the transformation from secular man to saint that was begun in the poem's initial section. As in the previous section, the persona's voice is altered; Francis is now even more self-assured and knowledgeable than he was previously, and his message is more compressed, a bit cryptic, and certainly more profound and explicitly mystical than it was in Parts (I) and (II). This section's first quatrain acknowledges the paradoxical nature of being a saint or 'prophet', a 'man of the cloth' (though a cloth of a different ilk than the kind with which Francis's father dealt) – it asserts that such a life is one both of 'joy' and 'stigma'. The quatrain's next sentence, which is syntactically strained, posits that the wisdom gained from such a life is sometimes ephemeral and easily diminished or 'dimmed'. Interestingly, what follows next is this simple and direct exclamation – 'Only a while, my brothers!' – as if his own and Francis's followers' exertion and difficulty in pursuing spiritual 'wisdom' will undeniably be rewarded with eventual understanding.

The last line of this first quatrain is enjambed so that it flows grammatically into the second and final quatrain; indeed, the last sentence of the poem comprises the final five lines of this section, and they maintain (through an elaborate and complex metaphorical structure) that, in essence, the visionary—as well as the saint, and, I would add, the *poet*-labour to see beyond the 'knots' in 'the net of time' in order to 'glimpse the image-god hidden in the thoughts of man'. Ultimately, Francis claims that he 'tied [his] love-knot, hitched a thread to the work', thus asserting that he is both the master and servant of his own destiny, and inferring that devotion to God is both a matter of love and labour. So it is and was for the saint, and so it remains for this poet who devotes himself with such brilliance, like St. Francis, to glimpsing 'the image-god' in our minds and hearts.

6 | In Love with the World: O'Siadhail and the Sonnet

Kim Bridgford

While Micheal O'Siadhail is skilled at a wide range of fixed forms, one might argue that his true form is the sonnet. Because O'Siadhail's main subject is love – romantic love, friendship, and love of humanity – this choice is fitting, as it is still the poetic form most closely allied with love. O'Siadhail uses a range of sonnet forms to address his subject matter: the Shakespearean sonnet, the combination Shakespearean/Italian sonnet, the Italian sonnet, the sonnet series, and the embedded sonnet. These forms show a supple awareness of the craft of the sonnet, as well as a growth from individual sonnets to more complex renderings of theme in the sonnet and embedded sonnet series.

The Shakespearean Sonnet

The Shakespearean sonnet is, by far, O'Siadhail's favourite form, no doubt because of his tendency to build poems by argument and his facility with the final couplet. For example, as early as *Springnight* (1983), he was illustrating his facility with the form and his key subject. In 'Seepage', the speaker discusses how betrayal can drain the trust from a relationship, and yet, at the same time, there is optimism. 'I covet this chance. We've no time to waste!,' says the speaker.

> Beginning the slow penance of a seeped devotion,
> We spoon-feed trust, thimble back the ocean.

It is rare for O'Siadhail to choose despair over possibility, and this gives even his saddest poems a buoyant underpinning.

In *The Image Wheel* (1985), his deep interest in the Shakespearean sonnet became established and with it a belief that human connection is essential. The Shakespearean sonnets in the collection circle from aloneness, to friendship, to the need for friendship, and then back to aloneness, mirroring the book as a whole, which plays with the idea of circling back. In 'Self-Portrait', O'Siadhail writes of the poet's task:

Intense, yet stooped, he walks as though weighted
Down by unfinished thought ablaze in the rubble
Of his mind.

Yet in his aloneness and burden – emphasized nicely by the line break between 'weighted' and 'Down' – he is not cut off from humanity:

Light rays fuse the perpetual in the transitory,
In the lover's lens through which he views the story.

While one could call these rose-colored glasses, a more appropriate way to describe these would be in O'Siadhail's own words: 'the lover's lens'.

Typical of his early sonnets is a controlling image, often illustrating his theme of connection. This is true in 'For My Friends', which uses weavework to illustrate how the speaker's understanding of friendship has changed over time, from 'Spendthrift friendships once ravelled and unravelled' to 'the fabric of a common story'. This image is useful in describing the conversational way in which O'Siadhail lets his lines run over from one line to the next. In addition, the caesuras in his lines are not predictable, giving a complex feel to the technical weavework of his sonnet.

In 'Absence' O'Siadhail picks up the imagistic thread of 'For My Friends' by speaking of his lover's absence: his 'plans [are] threadbare', 'a sacred thread is broken'. 'Absence' is O'Siadhail's 'A Valediction: Forbidding Mourning'; he like the speaker of Donne's poem is still connected through the mind to the other. This poem is more melancholy than most of O'Siadhail's work; while Donne's compass is more sturdy, O'Siadhail's threads are, by their very nature, more vulnerable. Although O'Siadhail lets himself be more pessimistic in personal situations than in public ones, he never remains gloomy.

These Shakespearean sonnets are the underpinning, both formally and thematically, for the sonnet and embedded sonnet series.

The Combination Shakespearean/Italian Sonnet

While not as common as the Shakespearean sonnet in O'Siadhail's work, the combination Shakespearean/Italian sonnet enables O'Siadhail to vary his poetic argument. In the poem 'Transit' from *A Fragile City* (1995), O'Siadhail can juxtapose his own experience – that of the lover's eye – against the world of leavetakings and reunions. Typically O'Siadhail builds toward the couplet, but in this combination sonnet he zeroes in at line 9, the turn, focusing on the woman who is left behind. (He is playful in the poem in that the woman actually physically turns at the beginning of line 10.) The concluding sestet, while still containing an O'Siadhailesque pronouncement –

Tell me we live
for those faces wiped into the folds of our being

– has a more muted delivery, made more conversational by the lack of concluding couplet.

Since O'Siadhail is one of the best living practitioners of the Shakespearean couplet, it is important to understand what one does not hear in the Shakespearean/Italian combination sonnets and in the Italian sonnets. Because of his facility with enjambment, his skill with both full and slant rhyme, and his ability to weave the lines in a conversational way over the grid of the poem, the poem feels more muted in its sestet than it might in the hands of a different poet. In the work of O'Siadhail, these alternative sonnets, while still retaining their own music, feel in their sestets a little like blank verse. In fact, O'Siadhail is to the sestet of the Italian sonnet what Browning is to blank verse.

The Italian Sonnet

O'Siadhail has few freestanding Italian sonnets. One such example is 'At the Hairdresser's' from *A Fragile City*, which, while still emphasizing his characteristic themes – connection to other people, his love affair with the world – has a different feel. Part of the reason is that, on the surface, the relationship with the hairdresser is not as intimate as that with a friend or a lover, and yet what O'Siadhail finds curious is that, even in this service relationship, there is an intimacy: 'Surely a world is safe in her hands.' Part of the reason is that, in a typical O'Siadhail sonnet, the couplet rhyme is at the end. Thus, there is a feeling of surprise in the initial rhymes of the octave: unbends/water/daughter/hands, radio/dug in/domination/*sea-sparrow*. With the water/daughter rhyme, it feels as if the usual music of his sonnets has been reversed. While there is still the feeling of pronouncement at the end of the poem —

> Above all, don't cry.
> My clogged maleness loosens in her determined fingers.
> Those helmeted faces so boyish with their unspilt tears

– the slanting of the rhyme stands in stark juxtaposition to the more resounding rhymes of the octave. While O'Siadhail is adept at all forms of the sonnet, this feeling of discombobulation in the Italian sonnet may partially explain why the frequency of his sonnets moves from Shakespearean, to combination Shakespearean/Italian, to Italian.

The Sonnet Sequence

– Book Sections Made of Sonnets

O'Siadhail includes two types of sonnet sequences in his work: sections of books with individual sonnets that can also be read as part of the larger sequence; and individual longer poems made up of numbered sections of sonnets. That O'Siadhail would be attracted to the sonnet sequence is not surprising, given his facility with the form and the need of most poets to move from a smaller form to a larger one; yet the way in which he introduces the sonnet sequence is. Because of O'Siadhail's supple awareness of the form, from slant rhyme to the weavework of rhymes, it is surprising that he does not have sonnet crowns in this work, or, on a larger scale, the sonnet redouble or magistrale. Yet so important is the feeling of conversation and connection in his work that at the very point at which the repetition of lines might be too self-conscious, he resists them (he is certainly capable of *tour de force* rhymes and repetitions in other rhyming poems). His chain of sonnets has a lighter touch. Perhaps, from O'Siadhail's point of view, it might be the very point at which the garland feels like a chain.

The 'Rerooting' sequence of *The Chosen Garden* is the first place O'Siadhail uses the sonnet section. It also begins his strategy of framing his series with quotations. This one, by Anne Stevenson, introduces both a motif of journey and a motif of light. O'Siadhail picks this motif by writing a Shakespearean sonnet entitled 'Journeys' to frame the series, with this thematic couplet:

> *a wheel is the rim of many ways,*
> *spokes of intensity, journeys to the blaze.*

It is noteworthy that some of O'Siadhail's rhymes are more slant than usual, '*muse*' and '*moods*', '*left*' and '*met*'. As the poem plays with the idea of exploring the rim, this extra slanting of the slant rhyme does so as well by exploring the limit of rhyme itself.

The ten poems in the series have simple titles, 'Beginnings', 'A Presence', 'An Unfolding', 'Squall', 'The Other Voice', 'Out of the Blue', 'St Brigid's Cross', 'While You Are Talking', 'Hindsight', and 'A Circle'. Six of the poems are Shakespearean, and four are Italian. Since O'Siadhail rarely uses the Italian sonnet, and especially in combination with the Shakespearean, this fact in itself is noteworthy. Moreover, they are introduced in distinct patterns: two Shakespearean sonnets, two Italian sonnets, four Shakespearean sonnets, two Italian sonnets. The question is why.

If one reads these sonnets not as individual poems, but as members of a series, this question is answered. The shift in form heightens the shift in argument. The first two poems, 'Beginnings' and 'A Presence', emphasize a beginning, while the second two poems, 'An Unfolding' and 'Squall', emphasize both twisting and misunderstanding, so that O'Siadhail shifts and twists the forms themselves. At the fifth poem, 'The Other Voice', the halfway poem in the series, the speaker announces 'No half measures then', and in its concluding couplet says,

> My love is your freedom. Do or die or downfall,
> it's all or nothing and I have chosen all.

The next three poems, 'Out of the Blue', 'St Brigid's Cross', and 'While You Are Talking', underscore the various stages of the love journey, from joining one's life to another and blending it, to watching the loved one, to being jealous of the loved one. The last two, 'Hindsight' and 'A Circle', shift to images of light. The speaker admits in 'Hindsight', 'it's all summer now'. 'A Circle' fittingly brings back the journey motif of the framing poem, and in its use of the Italian sonnet brings a more conversational feel to the end of the sequence, which in its soft emphasis of the present moment sounds like whispering in the dark:

> Now I love to watch the lighthouse at Howth
> flash its codes to steer ships past our gable,
> to gossip in the dark with you my bed and boarder
> and marvel at how, like tortoises in an Aesop fable,
> our years have coiled their slow circles of growth;
> a world brought back to scale, a house to order.

The 'Filtered Light' sequence of *A Fragile City* is another sequence that serves as its own section of a book. The section is framed by a Rilke quotation, which uses literal light as a way to describe the feeling of human connection. The thirteen poems in this section all have one-word titles and do not reveal much about the poems they frame: 'Transit', 'Folding', 'Beyond', 'News', 'Quartet', 'Flare', 'Focus', 'Tension', 'Casualty', 'Revelation', 'Translation', 'Light', and 'Aversion'. What breaks through these generic titles is the connection that O'Siadhail seeks in all his work, revealed through gestures, faces, and light. If one reads the poems with these topics in mind, the kaleidoscopic shifting of the patterns – Shakespearean, combination Shakespearean/Italian, Italian, and even one ('News') mostly written in couplets – carries out the theme of connection in the way that it does in human life, through subtlety, not fireworks.

One poem in the series that might sum up the way in which the series operates is his poem 'Quartet'. The musicians, who are in harmony with each other and the audience, 'nod and gleam'; the speaker watches and listens to them. Transfixed by the music, their faces seem to glow with light. As O'Siadhail writes,

> I grow in this mutual succumbing:
> Bow and pluck, phrase and breath of an earned
> And watchful passion, our face to face becoming.

Just as there is a connection among musicians playing a piece of music together, so is there one between people in relationships: 'A shining between faces, a listening inward and open.' The *tour de force* feminine rhymes in the poem – 'seeing' and 'being', 'leaning' and 'meaning', 'succumbing' and 'becoming', 'matches' and 'over-reaches'—emphasize the sense of process and connection in the poem.

One other striking sonnet series is the 'Figures' series in *The Gossamer Wall: Poems in Witness to the Holocaust* (2002). The sequence is framed by a quotation from Shmerke Kaczerginski:

> Still, still let us be still.
> Graves grow here.
> Planted by the enemy,
> they blossom to the sky.

The fourteen poems in this series are one shy of the fifteen needed for a sonnet redouble or magistrale. This missing sonnet or sonnet of absence is noteworthy, given the overwhelming loss this series addresses.

As in his 'Filtered Light' sequence, O'Siadhail is drawn to simple titles, 'Summons', 'Figures', 'Arrivals', 'There', 'Here', 'Qui vive', 'Threads', 'Night', 'Ensemble', 'Ravens', 'Elite', 'Lily', 'Chinks', and 'Alone'. The muted approach matches O'Siadhail's struggle to communicate the incomprehensibility of what occurred in the death camps. With this in mind he brings back his strategy of glintings in gestures, faces, and light. Particularly important is the use of eyes in the series, the necessity of witnessing. As O'Siadhail writes in 'Summons', the first poem in the series:

> Out of the cone of Vesuvius their lives rise
> To sky-write gaunt silences in the frozen air.
> A summons to try to look, to try to see.
> A muted dead demand their debt of memory.

Nine of these poems are Shakespearean sonnets; five are not. The discombobulation of the mixture of the forms adds to the sickly unease of the subject matter. As argued previously, when one knows O'Siadhail's work, especially the sonnets, one grows to expect the Shakespearean sonnet, and his masterful couplets. Since the first three poems in the series are Shakespearean sonnets, they imitate the development of an individual Shakespearean sonnet, with its three examples, followed by the couplet. However, in this case the couplet does not come. The Shakespearean sonnet is pulled out from under one, so to speak. It cannot be chance that this shift happens in this series with the poem 'There', accompanying the realization that the showers in the death camps are not ordinary showers: 'In every heart one moment when it knows?'

The argument that the Shakespearean sonnet is the point for which the combination Shakespearean/Italian sonnet is the counterpoint is furthered with two other considerations. One, the reader is continually set up for the Shakespearean sonnet, only to have the poem turn into something else, which is, of course, the eerie subject matter of the poems, the disbelief at the horror and shifting play of human experience. Thus, the ever-shifting sestet after the Shakespearean octave serves as a continual reminder. Two, when the Shakespearean sonnet does return, its couplets are noticeable because they are written in true or nearly true rhyme. The couplets range from the more subtle, but moving

> Just somebody to pass another's story on;
> Tiny threads of time loop beyond oblivion ('Threads')

to the vivid

> Short fitful hours when a Tantalus replays
> In feverish stereo broken nightmares of days ('Night')

to the horrific

> Pity these ravens for what driven ravens do;
> Bitter complicity that Jew should oven Jew ('Ravens')

and

> Thrilled by quivers of fear in lives they own,
> They crunch paths gravelled with human bone ('Elite')

to the hopeful

> For some, for a while, bitter and sweet parallel
> As rifts of light blink through the walls of hell ('Chinks')

to the concluding

> Endure to witness through one memory's lens.
> The silent alone fathom the depth of silence. ('Alone')

– Poems with Sections Made of Sonnets

'Perspectives', from *The Chosen Garden,* is a good example of how O'Siadhail uses multiple sonnets to his advantage, but on a smaller scale. This poem, made up of four sonnets, employs a knitting image to frame the way in which people transform others and the earth:

> Plain stitch and design, point and infinity.
> Who changes the world? Oh, this and that,
> strands as they happen to fall, tiny ligatures,
> particular here-and-nows, vast loopings
> of pattern, the ties and let-goes of a knot,
> small X-shapes of history; our spore and signature
> a gauze of junctures, a nettedness of things.

This poem moves from its initial combination Shakespearean/Italian sonnet to three other sonnets that show the way in which we are connected to other people and are changed by them. How fitting that shifting sonnet forms would underscore this 'nettedness of things'.

The second sonnet in this four-part series is atypical in form for O'Siadhail, although not in content. The rhyme scheme of the poem, ababcbcdcdedff, is a variation of the Spenserian sonnet. The repetition is suitable for the transforming qualities of music, and sets O'Siadhail up for his signature couplet:

> Possessor of everything, owner of nothing.
> Whose bow shivers its music in my string?

Sonnet three returns to the combination Italian/Shakespearean sonnet. In looping back to the form of the initial sonnet, O'Siadhail shows the interconnectedness of sonnet three with the knitting/nettedness image of stanza one. Sonnet three is about Dietrich Bonhoeffer and how, in his resistance to the Nazis, he set an example.

Finally, in sonnet four, O'Siadhail uses a childhood bullying example to show how young people think in terms of 'black and white', but need to have a larger perspective:

> ... the schoolroom globe, a balloon viewed
> with a spaceman's floating glance ...

The form of the poem, while it has a Shakespearean introduction, varies its sestet: cdedce. As the sestet brings the poem to a close, it reinforces the shaking loose of a small perspective while illustrating that in such differing ways – music, heroic example, childhood bullying – we change the course not only of our own moments, but also the weavework of humanity.

While 'Perspectives' uses four sonnets, one to establish the theme, followed by three examples, 'Summerfest', from *The Middle Voice* (1992), uses its three examples to show the passing of time. The first sonnet, 'Open Air', a Shakespearean sonnet, illustrates an evening party, with unusually hot weather, at the end of August. In the 'Shadows' section something has changed. For one thing, darkness has fallen, but, in addition to that, the party-goers have been drinking, moving to an in-between state. To emphasize this shift, O'Siadhail moves from the Shakespearean sonnet to the combination Italian/Shakespearean sonnet, writing 'A mood seems to blur our lines of joy and sorrow.' Lastly, in 'Sway' the mood shifts, and so does the sonnet form – to the Italian. Reminiscent of William Carlos Williams's 'The Dance', this poem through its ecstatic playfulness also hints at the change in its sonnet form, through 'wild variations on what we're given'. However, the ending of this Italian sonnet – effegg – enables O'Siadhail also to use his signature couplet to bring the sonnet to a close:

> Swirl, let-go, comback. A flirtatious liaison.
> Some dream in the dance's sway goes on and on.

Sonnet series become increasingly frequent in O'Siadhail's work, particularly the poems in sections and embedded sonnets. In *Our Double Time* (1998), there are five poems in sonnet sections alone: 'Ageing', 'What If?', 'Three Wishes', 'Trio', and 'Triptych'. All five poems use sonnets in threes. All five use sonnet variations, with the combination Italian/Shakespearean as the base sonnet. All have a musing tone, and all make only subtle differences among the sonnets in the series, as if to illustrate the murkiness of age and time.

In 'Ageing' the three poems seem to spin out of each other, subtly commenting on the fact that aging takes us by surprise, the paradox of existence: 'Each memory and hope woven in a dying now.' 'What If?' has the same tone, but the sections work to elaborate upon the layerings of memories and moments. As O'Siadhail writes, 'I know the layers of things unconscious and hidden.' 'Three Wishes' examines the nature of rituals to shape life, and how in human existence there is a 'need for patterns', 'Some overarching design'. While the poems lead easily one out of the other, the very structure of the poem, with its three sonnets, imitates this urge for an underlying pattern to life. 'Trio' has more clearly delineated sections—they are labelled 'Millennium', 'Recorder', and 'Nocturne' – but underneath the subjects of all three, New Year's, music making, and music listening, there is the sense of longing, which as O'Siadhail notes, only seems to increase as one grows older: 'A music grown richer in disciplines of yearning.' The last of the five poems, 'Triptych', reinforces the notion of an underlying pattern, but with a blending that sums up everyday experience:

> I think of an old man telling a college researcher
> How the fabric of existence was all of a piece,
> Just one seamless garment of nature and nurture.

Or, as O'Siadhail writes in the last sonnet of the three,

> I wonder is it youth's brimming urge to divide
> Their world from ours, as if the great leveller
> Sealed us from them. Our side and the other side.
> Have all the boundaries already started to blur?

'Traces', from *Globe* (2006), also explores this blurring, but in terms of our contributions to humanity. With three combination Italian/Shakespearean sonnets and two Shakespearean, this poem traces this 'tangle' and 'looping' of form. While there will be the Galileo and Bach, there will also be the rest of us:

> Just some trace laid down, our mark made
> In the give and take of lives, a loan of a loan
> Passed on as mention of our names will fade.

Yet these traces are important and resurface just as a recessive gene can resurface. In this way we blur our boundaries with each other.

– The Embedded Sonnet

This blurring of boundaries is another way to view O'Siadhail's gradual movement to the embedded sonnet. The term is apt in that the sonnet maintains its integrity while being part of a larger structure. Also 'embedded' as it applies to memory is fitting, as so much of what O'Siadhail does is to use the poem to hold on to a memory and make sense of it.

The strategy of the embedded sonnet underscores O'Siadhail's project of bringing together diverse experience. Music, friendship, love: these are ways to transform moments. However, moments do not always have the same shape or texture, and it is difference that O'Siadhail wishes to examine. As O'Siadhail writes in the introduction to *Poems 1975-1995*, 'we both need our boundaries and need to transcend them'.

The first use of the embedded sonnet appears in *Our Double Time*. 'Rehearsals', using a mirroring technique, is more predictable than his embedded sonnet series would grow to be. Still, there is a departure from previous uses of the sonnet. The rollicking framework of the poem – with multiple variations of dactyls, trochees, anapests, and spondees – not only has a more heavily substituted metre than the rest of the poem but a different, sparser set-up. The brief frame is about the past and the speaker's relationship with his father. The speaker has travelled in place by bouncing on his father's knee. The initial quatrain comes from the Italian sonnet and the concluding quatrain comes from the Shakespearean sonnet, and the two sonnets that are embedded are the Shakespearean and the combination Italian/Shakespearean, respectively (although one line short), so O'Siadhail can have his cake (Shakespearean) and eat it too (Italian). In addition, there is a mirroring effect but it is mirroring *with variation*, just as the subject matter (travelling in place) is mirroring but with variation. The sonnets embedded within show how one may also travel in place through literature, and through gender, first through the Norse story of Kristin Lavransdatter and, secondly, through the Greek story of Antigone.

'Orchard' from *Our Double Time* also uses the mirroring technique but in a more complicated way, using quatrain variations from the Italian and Shakespearean sonnets. Naturally the embedded sonnet is the combination Italian/Shakespearean sonnet. The poem, which is about the doubling back upon remembered time, uses the embedded sonnet as a way to speed up the doubling effect in the poem, to emphasize 'A looped story where the start and finish blend'. In addition, the embedded sonnet underscores the moment that resonates through time and remains 'Deep in the core'.

Thirdly, 'Etty Hillesum' discombobulates the mirroring technique by using thirteen tercets with an aba rhyme scheme to begin the poem and ending with ten such tercets. The three embedded sonnets – one Shakespearean, one combination Italian/Shakespearean, and one picking up on the tercets with an abacdcd septet, followed by an Italian sestet (the poem is one line short) – serve then to balance in a rough way the missing three tercets. Yet in the sonnets there is a thickening, a slowing down, an interiority that replicates the intensity of life – and love – during WWII. As Etty Hillesum kept a diary that became almost as famous as Anne Frank's, this interiority is noteworthy for the way in which it replicates the keeping of a diary and the preservation of intense moments of experience.

Lastly, 'Secrets of Assisi' uses two framing stanzas of eleven rhyming couplets with three embedded sonnets: two combination Italian/Shakespearean sonnets and one Shakespearean. The framing stanzas, spoken by someone from the present who is walking through the gardens of Assisi, are fittingly in couplets, as the interior sonnets are about love. Francesco of Assisi is the speaker of these sonnets, and he speaks of his love for Chiara, which parallels Abelard's feelings for Heloise (moment within moment within moment). These sonnets have the same feeling of interiority as the sonnets in the middle of 'Etty Millesum'. What O'Siadhail gains from this is, again, the intensity of experience, a kind of thickening at the same time that there is an intimacy that the framing couplets lack. O'Siadhail plays with ways in which to affect rhythm in poems by juxtaposing a variety of forms, and in *Our Double Time* it is not surprising that these effects are experiments in mirroring, or doubling.

In *Love Life* (2005), O'Siadhail extends his rhythmic experiments with the sonnet by moving away from mirroring, and toward experimentations with breath. 'Concertina' is an excellent example of the way in which O'Siadhail experiments with the breath of the poem. The first two sections of the poem experiment with a three-beat line – with the first section in more traditional iambic trimeter and the second, like an accordion, shortening and extending the line. The third section, a combination Italian/Shakespearean sonnet, then begins wittily: '*Festina lente*. The love-maker's paradox.' The sonnet goes on to elaborate on the ways in which our moments in life rise and fall, and the last line sums up both the metrical set-up and theme of the poem: '*Paradise squeezed in folds of a concertina.*'

If O'Siadhail does use the mirroring device in this volume, it is in the opposite way that he uses it in *Our Double Time*. Because the sonnets frame the poem and are not placed in the centre, O'Siadhail can gauge the different way in which the poem breathes by his shift in strategy. In both 'Trimleston' and 'Dwelling' poems with quicker movements are at the centre. While in 'Trimleston' the effect is to have the first two-thirds of the poem feel more musical, with a melancholy, whispery effect at the end, in 'Dwelling' the effect is to have the framing sonnets emphasize design and patterning, while the interior stanzas emphasize crevices, creaks, and light.

'Guests', 'Study', 'Watch', 'About', 'Dedication', 'Ten to Seven', and 'House' play with variations in the embedded sonnet. These poems experiment with breath, the alternating of it – whether through varying accentual lines ('Guests'), haiku-like stanzas ('Study'), or rhyming triplets ('About'). The sonnet moves to different spots in the poetic order, sometimes framing the poem ('Shades'), providing the middle weightiness of the poem ('Dedication'), and at other times establishing order by concluding the poem ('Study', 'Ten to Seven', 'House').

'Settlement', 'Parkinson's', and 'Crimson Thread' are less important formally than thematically, since these embedded sonnet series participate in the tradition of the love poem, underscoring O'Siadhail's lifetime of love for his wife, Bríd. 'Settlement' is a Biblical love poem. Its three sections are echoed by the three sections of 'Parkinson's', from which Bríd suffers. The establishment of order in a Shakespearean sonnet is particularly touching in a world gone awry with the shaking of Parkinson's:

> I couldn't but see your half flirtatious sidelong
> Glance at me that both asks and reassures:

Even if I shake I think my spirit is young?
Our years side by side tongued and grooved.
A face is beautiful once a face is loved.

'Crimson Thread' ties everything together — both literally and metaphorically. The poem is framed by Shakespearean sonnets, with an Italian/Shakespearean sonnet embedded within the poem between two haiku. The poem is both Biblical and personal; it juxtaposes images of nature with a rich and resonant love relationship:

I come to my garden, my sister, my bride.
Eat friend, drink and be drunk with love
And every moment I think I'm satisfied
Wakes me to desires I'm dreaming of.
In Solomon's blue curtain a cord of covenant,
A crimson thread until the crimson moment.

In *Globe* (2006), O'Siadhail brings his project full circle, back to human experience. The poem 'Remember' is about the slaughter of Armenians during the latter half of 1915. In light of greater slaughters and collective historical amnesia, these 300,000 deaths may not get the attention that they should. Yet the poem, through its varying forms and breath, attempts to conjure people's lives out of silence. 'Remember' uses first tercets, then couplets, then a varying three-four beat accentual line, and finally a Shakespearean sonnet. In its effect as a sonnet, it recalls the 'Figures' sequence from *The Gossamer Wall*. Although the concluding sonnet is bitter, the couplet is the perfect vehicle for the litany of names:

Megerditch, Garabet, Touma, Shukri, Paul;
A name for each three hundred thousand to recall.

It is fitting that one of the world's greatest living practitioners of the sonnet is the one to speak these names, and that the sonnet, the form most closely associated with love, is the vehicle.

7 | Hail! Jazzman O'Siadhail: Form and Metaphor

Richard Rust

Reading Micheal O'Siadhail's poems like 'Hail! Madam Jazz' we are led to hail O'Siadhail himself as a jazzman, especially in his forms and use of metaphor. While a jazzman is a musician who plays or composes jazz music, the term 'jazzman' can readily be applied to a poet who produces jazz-like poetry. O'Siadhail does so to perfection!

Just as jazz is characterized by its strong but flexible rhythmic understructure, so O'Siadhail's poetry has a rhythmic understructure of a large range of poetic forms. The polyphony in jazz has its counterpart in the many voices we hear in O'Siadhail's poetry. Just as jazz has solo and ensemble improvisations, so we hear O'Siadhail's individualistic voice in company with many other persons, especially poets, through time. Ragtime and blues, from which jazz developed, have syncopated rhythms and varying degrees of improvisation; likewise, O'Siadhail creates uneven patterns over a regular underlying beat of traditional forms. Form and formlessness are combined in both jazz and O'Siadhail's poetry. Jazz originated as dance music, and as such has a strong foundation of rhythm; in like manner, a number of O'Siadhail's poems refer to dancing and dance music – showing O'Siadhail's mastery of different dance forms. The kind of spontaneous creativity that is a hallmark of jazz is exhibited prominently in O'Siadhail's metaphors. The theme-and-variations cyclic structures of jazz have a parallel in the subtle but highly effective architecture of O'Siadhail's larger works. As jazz is a music of inclusion, combining many influences and techniques, so O'Siadhail's poetry is richly inclusive of human concerns from the time of Eden to the present, and is marked by an exceptional array of epigraphs, phrases, and allusions coming from O'Siadhail's wide-ranging knowledge and experience. The histories and people of the earth are found not just in *Globe* but in the whole range of O'Siadhail's work. What jazzman Jelly Roll Morton claimed about the borrowing and adapting found in jazz could be applied to Micheal O'Siadhail as well: 'I transformed every style to mine. ... There's nothing finer than jazz music because it comes from everything of the finest class music.' For O'Siadhail, 'Transformation is everything' ('Rilke').

To be a highly successful jazzman, one has to know the rules in order to improvise. This is especially true of Micheal O'Siadhail; he is thoroughly versed in poetic forms through the ages which provide the understructures on which he creates variations in an individualistic and fresh manner. A prime illustration of this is O'Siadhail's poem, 'Hail! Madam Jazz'—which also provides the title of one of his books.

> Worship, hold her a moment in thought.
> *Femme fatale*, she shapes another face,
> unveils an idol. O Never-To-Be-Caught,
>
> O Minx beyond this mind's embrace,
> Hider-Go-Seeker, Miss Unfathomable,
> Demurring Lady playing at the chase.
>
> As stars or atoms we turn, fall
> towards each other's gravity. I spin
> in your love's nexus, Mistress All.
>
> Once a child of Newton's fallen
> apple, I'd the measure of your ways.
> My stars, my atoms, are we one?
>
> Mischievous Strategy, Madam Jazz!
> Old tunes die in metamorphosis.
> Rise, fall, reawakening. I praise.

As a 'jazzman', O'Siadhail in this poem engages in a spirit of improvisation while building on a traditional form. Unless one's attention were directed to it, a reader would likely never notice the poetic form O'Siadhail is using here for his own purposes. It is the *terza rima* – interlinked tercets in which the last word of the second line of the first stanza provides the rhyme for the first and third lines of the next stanza, and so forth. This is the stanzaic form Dante Alighieri used in his *Divine Comedy*. O'Siadhail's is indeed a 'Mischievous Strategy' in which 'Old tunes die in metamorphosis'. In O'Siadhail's poetry, these old tunes 'Rise, fall, reawakening'. At the end of this complex poem, the poet addresses Madam Jazz: 'I praise'. In turn, we praise 'Jazzman O'Siadhail' for his spinning in 'love's nexus'.

An even more intricate form upon which O'Siadhail plays the jazzman is the sestina. In this six-stanza French form, the first end-word provides the rhyme for the subsequent first and third lines of each stanza; the first and last lines of the opening triplet alternately become the last lines of the subsequent four triplets and the last two lines of the closing envoy; and the end-words of the first stanza are repeated in the envoy. O'Siadhail's 'Uncertain' in *Our Double Time* does this, with some variation (having a single last line that coheres to the last triplet). The poem bespeaks an improvisation upon traditional music:

> Are tune and rhythm one in the fullness of the play?
> My jazz, my jazz, will tomorrow be my dancing day?

Besides the form itself, a traditional element in this improvisation is the question, 'Will tomorrow be my dancing day?' which comes from an English folk song. (A similar sestina is 'How?' in *A Fragile City*.)

Proclaiming himself to be a jazzman, O'Siadhail says in his Introduction to *Poems 1975-1995*: 'A universe which might have narrowed became now an endless jazz improvisation. Madam Jazz had made me her own.' In respect to O'Siadhail's knowledge of poetic forms, that universe is great indeed. His writings are a *tour de force* of forms found throughout the globe and through time. Referring to some of his favourite poets such as Herrick, Jonson, Raleigh, Shakespeare, Herbert, Donne, Hopkins, Frost, Auden, and Kavanagh, O'Siadhail says: 'Such a tradition. Such a privilege to spend a life in this community. ... It seems we're tapping into something huge and opulent.' As shown by his epigraphs and by subsequent borrowed phrases, O'Siadhail connects with many other poets including Homer, Epictetus, Pindar, Mevlana Jalaluddin Rumi, William Shakespeare, Rainer Maria Rilke, Mirjam Tuominen, Karin Boye, Philippe Desportes, Abraham Sutzkever, Judah Halevi, and Tess Gallagher. 'But we're all part of a tradition', O'Siadhail says. 'I still have tucked away from my primary school four pages of *Poets and Poetry for Irish Schools*.' 'All my tinyness rejoices', he affirms in 'Our Double Time', 'That I'll have been a voice among your voices.'

While O'Siadhail has an intended connection to other poets, yet he launches out on his own:

> Gilgamesh, Odysseus, Mad Quixote,
> wanderers relive in us your daylight.
> And hey! what stranger down the line
> moves to this rhythm, whose moment
> twangs in the blood? Good morning, Segovia. ('Matins')

O'Siadhail, too, 'down the line', moves to the rhythm of Gilgamesh, Homer, Cervantes. Yet he does so with variations. As he puts it in his poem 'Apprentice':

> Traces of shades and revenants shape our becoming.
> Herbert's green and fresh returns. Rilke's Orpheus
> On saxophone playing his variations for Madam Jazz.

O'Siadhail, as he says in 'Tremolo', is

> Given a globe of boundless jazz,
> Yet still a remembered undertone.

That remembered undertone or rhythmic understructure of poetic creations through the ages is a community in which O'Siadhail is a 'middle voice'. He writes,

> It's good to stand in between, touching our coming
> and our going. Hinge and middleman. ('Three Rock')

In this manner, he connects with what a monk wrote about a blackbird a thousand years ago and says, 'We are brothers conjugate in ecstasy' ('Early Irish Lyric'). In a poem entitled 'Tradition' he affirms: 'All that was received I again deliver.' O'Siadhail has placed himself on a threshold between past and present:

> I travel
> Like Proust, a touch, a scent, a sound,
> Both past and present now refound. ('Passivity')

Appropriately, a section of *Our Double Time* is called 'Threshold'. As a jazzman, O'Siadhail draws on the past to reshape the future:

> All that's to come still jazz,
> An unknown latent in know-how;
> Our past a future we learn. ('Scenario')

His jazz playing is an 'Interplay of riff and debt' ('Tension'). He repossesses classical forms by weaving variations on them and responding to deeply felt creative works. As he says, 'It's almost as if, by repossessing the past, we redeem the present.'

Rerooting, which provides the title of Section V of *The Chosen Garden*, is an apt metaphor which suggests connections to the past, to tradition. 'Rerooting' appropriately is made up entirely of eleven sonnets. O'Siadhail extensively uses the sonnet, one of the most beloved traditional forms – putting him in company with poets such as William Shakespeare, John Milton, John Keats, Elizabeth Barrett Browning, Gerard Manley Hopkins, and William Butler Yeats. He ends *The Middle Voice* with three sonnets; *A Fragile City begins* with thirteen sonnets; besides containing a number of sonnets elsewhere, *Our Double Time* ends with five sonnets; *The Gossamer Wall* is enriched by sonnets; *Love Life* contains nineteen sonnets, with three of its four sections ending with sonnets; and there are seven sonnets in *Globe*. Yet the forms of O'Siadhail's sonnets are nearly invisible on a first reading. Why is this so? Often it is because Jazzman O'Siadhail turns 'wild variations on what we're given' with 'a pulsing frenzy of control'.

> Again and again this play of check and freedom,
> A jazz pulling against the sameness of the drum

– as he says in his sonnet 'Sway'. He also conceals his sonnets by interspersing other forms in between them; for instance, the poem 'Crimson Thread' in *Love Life* is made up of three sonnets with two haikus interspersed. O'Siadhail, in his own words, is 'fascinated both by the way old forms never cease to be renewed and by how there are endless possible variations and formal inventions'.

At other times, O'Siadhail clearly wants the sonnet form to be apparent. The third section of *The Gossamer Wall* is entitled 'Figures', with all of its fourteen poems being sonnets. The section title and the formal poems this section contains suggest that form is an attempt to bring some understanding to chaos. The sonnet form here is also ironic since these poems emphasize the external orderliness of 'Desolation's mad machine' ('Summons'), operating in 'a molten Pompeii' ('Figures') where there is 'no future or no past' ('Here') and where 'Phantom bodies move outside their mind' ('Threads') in 'broken nightmares of days' ('Night') and are destroyed in 'the walls of hell' ('Chinks'). In 'Ensemble', a sonnet about an ensemble's concerts, form ironically emphasizes the underlying horror of the concentration camps:

> In strict tempo marionettes in rags they slept in
> Jerk their stiffened joints and swollen feet.
> … A violin
> Is singing against the grain its hollow upbeat.

There is also irony in the poem 'Paradise' with its rhymed couplets giving us something slightly humorous and yet darkly chilling in the rhyme of 'pogrom' with 'crematorium':

> Down a corridor of history the booted pogrom
> Still echoes a broken rhyme with crematorium.

In this case, both the title ('Paradise') and the form signal the awfulness of it all. The people behind the gossamer wall are saying that

> Our stories become labyrinths of irony that turn
> On irony. ('Stretching')

O'Siadhail adapts his forms to the content of his poems. For instance, his tribute to William Shakespeare, 'Cue', in *Globe* is written in blank verse. The anapestic metre of 'Train Journey' captures the rhythm of the train, the 'train's undersong', as it opens with: 'As a boy I was sure that the track's anapest'. O'Siadhail's structure of the poem 'Our Double Time' is based on the musical composition the motet, and has this line:

> Across all the aeons, my one humming breath
> Poised in this motet.

A poem about music known as the blues, 'Shuffle', takes on the form of blues:

> The counterpoint, the taken chance,
> As discord by discord we recompose
> And for the music's sake extemporise
> Bluesy scales of how we cope.
> Neither returning or losing the way.

Again, in 'Doggone Blues', O'Siadhail captures the rhythm and the feeling of blues:

> In mumble, holler, scat or groan
> Go *tell 'em ivories* how to groan.

A verse form that connects with O'Siadhail's longstanding interest in the Japanese language, culture, and poetry is the haiku. As in the following instances, O'Siadhail employs this form in fresh ways:

> A fresh turn of phrase
> The flurry and throb
> Of words tuned for a first time. ('Watch')

> Bird flight at sundown.
> Afterwards the aftershine.
> Infinite moment. ('Ceremony')

> Yoked we throw our light.
> That one will be first to go.
> A twin star untwinned. ('At Sea')

> Our love spooling out
> Sun-up-ness and sun-down-ness.
> Wisdom's crimson thread. ('Day')

> Deep deeper yellow
> Prepares a crimson moment.
> A sumac's leaf falls. ('Crimson Thread')

While O'Siadhail 'works in skilful verse forms', as poet Louis Simpson observed, 'yet his language is so suited to the thought as to seem perfectly natural'. It should be noted, too, that while O'Siadhail engages with a variety of traditional forms, he creates many forms that are unique to him. Indeed, his poetry is largely made up of his own forms. Here are just three examples out of many: In the poem 'Butt' in *The Gossamer Wall*, four of the five six-line stanzas have the fifth line being two one-syllable words while the last stanza has but one striking word in the fifth place: 'rifts'. The poem 'Anniversary' in *Love Life* has three five-line stanzas in which the first and fifth lines have four to six beats each while the middle three lines have three beats. And throughout the poem 'In Memoriam Máirtín Ó Cadhain', made up of seven stanzas containing five lines each, O'Siadhail alternates first, third, and fifth lines that are long with shorter second and fourth lines.

Verse forms are themselves metaphors – they are a means of seeing one thing in terms of another. As an example, love in the haiku 'Day' is compared to a spooling out of Wisdom's crimson thread. The ending sestet in an Italian sonnet or couplet in a Shakespearean sonnet typically provides a metaphorical turn. Through his sonnets, and indeed throughout his poetry, O'Siadhail is regularly metaphorical. He alerts us to this in his 'Self-Portrait' in *The Image Wheel*:

> Falling for the pulse-music, a dreamer succumbs
> To the mind-expanding frenzy of word and metaphor.

Both form and metaphor – indeed the linkage of form and metaphor – are at the heart of O'Siadhail's creation of poetry. Poetry involves both form and feeling; it has been defined as 'the measured language of emotion' (*Easton's 1897 Bible Dictionary*). The word 'poetry' comes from *poiein*, to create, and 'poet' comes from the Greek *poiētēs*, maker, composer. To create is to give form to something, to bring it out of chaos. An initial act of creation is naming, the Adamic act, with the naming coming from a connection being made to something already known. By indicating what something is like, this naming becomes a form of metaphor. In 'Autumn Report', O'Siadhail identifies with Adam,

> the first to mouth, to feel the garden overflow
> in word and rhythm.

In his 'A Short Biography', O'Siadhail as poet recounts that

> passing through the garden gate,
> you turned forever into Eden.

He illustrates in his poetry Ralph Waldo Emerson's belief that 'poetry is faith. To the poet the world is virgin soil; all is practicable; the men are ready for virtue; it is always time to do right. He is the true recommencer, or Adam in the garden again'. 'A new Adam in the garden', Emerson says, is to 'name all the beasts in the field, all the gods in the sky'. In this spirit, O'Siadhail affirms:

> history has
> accumulated this moment, now funnels through me
> the urge to utter. ('Autumn Report')

And like Emerson, O'Siadhail shows that 'the whole of nature is a metaphor of the human mind'.

Drawing on close observations of nature and humanity, O'Siadhail creates many remarkably apt metaphors. Here are some of them: Daisies are 'Frail ballerinas poised in the dew' ('Daisies'). 'Just today winter flung off its coat' ('Of Course').

> Time is sand
> On a river's bed. ('Sand')

> We're born to betray the nest,
> to quit the brood, flutter alone. ('Nest')

> Framed by our window, trunks and branches
> of chestnut trees are handbook illustrations
> of arteries, veins charcoaled on a frosty sky. ('Springnight')

'Is life itself the burning bush?' ('April Soliloquy')

> Beyond the bowed colours the raindrops disperse,
> Do my outstretched hands tip the ends of a universe? ('Voices')

> Grafton Street is yawning, waking
> limb by limb. ('Morning on Grafton Street')

> Crossed, matted fibres long inwrought,
> Friendships prove the fabric of a common story. ('For My Friends')

'I feast on faces' ('Delight'). 'My friend. An oak for all the world' ('Oak').

O'Siadhail's favourite description of metaphor is 'the ability to speak of one thing in terms of another'. This is subtle in that it refuses the simplistic substitution of one thing for another'. In developing his metaphors, O'Siadhail sees the uncommon in the common. For instance, in tending oatmeal cereal he discovers, 'I watch again creation' ('Temperament'). O'Siadhail knows what Emerson observed: 'The world globes itself in a drop of dew.' Some of O'Siadhail's metaphors come from objects in and around his house; others are derived from his extensive experience with sailing and his involvement in drama:

> A timber's head nestles in another's,
> A mitred joint, this bevelled match,
> Two beams and their collar-beam which
> Shape a triangle, the tie and apex

Of togetherness. So easily one forgets
Couples are a liaison of two rafters. ('Roofing')

Floorboards worn to reveal
Planed, knotted parallels of love.
Honeymoon of tongue and groove. ('Settlement')

Warped threads of memory
dream a weft. ('Memory')

I take the gift of whatever gift I bring
To juice endless taproots of your longing. ('Tending')

Voyage we still dream.
Long perspective of desire.
Port's fugitive gleam. ('Passage')

We intersperse
For better, for worse
Our strands. ('Launch')

Love weathers to what is,
An ease and latitude,
Parallels that needn't meet. ('Watch')

'In every squall a heart's range and stretch' ('Ten to Seven'). 'High and low waters of mood'
('Watch').

Holding a delicate balance
Ad-libbingly you love. ('Tandem')

'Right from curtain-up a jangle of rapport' ('Selves').

To know our parts inside out,
To choose rehearsed naïveté. ('Duration')

Form and metaphor meet where O'Siadhail locates himself as a jazzman. Metaphorically
he places himself on the edge, at the threshold, or in the crosslight. These are intentionally
ambiguous positions between control and freedom, form and formlessness, order and chaos
– all of which are in the nature of jazz. O'Siadhail sees himself as a broker or mover 'in a
loose focus of betwixtness' ('Perspective'). He has 'been to the edge' ('Our Double Time')
where he experiences the vertigo of jazz:

A vibrato at the music's brim, my gift and privilege.
Lady Jazz, I'm your brinkman still dizzy at the edge. ('Vertigo')

In 'that interplay of melody and rhythm', he says, 'My jazz moves in between'
('Underwritten'). O'Siadhail is always cognizant of form yet delights in metaphorical detours:

Poem of becoming. Dance of detours.

> Boundaries fall and a radiance endures. ('Radiance')

This threshold location where boundaries fall is ambiguous:

> As a Chinese sign with a treadle hindering a gate,
> A single word for both barrier and concern. ('Guests')

Jazz itself is O'Siadhail's primary metaphor to show the relationship between his control and freedom. In jazz, 'a tune balances against its freedom' ('Cosmos').

> A beat poised, a crossgrained rhythm,
> interplays, imbrications of voice over voice,
> ... these riffs and overlappings
> a love of deviance, ... ('Cosmos')

Dance, out of which jazz came, is another metaphor of this interplay between form and freedom:

> So tables aside! Any dance at all.
> I'd loved our flight from the formal.
> ... But I yearn again for ritual, organic
> Patterns, circlings, the whorled dance. ('Dance')

A third metaphor comes from the stage where spotlights cross at a focal point. This metaphor gives meaning to the section 'Crosslight' in *Our Double Time* and is one of O'Siadhail's ways of explaining his intermediate position. He says, 'Our sign system is finite but the potential for growth in meaning is infinite; we stand in the crosslight of structure and freedom. ... And just as in language and metaphor, tradition and innovation are held in tension, so too in literature. There is both the desire to absorb the canon and to interrupt and subvert it.'

One way O'Siadhail achieves both structure and freedom is through the use of slanted or near rhymes as in 'Probing':

> And there is no knowing
> the weight that weighed, the agony that drove
> a mind beyond its edges. Although disavowing
> daylight, was he still begging love
> by that dark going?

In 'A Birthday', O'Siadhail rhymes 'our will' with 'circle'; in 'Becoming', he rhymes 'room' and 'rim', 'womb' and 'home', 'full' and 'whole'. This type of rhyming can be playful, as in 'Naked' (with emphasis added):

> In the morning light, her face harrowed and *ashen*.
> Hours in a garden where a chalice will not *pass*.
> Everything I know is nothing. Nothing but *compassion*.

Another aspect of form that O'Siadhail uses to carry the effect of jazz is enjambement or run-on lines. This is found in many of his poems and is nicely illustrated in 'Nakedness':

> Against the beat, between the throbs,
> our moments leap and fall, jazz
> notes of ecstasy, random arabesques
> of anguish, a hazardous melody of being.

This Irish poet for the world needs both the boundaries of form and the transcendence of them. As O'Siadhail put it in this comparison: 'How even in trust, like children playing hopscotch, we both need our boundaries and need to transcend them.'

In many of his poems, O'Siadhail explores the paradox of the coexistence of form and chaos. His is 'A music grown richer in disciplines of yearning' ('Nocturne'); 'Music of paradox. Music of now and metamorphosis' ('That in the End');

> Paradox of a steady passion ... Clearheaded joy, sober kick,
> Trembling music's arithmetic. ('Ten to Seven')

In 'Promise', 'An exploded star still travels down its light.' The music O'Siadhail presents in 'Motet' contains

> webs and layers of voices.
> And which voice dominates or is it chaos?

This is a central concern in 'Madam [Jazz]':

> Chaos in order, order at the heart of chaos.
> Theme and overflow and all that sweeps between them.
>
> ... Nourish me, my jazz. Play this tune to its close.

Another paradox of jazz is the discipline of form combined with improvisation. Both are found in 'Overflow':

> The jazzmen say to improvise is both to hear
> And answer at one time. Careless and austere,
> How a knitted music revels in its discipline.

There is also in jazz the

> Paradox of solo and ensemble in one splendid
> Line that knows the moment of ordered freedom. ('Clusters')

It is in his poetic music (or musical poetry) that we most see O'Siadhail's form and freedom. 'Music, always music', he says in the poem 'Music' – and then invents his own stanzaic form consisting of five lines, the first and last of which have six dominant beats, the second and fourth of which have three beats, and the middle one has two beats. His poem 'Rondo' exemplifies and is a tribute to a musical composition that alternates a main recurring theme with the poet's contrasting voice as he says: 'now it's my turn to respond'. The poem 'Dwelling' has three sections, the first and third of which are sonnets, with the middle section being O'Siadhail's created form being seven tercets celebrating 'Our daily rondo'. The word 'rondo' at the end of the first tercet sets up the rhyme for each of the last subsequent lines, ending 'Navaho' … 'as though' … 'and know' … 'tiptoe' … 'and flow' … 'window'. In the song 'Aubade',

> Secretly a season turns its rondo.
> … time and timelessness counter-subjects in this fugue.

O'Siadhail responds to both the fugue and the motet in his works because they are polyphonic; that is, they have independent but related melodic parts that sound together. Thus in 'Overflow', the first poem in a section of *Our Double Time* called 'Voices', O'Siadhail celebrates

> …discrete polyphony within,
> Where voices intersect,

where voices braid melodies of 'part and counterpart' in what he calls a 'double fugue'. His poem 'Motet' is jazz-like in its 'music of compassion, noise of enchantment'. O'Siadhail closes 'Voices' with reference to 'those fervent motets of William Byrd' as part of the 'counterpointed noises' in which O'Siadhail participates as 'a voice among your voices'. As a jazzman, he affirms: 'Never again one voice' ('Motet'), meaning only one voice. He is like a musician playing in his 'Late Beethoven Quartet':

> Motifs then fragment, configurations interweave,
> mix, shapeshift with maniacal precision –
> a reckless accelerando of distilled simplicity.

Just as a fiddle and viola in that poem 'interject a casual symmetry', so O'Siadhail's playing his musical instrument in connection with former poets is a 'casual symmetry'. If traditional forms are like the march of a band, O'Siadhail plays counterpoint to them, as in his poem 'Around the Bandstand':

> Man from the beginning has heard
> Above the tuba's grumble
> the gaiety of the unpredictable
> Rhythm run counter to his march;
> Through the force-house of a horn
> Blows the ragtime of our hopes.

To shift the metaphor, he knows well the dance, the expected form, but then courts

> … our guilty ecstasy of broken
> symbols, a dance along the precipice … ('Questing')

Looking at larger forms, we see that O'Siadhail's books have, in his words, 'an architecture, an overriding focus' revealing the interconnectedness of things. He moves through time and space with *Rungs of Time* and *The Image Wheel*. In *The Chosen Garden*, he traces his personal epic. As he says, it was his journey of 'setting out, challenging the world, ordeal and failure, the underworld, achievement, the delight of return and re-rooting to open to the world in a new way. A journey from the garden chosen for me by my parents, through boarding school, youthful excesses, ideologies, despair, learning to love and reconnect with society, to the garden I'd chosen for myself'. The volume climaxes with a universal return to Eden in the final section, 'Opening Out'. *Our Double Time* affirms progression through time and maturity, suggested by the section titles: 'Wakings', 'Out of Eden', 'Namings', 'Crosslight', and 'Voices'. Throughout the book there are developments of the multiple meanings of double time, with O'Siadhail persuading us that we, too, 'want to live in double time' ('Twofold').

The overall form of *The Gossamer Wall* is a movement from larger 'Landscapes' (O'Siadhail's section title) to a 'Descent' into evil found in the town of Northeim and in 'Battalion 101' with the horrific slaughter of people from the Polish town of Józefów. The book then moves through 'Figures' of the 'muted dead' who 'demand their debt of memory' to the third and contrasting town in *The Gossamer Wall*, the French village Le Chambon-sur-Lignon, Pastor Trocmé's 'City of refuge' ('Pastor Trocmé'). O'Siadhail ends with the section entitled 'Prisoners of Hope', which out of the horrific awfulness of the Holocaust reveals glimpses of hope:

> Dream and reality feeding circuitries of hope;
> a promise to remember, a promise of never again. ('Glimpses')

O'Siadhail the jazzman affirms

> The sudden riffs of surprise beyond our ken;
> Out of control, a music's brimming let-go.
> We feast to keep our promise of never again. ('Never')

This phrase 'never again' is echoed in three of the closing poems of the book: 'Imagine', 'Never', and 'Repair', with the closing 'Reprise' with its living spirits breathing 'behind a gossamer wall' bringing us full circle to the gossamer wall in the epigraph taken from Anne Michaels's *Fugitive Pieces*.

The architecture of *Love Life* is the history through time of a love relationship. It begins with a section called 'Crimson Thread', a phrase borrowed initially from the Song of Solomon ('Your lips are like a crimson thread') and made the epigraph. The work is then woven with a series of crimson threads such as: 'In Rahab's window tie a crimson thread' ('Sun');

> Funambulist on a crimson thread.
> Love's balancing act ('Cameo x 3')

and the closing lines of the book:

> In Solomon's blue curtain a cord of covenant,
> A crimson thread until the crimson moment. ('Crimson Thread')

That ending also connects sections 1 and 2: 'Crimson Thread' and 'Covenants'. At various places in *Love Life* are found phrases and sentences from the Song of Solomon. *Love Life* is also full of echoes found not only in repeated phrases but also in echoing words as in this stanza from the poem 'Echoes':

Harmonics of abode, geography of echoes
Embrace
A trace
Of daily footpace,
Fall and print on years of staircase.

Echoing words link one section of *Love Life* with the subsequent section. The last poem in the first section, 'Crimson Thread', is 'Covenant', with the next section being entitled, 'Covenants'. The last poem in 'Covenants' is 'House' – which leads to the third section, 'Seasoning', the first poem of which is 'Settlement', a synonym for 'house'. The end of that section is the poem 'Mistress', leading to the final section, 'Full and By', with the action of the first poem 'Gaze' reflecting back to the 'peeping' and 'glimpse' of 'Mistress'.

A system of linking words is found even more extensively in *Globe*. Permutations of 'globe' are found throughout the book, starting with the epigraph from Shakespeare ('while memory holds a seat in this distracted globe'). References to the earth or its geography are subtly placed in most of the poems in the first section of *Globe*, 'Shadow-marks'. The last poem in the next section, 'Knot-Tying', contains the phrase, 'A globe inferred' ('Unbroken'). The next section, 'Wounded Memory', starts with an epigraph from Cavafy that begins, '*Earth is a sanctuary of sorrow*', and contains phrases such as 'A seamless globe' and 'a globe shadowed' ('Eclipse'). The poem 'Eclipse' refers to

The sphere of living, the sphere of gone or unborn
A seamless globe where dead in dreams return.

'In eclipse peoples saw … a globe shadowed.' The last section, 'Angel of Change', is rich with references to the globe such as 'Giddy world', 'Criss-cross planet', 'globe-trotter', 'earth', 'world', 'pole to pole', 'sphere', 'earth's four corners', 'planet-girdling', and 'Worldwide'.

In *Globe*, O'Siadhail speaks of the 'thrill of connectedness' ('Butterfly') – which is exactly what he provides in the entire book. Very subtly, he interweaves the poems in *Globe* with looping end-words and beginning-words. For instance, the first poem, 'Overview', ends with 'wispy face' to be followed by 'Hovering' which begins with 'wisps of cloud' and ends with 'before our leap' which is followed in the next poem by 'teetering', and so forth. Additional creative but unobtrusive links include 'mesh of dreams' – 'mix and brew', 'cyclotron' – 'One-eyed market giants', 'jazz of things' – 'fellowship of jazz', 'Quarrelsome sessions of beloved noise' – 'White noise', 'has never been' – 'All that has been', 'quivering' and 'Crying' – 'Trembling, in tears', '*We can't forget*' – 'Never to forget', 'fragile city' – 'Global city', and 'the music's sake' – 'Music of a given globe'.

Considered as a whole, O'Siadhail's oeuvre is as expansive, varied, and entertaining as the jazz he loves and emulates. In the forms he uses and the range of allusions and ideas that enrich his work, he affirms,

My part
My own variation shaping this history
Of a theme as though one narrow heart
Contains the fractured voices of humanity. ('In Crosslight')

> In vast reaches and weaves of history my own knot.
> Gentle and alert. Just that one ligature in the plot. ('Sweep')

O'Siadhail is a virtuoso jazzman:

> Intrinsic and jazzy and so unselfconscious
> The fingers themselves begin to improvise.
> Braille of flair and skill. Our letting go. ('Virtuoso')

Knowing poetic forms so thoroughly well, he improvises beautifully upon them, letting us hear many voices while his solo voice gives expression to the paradox of freedom through form, of uneven jazz patterns over a regular underlying beat. A master of different dance forms, he

> sings
> And sways to a tune. ('Overflow')

He constantly brings his poetic music alive with apt and striking metaphors. 'I'm hooked', he said in an interview, 'on the wonder of experience shaped in words'. With all its rich connections to other voices, O'Siadhail's poetry is distinctly his own and comes out of his innermost being. 'I've always relished poetry that comes from the core', he said, 'that's written in blood.' For his part, as he says in 'Three Charms':

> Though I relish action,
> on purpose I've chosen a quarantine
> to try to reach the core of things.

The ending poem of O'Siadhail's *Globe*, 'Only End', beautifully sums up O'Siadhail's stance and also his accomplishment – both in *Globe* and in the full range of his poetry. Jazzman O'Siadhail gives us

> Music of a given globe,
> Off-chance jazz forever bringing
> More being into being
> Out of history's tangled knots and loops.

What he has done is 'Made, broken and remade in love' in an 'interwoven polyphony'. Admirers of O'Siadhail's work can take heart that his end in this most recent book of poetry is 'Only End', since 'The only end of jazz is jazz.'

8 | The Poetry of Musical Perception

Lorraine Byrne Bodley

The Double Face of Poetry

There is something about music that keeps its distance even at the moment that it engulfs us,' wrote composer Aaron Copland in his book, *Music and Imagination*. 'It is at the same time outside and away from us and inside and part of us.' The same could be said of O'Siadhail's poetry. Unlike purely musical poetry, which seals itself within its own enchanting domain, O'Siadhail's poetry is bound up with musical meaning and the power which binds us within its acoustic complex is the truth drawn from experience.

The representation of music in O'Siadhail's poetry unlocks a range of ways to explore the themes of love, death, friendship, the abuse of trust, the individual, and society. O'Siadhail is in primary ways an artist of the moment, with all of life's transitions, expressive intervals, speculative quests, and sympathetic projects. Music is central in this context, since for O'Siadhail, the response to music clearly constitutes one of the most fundamental revelations of human individuality and emotion. Musical responsiveness is at the heart of O'Siadhail's work, not merely as effect (whereby the writing provokes the composer to musical imaginings of his own) or as an aspect of his own creativity. Beyond and beneath these manifestations, musical pleasure operates in many interconnected ways. Above all, it works as a recurrent figure, within the scenarios of the poems, for those capacities of affective and imaginative expression that lie at the core of O'Siadhail's work. Musical experience offers O'Siadhail a dramatic equivalent of individuality, and the redemptive inspiration to which it is linked. This is why the significance and function of music in O'Siadhail's work goes beyond its biographical importance for the man himself or its dramatic importance as an element in countless poetic scenes. Such scenes hold binding fascination for O'Siadhail's imagination, since they offer him a dramatic paradigm for those creative, affective, and meditative augmentations of the self that his work repeatedly represents and produces. This remains the case even in 'Rubato', which holds the fatal discordance between its sense of such possibilities and the poet's recognition that the promise of such experiences are undone by the satires of circumstance:

'Rubato'

Here I am once more colloguing with her shadow.
Remember a nineteen-year-old callow, awe-struck?
Surges and *tremolos* of song, passionate bravado
That must soon consume her. My Piaf of Rosmuck.

A life drawn down on accounts always overdrawn.
Pageboy fringe and that singer's vulnerable gaze
Lamenting Barbara Allen or The Rocks of Bawn.
That I should be the one to survive those days?

Death has never danced so close to me before.
Youthful passion. A fling. Loneliness. A lust.
The blind led the blind in our need to explore.
That I should be the one to walk in her dust?

Rubato. Life wavered in intensities of a trill.
And it would be the first warm weekend in June
We'd lay her bones in the clay of a Dublin hill.
Rien de rien. O that defiant and giddy tune

Non. No regrets. Yet still a desire to lament.
A blossom dropped so stealthily in full bloom.
A star flared and faded across the firmament.
A thread stretched and pegged, a warp in a loom.

Who'd guess which of us would outlive our youth?
Her songs still croon in my bones. A hum. A buzz.
Me the survivor. May I grow wiser for us both?
Everything that happens must happen as it does.[1]

Although 'Rubato' addresses such a particular occasion of distress as the singer's untimely death, as long as desire is not disallowed, as long as its tune plays into the prepared expectations of our ear and our nature, then the poem's effect is to offer an affirmation of her life and a sense of possible consolation in its closing lines.

There can be few poets with O'Siadhail's capacities to evoke musical transports and intensities. His gift in this area is innately musical and his anthologies are laden with poems that betray his fascination with musical moments or experiences. Musical experience offers O'Siadhail himself both an important source for his own poetic inspiration, and a template or analogue for his thinking about it. In 'Quartet', the poem floats parallel to the musical moment:

These players nod and gleam as if they're seeing
And hearing the other's expression, each leaning
Into the fine-nerved strings, their whole being
Vested in this interplay, this gamble on meaning.[2]

What happens to us when we read the poem depends upon the kind of relation it displays towards our musical life; our sense of what it is to be alive to musical experience. While the poetic structure can be seen as an equivalent to musical form, 'Quartet' is shaped by O'Siadhail's inner ear in a way that also revives the inner ear of the reader. Although inspired by experience, this sonnet does not fall into step with the performance. In the second and third quartrain the poem presents us with a new form, which is adjacent and parallel to lived experience but which, in spite of perfect sympathy for that living experience, has no desire to dwell among it:

> I remember a crescendo dream. We burned and burned.
> Maybe it's age. I grow in this mutual succumbing:
> Bow and pluck, phrase and breath of an earned
> And watchful passion, our face to face becoming.[3]

Here the associations of sound open up past lives and time, and offers the poet a way of banishing the present. Music becomes a privileged vehicle and analogue for the poet's memories that eclipse determinations of consciousness and chronology. As O'Siadhail re-enters the performance: the closing couplet affirms the power of transformative expression, occasioned by music, that the sonnet explicitly aspires to reproduce.[4] The sonnet appeals because the response it provokes is innately artistic: there is an inwardly expanding sense, for O'Siadhail and for the reader, of how the art of another person can become the condition of a creativity of one's own. In 'Late Beethoven Quartet', the poet again finds the means of musical expression in this genre as he is inspired by the combination of surface simplicity and fathomless depth of Beethoven Quartets. He returns to these late works with a second 'Quartet' in *Our Double Time*[5] – inspired by Beethoven's Opus 127, no. 12 – which he scores in four movements and in which he captures a range of rhythms, tempi, and dynamics, as well as an exploration of tonality and mood. While poetry is often the source of musical inspiration, O'Siadhail reverses this process in 'Quartet' and the interanimation of musical expression plays between player, poet and reader.[6]

In ways reminiscent of poetry, music is itself described as something that passes from one person to another, catching up both in a common movement or accord that surprises the poet's sense of physical and subjective separation. A song that provides a precarious, but genuine, connection between poet and performer is 'Folksong'.[7] The title of the poem announces that the mutuality that exists between poetry and music is not something new. By blending music and poetry O'Siadhail acknowledges his debt to the attitudinal significance of our national culture and its influence on poetry, and lends permanence to the fleeting nature of one performance, privately replayed in the poet's memory. This division between poetry and musical lyric is evoked as 'the singer winds down to the final spoken words' and 'A loneness in the shaft of song refuses to end'.[8] Here O'Siadhail captures the transition from singing to speaking in sean-nós which marks the end of the song. Yet the actuality of the performance described is less the issue than the emotional quality of the voice which takes hold of the poet. 'The voice is the only music that says what it tells',[9] the poet begins, and throughout the poem language makes available, and produces, the essential affects of truth around which the poem is organized. O'Siadhail's words share the qualities of inconclusiveness and promise that the poem's content presents in association with music's power to connect people. Such incidents are accidental, 'forced upon us', yet deeply significant. There is a different correlation between lived time and musical time in 'Rowan' where the protagonist's final days are accompanied by:

Hours listening to a late Beethoven adagio,
Latticed yearning for a peace she wants to win.

... He's now ghostly thin

And speaks of when she's gone. Must it be so?
The long struggle to joy of a quartet's violin.[10]

The resonance of the late quartets with the events of human life identifies music with a power to overcome time. Here music is linked not to an escape from individuality but to a lifelong modification of it and expression arising from it. Such musical scenes in *Crosslight* produce effects of sympathy which in turn condition ethical responses and enquiries; like music, the poems offer expansions of thought and sympathy.

One of the fascinations of music for O'Siadhail, is that its experiences of joy are undeniably physical, even though they carry a metaphysical import. In 'Music', aesthetic experience is also implicitly ethical, because goodness and joy are inseparable from the reanimating events and processes of self-expression through which new horizons open and old wounds disappear. A memorable poem which allows for a development of these ideas is the closing stanza of 'Our Double Time' where the poet imagines a musical encounter, in which music is both a means of, and a figure for, ecstasies of the common-place:

Here is my life. ...
No fixed measures. Just moving with a word
As though I belong in counterpointed noises,
One of those fervent motets of William Byrd.
Across all the aeons, my one humming breath
Poised in this motet. Steady, even sublime.
To think this year will have been my fiftieth![11]

O'Siadhail's artistry resides in his ability to turn back and capture such fleeting moments and place them at the heart of his writing. As with the plaintive song of the bird anticipated in 'Springnight',[12] the dawn chorus at 'Easter' sets up an oscillation, between the literal and inspired, that is evident in various ways in the poem.[13] What becomes important is not what the song means to the poet as music, but what it does to him. And what it does, above all, unsought, is to evoke an affect of joy which in turn passes into the writing. Music binds together the natural music, poet, and audience through transmissions that are as indubitable as they are unaccountable. In 'An East Wind', the wind sets up an exchange of responses; the cherry trees answer:[14]

The wind's blowing its scruple,
a long pleading of oppression
eddying from gable to gable
around this Maytime Dublin.
Like rounded fists of confetti
blossoms cluster on cherry trees,
handfuls of memories to scatter.
What did the wind's voice say?

Did you hear the policeman's tap?

...
Did you feel Siberia's frost
Turning bitter, a heart tightening? ...

I hear it whispered in my ear.
Does anyone hear the wind's rustle? ...

Here music suggests, if not harmony, then a rapport or commerce of sound which effectively binds together the divergent elements of the scene, and draws the reader and poet together within the intent physicality of each moment. In 'St Stephen's Green', the scene as event goes beyond and between the various individuals and elements in it:

Only a stone's throw from here I was born.
As though pulled by navel gravity I return

To a first fountain, a gift from post-war Germany,
Three bronze women measuring out man's destiny.

Fateful spinners: What was, What is, Will be.
The three Norns Urður, Skuld and Verðandi.

Or a childhood's gentle women in German counterparts;
Roethke's Frau Baumann, Frau Schmidt, Frau Schwartze?

Yet I think I still know them by their cut and poise.
I imagine I hear their laughter bubbling in a voice

That wells underneath this fountain's fall and hiss.
I think I hang by their thread of golden promise.

That *all shall be well*. A gift I'm trying to accept.
To believe that promises given are promises kept.[15]

In 'St Stephen's Green', O'Siadhail sets the components as melodies in counterpoint, each of which serves as a motif for another. Under the sway of poet's music, the individual moves from the actualities of lived experience into an even remoter past. Poetry repeats that orientation to the future which gives this scene its meaning: 'the laughter bubbling in a voice that wells underneath' the fountain, the 'golden promise that all shall be well', are essential to the poem's transcendence of time. One could multiply examples of such incidents, involving the animating power of sound, from O'Siadhail's work: the urban music of a 'Streetscene'[16] and 'Morning on Grafton Street';[17] the songs which accompany children's games in 'Underworld'[18] and 'Perspectives';[19] the music of guests arriving in 'Embrace';[20] the juxtaposition of bawdy pub singing slipped into the second stanza of 'Arrival', a Christmas lullaby[21] or 'the train's anapaest' which narrates each passenger's tale in 'Train Journey'.[22] Such images are descendants of the ancient *musica humana*, part of the medieval tripartite division of music.

The Richness Of Possibility

Hail! Madam Jazz reveals a philosophical and deeply poetic mind, in which music forms a sonic image for the constant striving of life, the manifold fluctuations, the accidents of passion and feeling. In this collection, O'Siadhail's jazz imagery reveals a cast of mind characterized by his vision of experience as rich in possibility and yet undivided: life buds and burgeons, changes and creates. The dominant tenor of its imagery is characterized by this perception of jazz as figurative of this innate vitality in life. The figure of Madam Jazz is a symbol of radiating musical power in its most energizing and transcendent aspects. In the title poem of this anthology, 'Hail! Madam Jazz', O'Siadhail refers to her illusive nature as he coins a series of names for his *femme fatale*:

> ... O Never-To-Be-Caught,
> O Minx beyond this mind's embrace,
> Hider-Go-Seeker, Miss Unfathomable,
> Demurring Lady playing at the chase.
> ... Mistress All.
> Mischievous Strategy, Madam Jazz!

The poet's celebration of his Mistress Jazz embodies the poet's quest for knowledge of life which inclines away from the perplexed, to the proffered alternative, to be perplexed and exultant. In the musical persona of Madam Jazz life is concentrated into something rich rather than something strange: like Ariel and Prospero she embodies poetry's enchantment and the countervailing presence of human truth. This duality of sound and sense pervades *Our Double Time*, where she takes the stage eight years later. In this anthology O'Siadhail celebrates her precarious presence in 'Dread':

> I ripen now daily beyond my prime.
> A fiftieth year. ...
> All the more I live in double time.
>
> A precarious joy. The tear and let-rip,
> Sweet compulsions, obsessive innovation,
> As Madam Jazz improvises to seduce
> One heart still glorying in its courtship.[23]

In 'Passivity', the poet travels

> like Proust ...
> to trust the jazz of Madam's dark[24]

and he returns to celebrate her multiple voices in 'Light':

> All-loving Madam Jazz I've second-guessed, betrayed
> My trust. Let me take up my tune again, so finite
>
> And full as all the undreamed-of echoed and relayed.
> Fountain of life in thy light shall we see light.[25]

Such webs of meaning recur in 'Vertigo',[26] 'In Crosslight Now',[27] and in 'Madam', where 'an uncontainable theme spills out its tunes' and he addresses this 'insatiable Madam of variations'.[28] In this anthology the centrality of music is used as an anchor from which to pivot through an impressive range of human discourse. Such variations resound in *Globe* where O'Siadhail manages the reader's responses, taking us back and forth between the vibrant public and private domains of musical experience.[29] As in earlier anthologies the poet portrays Madam Jazz as an affair of resonances, reverberations, correspondences, expressive traits. Drawn in by her music like a moth a the candle flame, O'Siadhail reproduces such counterpoint between self and world and places it before the reader.

Music, configured as it is in terms of counterpoint, is an important contributory factor to the rhythm of experience. In 'Cosmos', 'a cross-grained rhythm' creates a new plane of counterpoint between two musical phrases, passing between each and holding them together, while elevating them to a new common power.[30] Such musical moments are symbolic of the natural processes of becoming found in 'Apprentice'.[31] In 'Aubade', a new rhythm is a new life given to the world, a resuscitation not just of the ear but of the springs of being:

> The sun has outdated darkness, another morning
> pacemakes history, man the word-bearer reawakes
> and dares to praise. Begging my tongue of fire
>
> I proclaim a motto theme, naming in ecstasy
> mysteries of time.[32]

Against this motto theme, this aubade as overture to another year, 'the metronome's remorseless beat' reminds us of music's rule-governed nature and stands in contrast to the passage of time:

> Although I celebrate, I still hear the metronome's
> remorseless beat. No rubato here or emancipation;
> accomplices in the scheme, each day is our biography.
>
> It's January. Secretly a season turns its rondo.[33]

This recognition of life's transience inspires the poet to dance, to live more fully in 'Invocation'[34] and 'Summerfest'[35]: music's counter-image of the dance of death in 'Rubato' or the demons which dance in depression in 'Blues'.[36] As with music, 'Dance' provides a trigger or means for the individual and collective expression:

> Limerick's Walls, The Siege of Ennis.
> Side-step and stoop under the arch.
> Our linked arms. A scent of dizziness.
>
> Openness. Again and again to realign.
> Another face and the moves must begin
> Anew. And we unfold into our design.
> I want to dance for ever. A veil
> Shakes between now-ness and infinity.

> Touch of hands. Communal and frail.
> Our courtesies weave a fragile city.[37]

In the third movement the charm of this céilí dance, 'a ballet of intimacies' and the dance of the spheres suggest how the microcosm and macrocosm exist in counterpoint, indivisible in themselves and in their correlation, like an individual line or phrase of music and the larger whole that it introduces or into which it is interwoven:

> A few are sitting this one out: ... catching a glance
> Of how the dancers turn like Plato's stars.
>
> Dance in a cosmos, cosmos in the light of dance ...
> Harmony, music of spheres, the mystic's trance.
>
> The whirl of it! ...[38]

To reap joy from multiplicity is the province of this poet and there are multiple examples, musical and otherwise, where O'Siadhail places unconscious elements of joy or ecstasy in counterpoint with the commonplace. 'Matins for You' gives a dual sense of the scene: as unremarkable, ordinary and inconsequential in one respect; while being also memorable, mysterious, even profound, in another.[39] Accordingly, 'Uncertain' renders the affective power of a musical encounter:

> Are tune and rhythm one in the fullness of the play?
> Art Tatum is fingering *Someone to watch over me*.
> My jazz, my jazz, will tomorrow be my dancing day.[40]

Typically, it is part of the force of the poem that it can accommodate and do justice to such questions, while maintaining its careful intensity of focus. So too 'Clarinet',[41] 'That in the End',[42] 'Underwritten',[43] and 'Overflow'[44] all skilfully counterpoise various differentiated elements of musical meaning and feeling, while preserving, through their seeming artlessness, a direct emotional concentration. In this anthology, *Our Double Time*, the poet characteristically employs the musical metaphors of polyphony, improvisation, and variation to suggest how we interact with each other and the world, the multiple and modulating aspects of our momentary experience, our antipathies and sympathies. Like music, every bit of experience has its quality, its duration, its extension, its urgency, its clearness, no one of which can exist in isolation: they exist only through each other. Reality is portrayed as a conflux of the same with the different: they co-penetrate and telescope; just as in counterpoint distinct lines can and do commune together.

Music and Individuality

Throughout his poetic career, music is associated by O'Siadhail with a mode of self-expression that is both physical and ideal: physical in that it relies on accidents of sensation and feeling, but also ideal in that it reveals essential human qualities. O'Siadhail uses musical metaphors for the descriptions of his poetic character's emotional capacities, coining a whole vocabulary of the vital passion for sound and the ability to resound and respond. In 'Rubato', O'Siadhail writes of a woman in terms of the characteristic musicality of her voice.[45] It is her singing, 'the surges and tremolos of song', which provides him with an aural image which he can replay endlessly. In 'Rubato', a sense of the singer's expressive possibilities comes alive, as does O'Siadhail's creative intelligence, and the listener's imagination. The poet's virtuosity is further evident in the way he weaves a living presence into the story of her passing; where recollections of a shared past expand into the most subtle and flexible accommodation of her divergent qualities. The rich timbre of the singer's voice, and the rich emotional depth it carries are an essential feature of her individuality: music is used once again as a trope for the expression of individuality, the singer's and the poet's: 'her songs still croon in my bones'. The poet's vitalism unchains our description of Caitlín Maude's individuality from the limiting, formal, concepts of person and time and allows us to glimpse the *élan vital* of a singer by living empathy. The scene is unredeemingly sad and provides a poignant example of O'Siadhail's use of music as tragedy.

In 'Rubato', O'Siadhail found inspiration in the voice of the dead, becoming a medium for her. In 'Elegy for a singer', the voice which conditions O'Siadhail's art belongs to this muse, someone from O'Siadhail's own past, whose tender influences still exert a powerful effect on his mind:

> Fevered woman too quick afire,
> song-queen too giving glowed
> over, fuelled a chiller world. ...
>
> Mastermind demands you leave,
> quit the dance in swing and drive,
> lonely take the last route home.
>
> Still a little my once sweetheart,
> rest a while and then farewell;
> travel gently the forever zone.[46]

The poet's lament for this fellow-traveller in 'Train Journey' plays on the similarity of musical strings and human nerves – her constitution is like a fine violin which vibrates to the lightest touch:

> ...I grieve
> For a fellow-traveller, a woman taut
> as a violin, lavishing her girth of life
> into song. Too near to the edge and overwrought:
> But how should I sing unless I burn? ...[47]

This motif is brought in concert with his own experience in 'Music',[48] and in 'Perspectives', where the poet asks:

> Whose music? ...
> Whose bow shivers its music in my string?[49]

Musical incidents in O'Siadhail's poetry set up scenes of identification where music creates a powerful way of feeling with another person. In 'Handing-On: Prelude', musical experience provides a key for unlocking fundamental revelations of the doctor's character.[50]

In 'In a New York Shoe Shop', the protagonist's delight and confidence in his musical power
has its roots in the origins of jazz:

'In a New York Shoe-Shop

Canned blues rhythms hum the background.
Air-conditioned from the swelter, a choosy
clientele vets the canted wall-racks

of new-look summer shoes. Unbargained for,
a handsome inky coloured man catching
the snappy syncopation, jazzes across the floor

to proof-dance a pair of cream loafers.
Beaming, he bobs and foot-taps; pleased
with his purchase, he jives a short magnificat.

A friend from Maryland had once described
seeing in his grandfather's cellar rusted irons
that had fettered a chain-gang of black slaves.

Behind the ployrhythm, the scoops, the sliding
pitches and turns, I hear the long liquid line
of transcended affliction; women with gay

kerchiefs are prayer-hot in the praise-house
or whoop in Alabama's cotton-fields. Life ad libs
with a jug and washboard; sublimity forgives.

In submission to the pulse, this customer lets go,
swings low to the bitter-sweet quadruple
time, unmuzzled, human and magnificent.[51]

Here the poem comes to accommodate, at its margins, the counter-knowledge of experience.
To acknowledge this is not to deny the happy reality of the moment, but merely to indicate
that joy and suffering are for O'Siadhail two inseparable tendencies, or viewpoints, or
moments of being.

Lyrical Imagery and the Semantics of Desire

Released in 2005, *Love Life* is a collection of poems of a highly lyrical nature. The anthology
begins with an enchanting musical prelude: three poems which invoke the themes of Eros
and Amor. In the following 'Long Song', the seductive arabesques of sound entangle the
reader, inspiring an intense connection to the scene:

Fragrance of your oils.
L'amour fou. Such sweet folly.
Your haunting presence
Distilled traces of perfume
Resonances of voice

Dwell in my nervous body.
My skin wants to glow,
All my being glistens.
Divine shining through.
Your lips like a crimson thread,
Your mouth is lovely...
You're all beautiful, my love.[52]

In 'Concertina', the body is converted into a musical instrument of sorts, at once expressive and pliable:

Taken by the folds of skirt
Which like a Japanese fan
Flicker accordion pleats,

Sways of silk redundancy
Whose melody's fall
Of light and dark caprices

Concertina creases
To play my nerves and call
A rousing tune I fancy. ...[53]

Here, as in many poems of this anthology, music provides a kind of topos for the scene and plot which plays out and arranges concordances of different qualities of feeling and of thought. In 'House', everyday life is crafted in musical terms;[54] in 'Voyage' this repetition is portrayed as 'a life's canonical rhythm'[55] and the ease of repetition is suggested by the memory of music in a pianist's hands – a motif which recurs in 'Ceremony'.[56] In a similar way rhythm is used to suggest the beats of being: the 'double rhythm' of life together in 'Tandem';[57] the use of tempi to describe the play of lovemaking, and the metaphor of dance to describe the glory of living in counterpoint. The celebration of spontaneity recurs in 'Selves', where improvisations on a daily theme capture the poet by surprise;[58] and the art of improvisation recognized in 'Overflow', from *Our Double Time*,[59] re-emerges in everyday life in 'Duration':

Chameleon days ...

The constant edits, rewrites or redirection ...
And yet to believe we haven't lost the plot

But keep on relearning and switching role
As if to follow a plot but not the plotting

As if forgivingly we go improvising on
A performance art still beyond control[60]

Despite such shared imagery, music has a particular status in *Love Life*: at the same time as being a stimulus to self-differentiation, it is often instrumental in producing new arrangements of feeling between the protagonists. Music both binds the couple together and mirrors the changes that take place within. In 'Caprice', this reciprocity is staged in terms of a giving and receiving of sound that is often explicitly musical;[61] in 'Anniversary', their first encounter is described as a tuning fork, exquisitely capturing those moments of tension before a performance;[62] while the recollection of a harvest song in 'Question' evokes the richness garnered from those years:

> a minor keyed harvest folksong ...
> what I cut down, you rake in ...
>
> ... In the falling tones
> of a melody again the low warm
> swish of a scythe. ...
> In the shadow an angel gathers in. [63]

Not only in *Love Life*, but in all his work, the poet's beloved is like a theme hidden in variations, and capable of a number of different manifestations. Her presence continually recurs like a musical motif as he returns to rest in her. In 'Nocturne', written twenty years earlier, music's ability to go to the heart provides the perfect trope for the intimate closure in love at the end of a day. 'Quartet', from *A Fragile City*, celebrates a seemingly transient musical event.[64] For O'Siadhail, the music inside answers the music outside, both natural and man-made, as the interplay between the musicians in mirrored in the couple's lives. Music takes on an extraordinary intensity in this context: here, as in *Love Life*, music is literally part of love, as well as a metaphor for it; love-in-flux, always being modulated, changed, transfigured.

Music and Transcendence

Throughout O'Siadhail's poetry music offers potent and irrefutable signs of transcendence through physical connection. The captivating effects of rhythm and melody may be impermanent, but they return, and in doing so, repeat life's inexhaustible possibilities. Vlado Perlemuter's playing in 'Homage' is valuable because it transforms everything. However, modestly and fleetingly, harmony occurs within the forlorn detail and momentariness of the scene:

> Nearly eighty, slow-paced,
> stooped, he enters. Even his suit
> has seen better days; but touching
> that instrument, his face is chamois
>
> which puckers, ripples each phrase;
> a smile inscrutable, ears pricked
> for an inward zing, heard deep
> in the calm of age. This virtuoso
>
> Vlado Perlemuter a half-century
> ago, Ravel's apprentice, played
> these pieces for the maitre whom
> in his turn Fauré had fostered. ...[65]

Here the musician is a positive type of the human spirit: through music, through his musical forefathers and protégés, he transcends the material conditions of his life, and in so doing reawakens the ethical imagination of the reader and poet. To talk of transcendence is not to talk of any secondary or enchanted domain. It is rather to talk of extraordinary physical encounters, dislocating events, which raise the various capacities of the spirit – perception, memory, imagination – to autonomous expression. Many of O'Siadhail's best lyrics contain moments of vision that have found their objective correlative in something close to common experience but yet evoke the underlying deeper reality that he celebrates in *Love Life*. Such inspiring augmentations of identity are found in the unremarkable and usually unremarked aspects of routine life which are brought into consciousness by the poet's penetrating search for the attainable significance that aspires beyond the world of here and now. Music, because it fluently resists cognition, retains an inwardness with such immanent conditions of experience. The more one contemplates O'Siadhail's 'moments of vision', the more musical experience appears to have an exemplary status for the poet as he focuses on the experience of transcendence that it carries with it. The emotional intensities, linked to possibilities of renewal afforded by music, are suggested in 'Psalm in the Night', where night-time anxieties recur like a responsorial psalm so that music propounds rather than allays anxiety.[66] In 'In the End', a soprano voice within expresses a surge of joy[67] which fills the spirit's vault like the echo of a chorister reverberating in a cathedral. Such poems exemplify the hymn-singing effect of poetry, its action as a dissolver of differences.

O'Siadhail's fascination with the paradoxical effects of music is evident in *Our Double Time*. In 'Whatever Else', music is seen by O'Siadhail not merely as another vehicle for the transports of the soul, but also as an analogue for it.[68] In the closing stanza of 'Our Double Time', music works as a sort of binding agent, providing a means of relatedness and individuation. It can also be said to be a revealing agent, as the poet engages in 'a deeper listening to a music's densities':

> Here is my life. These my friends and voices.
> No fixed measures. Just moving with a word
> As though I belong in counterpointed noises,
> One of those fervent motets of William Byrd.
> Across all the aeons, my one humming breath
> Poised in this motet. Steady, even sublime.
> To think this year will have been my fiftieth!
> From now every single moment our double time.
> Not that I've grown blasé or no longer care,
> More a deeper listening to a music's densities.
> No matter how or when, no matter where,
> The feel of a line sung with consummate ease.
> I love and am loved. All my tinyness rejoices
> That I'll have been a voice among your voices.[69]

The poems abound with these sorts of episode, where music acts as a catalyst, drawing together the accidents and touches of experience. In many ways, musical symbolism indicates how O'Siadhail's poetry itself has the power, in common with music, to transcend the constraints of identity and time.

O'Siadhail's poetic meditations on music can be said to be implicitly philosophical to the extent that they open up such complexities of temporality and identity. Music has the power to reanimate periods and traditions from the distant past, as in the many poems that follow musical trails into the culture and history of O'Siadhail's family and elsewhere. This leads to a more personal case of individual memory, where music is endlessly and variously employed by O'Siadhail as a link between the different temporal dimensions of experience. A piece of music can act like a genie's lamp releasing a cloud of significant emotion which generally takes on definition and intelligibility as the poet translates it into poetry. Countless poems originate with such moments of musical inspiration as enhancements of and renewals of the self. In many poems, O'Siadhail probes this plight of memory, where the poet, as the medium of the influences, voices and ghosts of the past, intensifies his division from the present. In 'Clarinet', music criss-crosses actuality with the memoirs of Etty Hillesum and the poet uses music to catch and revive the echoes of past innocence in the self.[70] To O'Siadhail the commonest song can have tremendous significance, may carry memories and associations of a lifetime's love with all its joys and sorrows. The ability of music to make the past a living present is evident in 'Rubato' which gathers up the emotional experience of years and recalls the radiance of Caitlín Maude, yet suggests the whole course of a poet's life since then.

Music and Silence

Dissonance, even cacophony, has its place in poetry as in music. In a poem of any length, there must be transitions between passages of greater and less intensity, to give a rhythm of fluctuating emotion essential to the musical structure of the whole. The rhythmic disjunctions in O'Siadhail's lines in 'Forebodings' and 'Signals'[71] from *The Gossamer Wall* and the correspondingly fractured elements of narrative or argument are wakenings to a new reality, lyric equivalents of the fault the poet intuited in the life of his times:

> Scatterings. Ghetto. Yellow badge. Pogroms.
> Who was it poisoned wells to spread
> Black Death among Christian folk? *And they spit*
>
> Upon him and took the reed and smote him
> *On the head*. So Europe at fever pitch.
> Crusades. Over again the Goyim's fall-guy.
>
> Outside inside. Love-hate's merry-go-round.
> Blood-baker, healer, *Jude Süss*.
> Even while the myth sleeps, a waiting victim. ... [72]

While this volume stands apart in the poet's oeuvre, it is at once characteristic of all his writing: from the beginning O'Siadhail has been eager to make a connection between what was happening outside Ireland and what was being shown inside himself. *The Gossamer Wall* is both historical and parabolic; it has gone far past the simplicity of historical record and is a cry of human depths. In this anthology, O'Siadhail has testified at different moments and in different registers in his poetry to the horror and fury of the holocaust. The adroit use of music in this poetic pavan is evident in the disturbing, violent implications of the recurring motif of Macbeth; in the staccato imperatives of 'Schnell! Schnell!' in the 'still violent round-ups' of 'Measures';[73] in the abuse of music to mask violence in 'Culmination';[74] and in the 'gaunt silences'[75] of the third movement, 'Figures', broken by an 'Ensemble', where the musicians play for their lives:

In summer by camp gates an ensemble's concerts:
As squads of inmates are filing past in fives,
On stools in their pleated navy-blue skirts
And lavender scarves they play for their lives.
Chosen by an exam, many who'd been *virtuose*
Now grind a music complicit and empty-eyed;
A band conductor from a famous Vienna café
Parodies for all she's worth her life outside. [76]

As the poet looks over the shoulder of history, traces of music return: first as a metaphor in 'Dust-veil'[77] and then in the private performances of Anita Lasker for Mengele:

After a tough day selecting who'd live or die,
For light relief Mengele had a camp cellist
Anita Lasker play him Schumann's *Träumerei*.[78]

The gaiety of Klezmer, jazz, and céili which emerged 'out of darkest histories'[79] is soon recalled and closing music is granted to:

Eight hundred dark-eyed girls from Salonica
Bony and sag-breasted singing the *Hatikvah*

Tread the barefoot floor to a shower-room.
Friedländer, Berenstein, Menasche, Blum.

Each someone's fondled face. A named few.
Did they hold hands the moment they knew?

I'll change their shame to praise and renown in all
The earth ... Always each face and shoeless footfall

A breathing memory behind the gossamer wall. [80]

The poems in this anthology draw much of their mesmerizing power from the direct way in which they present and accumulate such affective violence and physical brutality. The movement through *The Gossamer Wall* is like a slow dirge: a musical performance, unstoppable until the end.

The Musical Image

A 'musical poem' is a poem which has a musical pattern of sound and a musical pattern of secondary meanings in the words which compose it, and these two patterns are indissoluble and one. The music of verse is not about metrical patterns and scansion; it is a question of the whole poem: only with this in mind can we approach the question of music in O'Siadhail's verse. In the poetry of O'Siadhail a formal design can be discovered in particular strophes, and in complete poems. *The Gossamer Wall* is a very complex metrical structure; the more easily grasped structure is the sonnet; the skilful and sensual deployment of rhythm in *Love Life* suggests a refusal of the conventional metrics and in 'If' form is broken and remade. The properties of music that concern the poet are the sense of rhythm and the sense of structure. For O'Siadhail rhythm is aesthetic. It draws on the reader's own susceptibilities and sympathies, so that he or she will also find, in reflecting on his or her response to the poem, that it offers possibilities of self-reading: through reflecting on one's response. With regard to O'Siadhail's structure: the arrangement of sounds and their flow, first in score, second in performance, transcends the normal aspects of rhetoric or narrative. Like the visceral impact of painting, music hits in the gut, or upon some super-sense, without further interpretation being necessary. O'Siadhail's poetry is another of these arts, yet the music of imagery as well as sound sets it apart and much dominant and recurrent imagery throughout the poems has to do with the total effect. Like music, the poems offer expansions of thought and sympathy and the melodious note of the lines is the result of a kind of wisdom which this poet portrays.

The use of recurrent themes is as natural to poetry as to music. O'Siadhail's treatment of the recurring themes of love, death, friendship, trust, bears some analogy to the development of a theme by different groups of instruments. Repetition of themes unify anthologies and the reappearance of motifs engenders new intonations, new interpretations. O'Siadhail scores his anthologies in movements: the transitions in poems are also comparable to the different movements of a symphony or quartet, and there is contrapuntal arrangement of subject matter within poems.

Bodley and O'Siadhail: Poetic Collaborations

While O'Siadhail's poetry displays a music that is inherent, that comes about through the dance of its own language and without the need for external support, there is room, as well as a tradition, for the concourse between the two art forms. In collaborating with Seóirse Bodley, O'Siadhail made ample use of irony, metaphor, imagery, and his poems gain energy, lyricism, and texture through the synergistic effect music provides. The energy and lyric modernity of Bodley's music and the musical intimacy between singer and pianist are a match for O'Siadhail's words and voice. For *A Naked Flame*, O'Siadhail chose poems which achieve a balance between conceptual and sensual expressiveness; and as a result, the emotional content of the poetry seems fortified, and the sensual expressiveness of rhythm and sound is shared by poetry and music.[81] Poetry is oral by tradition and is not fated to diminution in the company of its kindred art. Language in a poem set to music seems to work better if there is space for the successful interplay between the two art forms. In the poems written for Bodley's orchestral song-cycle, *The Earlsfort Suite*, O'Siadhail has left room for the music to manoeuvre.[82] That the song-cycle functions best as a unified piece serves as its own validation.

The Spellbinding Musical Line

Hearing O'Siadhail read his own selection of his poems in Maynooth in 2004, I was immediately struck by their tunefulness and their feeling, and the sense that here was an involuntary and yet necessary physical expression of that individual's inmost essence, an expression which carries creative powers of thought which are opposed to the mechanical and purely formulaic. The control of musical metrics is centrally important in O'Siadhail's verse and the poet's musicality shows in his sense of line, flexible metre, choice of word; tone colours ring out in the form of intermingling vowels and consonants. The emotional expressiveness of O'Siadhail's poetry is located in its use of musical effects. His poems contain the most subtle modulations, stresses, and changes, entirely reminiscent of musical composition. These variations, with their dramatic breaks in rhythm and emphasis, are used with almost infallible skill when they underline emotional states. Each new musical work brings with it new feelings, new themes. In O'Siadhail's *Poems 1975-1995*, each new poem's distinctive grammar of sound, and the feelings which it creates, are not extracted from life by art according to some principle of resemblance or artistic precedent. Instead, the artist essentially creates a new and individuating affect in each anthology and out of the simplest phrases of conversation he evolves a magical melody. In *The Gossamer Wall*, he replaces such resonance and mellifluousness with the rough colloquial diction and rhythms and the fragmented difficult music of modern lyricism. To hear Micheal O'Siadhail read from each of these works is a memorable experience in which the spoken, the rhythmical and the melodic would appear at moments to combine mysteriously. One realizes the progressive disclosure of the controlling form, and the fine consistency of the metrical counterpoint with O'Siadhail's ultimate assumptions about poetry and reality.

One of the great pleasures of a sensually sophisticated poet, such as O'Siadhail, is the strong musicality and physical pleasure of language that is capable of producing a frisson in the listener. The power of O'Siadhail's readings is due to the power and manipulation of the voice as well as the verbal energy of his language. Reading in an unadorned voice, O'Siadhail brings the sound into full focus as highly rhythmic communication; this is something one can say of very few poets. A poem's music marks it as different, and pulls the reader into the event of the reading. Immediately you begin an O'Siadhail poem your inner response begins to rock in time with the poet's rhythm: a musicality which is quite inimitable. The musical character of O'Siadhail's readings is also evident in his use of rubato: the slowing down and speeding up, which pulls the listener along, keeping him or her slightly off balance and ever attentive. O'Siadhail writes such rubato, or stretching of the rhythm, into his work and emphasizes it in live reading. His poems start out of speech rhythms that drift near to song, or they begin with metrical regularity and then modulate into cadences that imply speech.

In O'Siadhail's readings, the transitions of the lyrical or musical and the spoken imply a social drama, so much so that one can trace echoes of the ballad form and the fading context of time-honoured community. Although he does not write ballads, O'Siadhail's readings have a more or less submerged reference to and solidarity with this immemorial tradition: one finds oneself in the company of a poet with a story to tell, a poet who needs to create an audience for his acutely personal experience or to raise before its eyes the horrors of social upheaval. Poetry hopes most of all for knowledge of life yet in the retelling of human experience O'Siadhail inclines away from poetry's impulse to be all truth. What happens in O'Siadhail's musical lyrics is a concentration between emotions experienced by the poet and the emotions expressed in a poem. We are in the presence of such concentration when we read a poem like 'Interrogation'. This lyric is obviously not meant to fall into step with our common speech-gait; rather it presents us with a new form, adjacent and parallel to lived experience but with no desire to dwell in the midst of it. The poet's sympathy for living experience and his desire to transcend it is at once evident in his poignant question: 'What have you given?'[83] To proffer an answer, life has called O'Siadhail to song and he has given us a wealth of musical poetry; a *rerum Concordia discors*, a true and personal picture of the nature of the world.

9 | *Song for Soprano and Piano*

Squall

Micheal O'Siadhail

Seóirse Bodley

A mis - un - der-stand - ing

we should but didn't___ broach___ rank-les then flares.___ one

load-ed re-mark rocks our world.

Strang - ers   we stand stark and al - one   as   words

sweep   us   in   whirl - - winds   of   re -

proach.   Old_____ sores

15
glare.
Yet why
18
fore - stall
dark
with
dark?
20
Buff - e - ted
we
ride
the
21
storm's
pitch
and
lurch.
A

squall clears, the sky lifts___ our kiss - es ti-mid

to - kens of___ am - nes - ty as the pur - ged___ air___

breathes___ its___ sweet af - ter -

math.

Diff-id- ent we pledge ne-ver a- gain like fledge- ling lo- vers still a-ware how the great fluke of love poi - ses on a knife - edge: e - ven the tur - ning earth trem-bles on its a - - - xis.

sempre diminuendo

perdendosi

2' 32" approx.

Seóirse Bodley
Dublin
2006/01/20

10 | 'A summons to try to look, to try to see': Close Reading/s'

David Mahan

To celebrate a poet's life work draws us, above all, to recognize the quality of his voice and the excellence of his craft. That recognition emerges gradually as we converse with the poet through his art, learning from him new ways of reading, as well as new capacities of hearing and seeing. In the following reflections I invite the reader to overhear the results of my own 'conversations' with two of Micheal O'Siadhail's poems, with the hope that these close readings will both encourage the recognition I believe warrants the publication of this book, and enhance the reader's own appreciation of this poet's achievement.

By way of focusing my comments within a larger framework (since this book addresses itself to a diverse and decades-long achievement), I wish to advance the following observation. Among the many themes and subject-matters that Micheal O'Siadhail has addressed in his several collections of poems, one that stands out involves what poet and theological thinker Charles Williams called '*the union of history and the individual*'.[1] By this locution Williams meant to indicate, among other things, the interpenetration of the past and present within one's experience. For our purposes, the concept may serve as well to describe how an individual stands self-consciously within his or her immediate cultural-historical moment, and from this vantage point also comprehends the same in terms of a larger social, cultural, and historical context. By such a purview, we understand a person both as someone whose sensibilities have been shaped by other events and persons, and as a subject who acts as agent to negotiate his or her own place in, and sense of, the world – seeking to 'trace one's own tiny epic', as O'Siadhail summarizes his ambition in 'The Chosen Garden'.[2]

Micheal O'Siadhail's poetry bears the stamp of this outlook throughout, yielding two notable effects. One is the creation of a sense of timelessness in time and the tension which attends this intersection. As the closing lines of 'Aubade' aver,

> In the clue of our rhythm flickers an incarnation,
> time and timelessness counter-subjects in this fugue. (*HMJ* 48)

A further effect invokes the presence of others (of the 'other'). Against the grain of a certain 'confessional mode' in verse, which regards the private reflections and opinions of the poet as primary, through his verse Micheal O'Siadhail would have us understand our lives wholly in terms of interconnected relationships. In the vernacular of this anthology of essays, he affirms that our belonging-to consists of belonging-*with* ... others. This attitude obtains however much the poet stands within or at a remove from his focus of attention – even, and often especially, when the spotlight fixes on himself.

The stance of a poetry able to produce both effects requires above all an imagination infused with keen attentiveness – attentiveness to the larger contexts of history, to the particulars of existence, and to the other – all bent towards an expansive horizon of potential meaning. One thinks here of the poem 'Pond' from *The Fragile City*, in which the poet recalls a friend throwing a pebble into the water:

> I remember how he'd smiled and didn't say a thing,
> Just idly tossed a pebble to the middle of the pond.
> Its plump and sucking fall expanded ring by ring,
> A fiesta of hoops keeps swelling beyond and beyond. (*Poems*, p.215)

It is this ability to endow even the minutest particulars with expansive energy and scope that simultaneously grounds O'Siadhail's verse in the concrete, and from that 'humus' to train our eyes in ways of seeing the world and ourselves in the world. We will observe this capacity in the poems I have selected for our close readings, both of which generate a call to attention – 'a summons to try to look, to try to see', as a line from the second of the two announces.

Each of the poems I have chosen – 'Hands' and 'Summons' – in its own way and from radically different vantage points fosters the recognition that we inhabit a larger historical, and indeed spiritual, environment than that of our own immediate experiences. Each insists as well that, whether recognized or not, we stand as individuals in relation to others – those past and present, living and dead – whose experiences call for our remembrance, and beckon us to view our lives from new, and renewed perspectives. As we shall also find, the renewing effects of these poems, infused with O'Siadhail's own sense of history and the human condition, offer a perceptive engagement with another of his most prominent, and our most urgent, themes – the challenge and promise of hope and human flourishing.

Lastly, through this convergence of history and the individual, and individuals, there also emerges from these poems an acute awareness of the poet's role as a mediator: as one who stages an encounter between the experiences he reports and his reader. How through his craft O'Siadhail negotiates such a stance (the 'middle voice' of his, and we may say of all successful, poetry) adds intensity to the struggle for clarity of perception that both he and we feel. In this regard, the desire for the poem to be a living voice, and not an artefact only, acquires a peculiar urgency in the poet's quest to serve as both singer and 'healer'. 'Are poets in the business of repair? Invisible menders?', O'Siadhail asks in his Introduction to *Poems 1975-1995*.[3] It remains a question that a poet's careful readers ultimately must decide.

'Hands' (from *The Middle Voice*, 1992)

This poem places the poet, and us, before a text which is at once verbal and visual, an illuminated manuscript of the *Book of Kells*. It evokes in the poet-observer what it depicts, what first arrests his attention – '*Moments of illumination*' – that species of transport specially accorded to works of art. In this ekphrastic study, the poet finds occasion to meditate upon the themes of art and word, and their interpretation, as well as time and the journeys of individuals in time.

Journey, voyage, transport – the motif ferries and directs the poem's reflections as the poet-observer's eye roves across the page, and as his mind's eye imaginatively engages its presentation. In consequence of both movements, he encounters not only a text, but a *context*: the world of the 'Hands' which produced it. Assuming then the role of interrogator as well as observer (voicing the 'interrogative mood' familiar to O'Siadhail's stance throughout his oeuvre⁴), his persona asks this guiding question: *'Whose were the hands?'*(l. 9).

The answer emerges gradually, but never finally. These individuals inhabit a rarefied space, geographically (we later learn), in the stillness of a scriptorium; but in the envisioned landscape of the poem, by their vocation and their art they exist in

> spirals of days,
> pigments, washes, the evening satchel
> hung and the nights woken in a cell
> by vellum worlds creaking in the breeze.

Awakened in their monastic cells at night, so the poet imagines, their mind and their media conflate. They hear in the 'creaking' of vellum pages hung out to dry in the evening breeze (the products of their day's work), a sound like a ship at sea with masts at full sail. Beyond their small confinement, thoughts of their art transport them. Now,

> A voyage their image: longhanded cruises
> over scraped and pumiced calf-skin,
> the steer and yaw of these quill-driven
> crossings as a reed trails its juices.

'*[J]uices*' tells more than 'ink' ever could. The poem professes these scribes free spirits, subjects of a rigorous discipline, but also sailors in their own self-construal, voyagers through the lush deposits of their medium and craft. The status of their art, for them, seems a co-animation of soaring spirit and living text.

Are we, then, to see them as subjects of Promethean ambition or excess? The only evidence at 'hand' resists this estimation. They remain *'Anonymous seafarers'* (l. 9), their personalities now apparent only through their respective styles:

> A copyist loose-limbed, calm; another
> sedate and careful. Or there's Brother
> Extrovert's black and violet flamboyance.

We name them by their art alone. We know them only by their artistic traces,

> their being a hand just
> hinted in a margin. The face is lost,
> a traveler congeals in traces of voyage.

'*[C]ongeals*' evokes thoughts of dried blood, and so, of sacrifice. Yet theirs is a nameless legacy for all that labour, without signature, *'A nothingness of ego'* (l. 21): their selves displaced onto their text, their acts of inscription a self-effacement. Remembering the vocation of these men, the poem continues by re-inscribing our appreciation of their art under an alternative heading than that of individualistic self-promotion. The very being of these scribes and illuminators now coalesces around a singular absent-presence, '*a hand ...hinted in a margin*', but that hand, the poem reminds us, '*worships by work*' (l. 22). Their art represents an act, and product, of worship.

This perception does recognize an excess, but of a markedly different variety than self-assertive ambition. On the one hand, the poet-observer notes:

> And it seems the rim becomes
> a hub gathering spokes, the scriptorium's
> stillness a geography at its fingertips.

The illuminations of the artist, that space '*in a margin*' (l. 15), or at '*the rim*', reveals the presence of the artist in his individuality and freedom. It is here where the observer's attention is drawn ('*a hub gathering spokes*'), which would seem to foreground the aesthetic impulse in the creation as well as the contemplation of art. On the other hand, the impulse is born of a source other than mere self-expression. It arises within '*the scriptorium's stillness*', a hallowed silence and a contemplative mode, a '*geography*' (paradoxically) within which and from which the worshipping hand derives the expressive energy '*at its fingertips*'. In short, the 'hands' that produced the art are *praying* hands.

Accordingly, just as we understand these illuminator-scribes to have drawn their creative impulse from the well of a holy and silent devotion, the poem prompts a question, the answer to which remains open. Is it possible to respect the true nature of this art without honouring the provenance, and primacy, of that same devotional reserve? Hence, for the poet-observer no sensitive 'reading' of this work of [sacred] art seems fitting without in some sense entering into that same mode of contemplation. It is a disposition reminiscent of the injunction to the reader in Part I of *Little Gidding*: Upon entering that sanctuary, Eliot's persona enjoins the would-be supplicant, and the reader, to remember that

> You are not here to verify,
> Instruct yourself, or inform curiosity
> Or carry report. You are here to kneel
> Where prayer has been valid.

Likewise, the manuscript in 'Hands', when seen in its own context – which is to say, when understood in the terms *it* requires – cannot be reduced to the status of an interesting religious artefact, an aesthetic phenomenon, or a mere historical datum. Its yield consists of what has yielded it: acts of worship. A misreading amounts to a refusal of that invitation, recalling not only the context of the monastic brotherhood who produced the *Book of Kells*, but the community of faith as well, those communicants whose own engagement with these texts similarly involved religious devotion. Aesthetic fascination, historical curiosity, all give way to the promise announced in the poem's opening line – '*Moments of illumination*' – which is to be the reader's, as it is the poet-observer's, own mode of engagement – participation, of sorts, rather than analysis.

Reinforced by the global scope of the scribal imagination depicted in their text – a '*Byzantine*' Judas, '*Hebrew names*', '*Asia Minor faces*', '*Viking Brooches*', '*that Coptic Virgin*' – the poem continues with the image of voyage, which these '*Publishers of the word*' (l. 13) embody. The historical geography of peoples and places, prismatically disclosed through the rendering of these hands, arrives finally to rest on a temporal as well as a spatial plain. From here the poem unfolds in the direction of a broader meditation upon time – not time as a theoretical concept, but specifically *time as history* – and the problems which attend such an inquiry. We have noted the interest in this manuscript's status as a work of art in *its* time, and how within its own context we are to regard it sympathetically; how it, as such, establishes the contours of our own interpretation and reception of it. But what other potential relevance does this text hold for us in our own time? The poem marks the transition to this last series of meditations in the opening line of the final stanza.: '*The harbor is a scribe's last verse*' (l. 25). These '*Anonymous seafarers*', these voyagers of art, have finished their course; their time, in this respect, has ended. Their faithful 'hands' have left us only '*traces of voyage*' (l. 16). But of what benefit is their work in *our* hands? Do we discover in their art and the sensibility it expresses something that stands in continuity with our present interests and concerns? Furthermore, how does attention to this manuscript serve as a vehicle to address abiding problems regarding *reading*: the reading of time-as-history, and ultimately, of reading ourselves in time?

The poem proceeds to address these interests in its final movement by placing the line, '*The harbor is a scribe's last verse*', at the *beginning* of the last stanza, rather than at the end of the previous one. The transition which opens up this broader interest in time-as-history, therefore, does not mark a break from the manuscript or from the artists who produced it, but a bridge, effected within the structure of the poem. Both art and artists carry over beyond their time, even as the poem 'carries' over their presence graphically. It is a move reinforced towards the conclusion of this stanza when attention returns to the manuscript explicitly, and brings *us* to attention before it (a point to which we will return presently).

Concentration on the manuscript is suspended temporarily, however, as the poem steps into a larger narrative, punctuated by four figures from 'sacred' history. Two are from the Church's European history – Columba and Gutenberg – and two from scriptural history – the serpent and Lot's wife. The move represents a remarkable *tour de force*, as a mere eight lines survey an historical sweep from the primeval (humanity's garden fall), through biblical ages, then on to the Medieval and Renaissance eras, and even to the present with the reference to 'software' and the arresting '*Just look*' in line 32. The injunction not only brings the manuscript into the present, by addressing the contemporary reader, but makes it radically present to us, as we, its readers, are now inscribed into that space created by the poem, invited to stand with the poet as fellow-observers. The passage that follows returns us to the manuscript itself, not vaguely but in its details:

> Just look at Lot's wife! And how venial
> her about-face there, arched and faded
> under an *M*. ...

This return further tightens the poem's unity, as do repeated references to faces (cf. l. 15), along with the extension of the sea-voyage motif earlier in the stanza, as we are directed to '*Sail on seven centuries*' in line 29. In this way, the unity of the poem – also achieved, albeit gently and without imposition, by the repeated pattern of predominantly half-rhymed lines – in turn reinforces a sense of continuity.

But what sort of continuity is this, which is also to inquire about what sort of history is recapitulated here? Turning to the four figures, we notice that each is implicated in matters of the word. St. Columba, the sixth century Irish priest who founded numerous other monasteries in the British Isles, was also an accomplished poet, scribe and illuminator, and, more notoriously, an accused plagiarist.[5] His 'history' as a plagiarist, whether believed or not, complicates our reading of him. Who was Columba really, we may ask? How are we to regard him? Was he the saint, sailing off bravely on a glorious mission to save the souls of the Scots (as his traditional image valorises him), or the plagiarist, banished to Iona because of his crime? Or both? His presence in this poem, here made explicit, but implicit throughout because of his likely participation in the production of the manuscript at Kells, 'figures' a view of history itself and our interpretation of it. In time-as-history there is continuity, as the poem emphasizes; but its meaning over time from whatever vantage point is not stable (a continuity that discloses a habitual discontinuity). Columba serves as ironic *figura* of this position.

The added figure of the serpent makes explicit this sense of irresolution. Its '*coiled/ question*' (lines 27-8) insinuates the ambiguity attending the mention of St. Columba, and, more broadly, the instability of historical certainty itself. The word 'coiled' connotes endless return as well as a lack of resolution. Time, in other words, does not inevitably disclose clarity of meaning, but only extends an abiding problematic, which attends the pursuit of meaning. In addition, within the Christian *mythos*, the serpent represents the originary distortion and corruption of words ('*coiled*' as 'twisted'), which provoked another endless return: among other effects, the tendency towards deception and instability of meaning constitutive of the human condition.

Notions of human progress are thus called into question, along with the effort to stabilize meaning in/over time. The figure of Gutenberg, another of history's '*Publishers of the word*', carries this theme further. What we typically regard as a major advance in human ingenuity – the invention of movable type – is not at all evident as a boon when viewed, as it is in the poem, against the backdrop of the illuminated manuscript. Nor is the even more radical development of word processing in our own day. Did such inventions, we are prompted to ask, demonstrate progress of such a kind that medieval scribes and illuminators would have welcomed their appearance? The poet queries:

> Did they dream
> warm presses, the software of memories? (lines 31-2)

The poem does not answer the question directly, but invites the reader to decide (a further refraction of the poet's 'interrogative mood'). We are urged only to

> Think of a lifetime
> inked in a concordance. (lines 30-1)

The choice of '*inked*' contrasts sharply with '*juices*' in line 8, indicating a loss of vitality, a lack of richness, and a flattening of presentation. Taken as a whole, the phrase '*inked in a concordance*' reinforces this attitude, leaving us to 'think' the stark difference between these respective projects.

Under the sway of the poem's suggestiveness on this account, what, we might ask further, has been lost? Not words *per se* – they remain, now capable of being multiplied interminably. Words we have, but under what possible diminishment? Have we, then, lost the 'hands' of those who were materially and spiritually invested (over '*a lifetime*') in the careful preservation and enhancement of the word? (Does the poet himself worry that this may be his own fate?) Have we, in other words, traded the consanguinity of their *juices* and sacrificial devotion for the inky remains of a concordance?

The following line – '*warm presses and software memories*' – strikes the same note of discord. The phrase sounds like a slogan for a publishing or computer advertisement. '*Did they dream*' this, the poet-observer wonders? Would it be *our* dream for them? Certainly the promise of warmth, speed, and easy preservation may have been the longing of scribes and illuminators who laboured tirelessly in notoriously cold and damp scriptoriums. But, again, what would be lost? For one, '*the scriptorium's stillness*', that space of holy silence which animated their very fingertips. As inviting as 'warm presses' may seem, they are noisy machines, and their operation displaces the worker from the '*pigments*' and '*washes*' (l. 2), from that visceral contact with '*scraped and pumiced calf-skin*' (l. 6). And '*software memories*', also teasingly inviting, nonetheless entail loss, a removal from the sense of vocation these artists felt as preservationists, and, most regrettably, from their dreams. In 'software memories' gone are the '*Moments of illumination*' and '*spirals of days*' – that enraptured swirl and interplay of work and worship; and gone too is that singular, world- and life-defining image of voyage, '*their image*' (l. 5). Moreover, 'software memories' indicates an even deeper potential loss, one of keen relevance to the theme of time-as-history, considered here under the auspices of remembrance – of time as *concrete*, rehearse-able history. The storage of memories by machines displaces, and potentially replaces, *us* as rememberers, thus removing us from the kind of vital contact with the world so materially manifest in the art of these scribes and illuminators.

The final stanza effects all of these remonstrations: the themes of loss, the diminishment of the word by virtue of our removal from the art of the word, the duplicity of notions of historical 'progress', the potential evacuation of remembrance. But is this all a form of nostalgia, an idealistic chimera proffered as a means to manage our uneasy relationship to the past in the present by selective anamnesis? Such a strategy, although common to our enduring romanticism, is too simple and too naïve for a poem that proceeds through a sophisticated weave of two intermingling strands. On one hand, it insists upon the evasiveness and ambiguity of meaning in our treatment of time-as-history, and on the other hand, upon the continuity of the past with the present, a continuity that relies upon vital, bodily contact with the world.

The presentation of the fourth figure – Lot's wife, who does double duty as an image in the manuscript as well as an image appropriated for O'Siadhail's poetic redress – brings these strands to a point of greater concentration, and, in the process, subverts the charge of naïve or idealistic nostalgia. For one, the image depicted in the manuscript and now brought to our attention portrays Lot's wife at the moment of decision. She is beyond Sodom, but not yet salt. Still, even in this in-between moment she is culpable – '*how venial her about-face*'. She has in fact already made her decision, and merely awaits its consequences. Secondly, the character of the manuscript has changed. No longer does it bear the suppleness and definition portrayed in the first two stanzas. Now its presentation is '*arched and faded*', resembling a relic of a distant past. How are we to interpret this shift against previous efforts to emphasize the manuscript's vitality and enduring promise as a vehicle of illumination, so expressive of vocation and communal creativity and receptivity? The answer comes by subtle prompting, found in a question, or in this case, two questions.

The first, raised earlier, is the '*coiled question*' of the serpent: '*Is patience a trust to rehearse/ such detail?*' (lines 27-9). The question as asked seems peculiar, contrary to our expectations (and perhaps in keeping with the character associated with the serpent – as a distorter). Concerning the labour of the monks who produced it, we might rather have asked, 'Is *trust* a *patience* to rehearse such detail?', inquiring after their sustained motivation in the painstaking process of artistic production. What is the significance of this inversion? At stake, as the question is ordered, is the matter of trust more than patience, understanding patience as the waiting, and trust as the thing waited and hoped for. But *whose* 'patience' and *whose* 'trust' are at issue here, and in what way might the former be synonymous with '*a trust to rehearse such detail*'?

Trust here operates at many levels. There is the trust of the manuscript's artisans, that what they have rendered is faithful to their calling as God's missioners, and that what they sought to preserve will be preserved. There is the trust required of the poet-observer that his own act of remembrance, his rehearsal with respect to this manuscript and its creators, will vindicate the vision it, and they, manifested. And in this, there is also the trust that the legacy of the past, for all of its admixture of motives and deeds (as with the legacy of St. Columba) will yet yield the recognition we nonetheless wish to bestow on it. (Does the poet have his own legacy, and that of any who would make a contribution to art, in mind here as well?) Finally, there is the trust between the poet and his readers, upon whom he has made the demands we have noted, and to whom he implicitly appeals in seeking to justify the importance of those demands. In all of the above, patience *is* a trust since in none can a final outcome be known. Thus, trust, as it operates within the particular way the serpent's question is rendered and under the auspices of the poem's reading of time-as-history, must not be understood as another effort to stabilize meaning. It is, significantly, the opposite; for in the absence of fixed and certain meaning, as is the case at least with respect to the interpretation of history (as well as art), trust is to be found always and only in the waiting, in the space of the 'in-between'. It is, in short, that very mode of existence distinctly proffered by a religious outlook: faith.

The second question – posed in response to the figure of Lot's wife now '*arched and faded*' – asks,

> ... Who watches too far ahead,
> *or behind?* (lines 35-6).

The past portrayed is now a distant past, but this image of a crisis enacted prompts a present concern. The choice Lot's wife has made, her '*venial about-face*', is already consummated in the moment of her depiction; but for us, who receive the exhortation '*Just look*', we remain in that tension of decision as we are now directed to place ourselves both before her, as well as, implicitly, in her place. We, the poem's readers, are the ones who now inhabit the space of the 'in-between'. The identity proposed by the question 'Who watches?', to whomever else it may apply, applies to us presently. And in such a position, we too encounter peril of some kind.

Of what kind? Taking the poem's cue from the story of Lot's wife, it seems one peril we face is that of longing; and in this respect, as previously introduced in connection with the serpent's question, the lack of trusting patience. Might we call this the danger of impatient desiring, and, in that, the danger of looking askance ('just look' also implying 'looking *justly*'); hence, *not* waiting, or in the parlance of faith, not *abiding*.

What creates such longing '*too far ahead,/or behind*'? The story of Lot's wife signifies a theme found throughout Scripture. On another figural plane, it is the habitual repetition of the longing for 'Egypt', for the security of a familiar place, however horrible, in resistance to a future destination promised but unknown – a resistance that a host of present insecurities exacerbates ('Where will we get water? How will we feed ourselves?'). It is this quest for security *for* the present but *in* the past or, as may also be the case, in the future, which comprises a view of how *not* to live in time. One form this takes is the drive to stabilize meaning, and so to moor ourselves in the present. This will not do, however, as the poem has insisted. In its vision, time-as-history is subject to continuous discontinuity, the flux of events that neither art nor technological 'progress' nor even memory itself can fix (in both senses of the word). As we find expressed in another poem from this collection ('Rhapsody'), '*Nothing will stay still*' (l. 1). Where, then, and how, do we locate ourselves meaningfully in time, as time's travellers?

We find ourselves, as the last line from the poem 'Voyage' (also from this collection) affirms, in the '*Middle of nowhere. Middle of everywhere*' (l. 24). In this same poem two questions appear that are relevant to our reading of 'Hands':

> ...How can we seek
> if we don't know where the harbor is?
> But if we knew, how could we've sought? (lines 3-5)

The questions echo the sentiment evoked in the final plea of our poem: '*Tell us the voyage is all*'. It is neither in the illuminated manuscript, for all of its sumptuous beauty 'now faded', nor in the world of its creators, for all of their dedication to their vocation and art, nor even in the vision they manifest of a fidelity to the word and its publication now lost, that we find our edification. To look there in order to situate ourselves would be to 'watch too far behind'. The consummate yield from the example of these artisans and monks, preserved for us in their work, abides rather in the image, '*their image*', the poem attributes to them: a voyage. The final plea – '*Tell us the voyage is all*' – returns us to that attitude, and to a way of envisioning our lives in time.

Still, the sentiment evoked here may strike us as sentimental. It may seem a romantic appeal as antidote to the discomfiting vagaries of time-as-history, leaving us only vaguely situated in the 'in-between', buoyed by equally vague reassurances. What rescues this plea from such possible capitulation regards another potential addressee for 'Tell us'. Who is it also '*Who watches*'? Who holds the past and the future in a single gaze without imperilling the present, and who holds our times in his 'hands'? The poem's interest in worship, devotion, and faith suggests the presence of a candidate who sustains our voyaging with both freedom and purposefulness: '*Just look*'.

'Summons' (from *The Gossamer Wall: Poems in Witness to the Holocaust*, 2002)

Among the many facets of Micheal O'Siadhail's *The Gossamer Wall*, its five chiastically related sections disclose an insistent redress of history and historical analysis. At stake is how we remember others, not in our own terms but theirs, and how we honour their experiences, in this case of profound suffering. As this 'poetic suite'[6] spirals towards its epicentre in the central section 'Figures', set in the concentration camps, the summons to remembrance advanced throughout – of persons, and not merely anonymous events – gains its greatest intensity.

   In this sequence of fourteen, fourteen-line sonnets, the poet deploys prosodic devices and images to create a thickly-tissued presentation, variously musical and angular – at times striking and eloquent, at others intentionally banal.[7] As elsewhere in the suite, the emotional proximity to bigoted destruction and human suffering achieved by the poetry in its resistance to time *in time* (by way of overcoming forgetfulness) bears with it the complexities of discernment and of reading – ourselves as well as the actions and experiences of others. In 'Figures', that challenge increases, and, with it, the expectations of an ethics of form.[8] Following the 'descent' of Europe into the atrocities of the Holocaust in 'Northeim' and 'Battalion 101' (doing so, notably, in a most particularistic manner, by naming names without hesitation), and then pursuing a line of ascent out of that mire by tracing the acts of resistance performed by victims and their sympathizers in 'Spoors' and 'Le Chambon', the poem situates the experiences of the concentration camps in this poetic journey at the furthest remove from the margins.

   Those experiences, of course, also stand at the furthest remove from the poet's experience, as well as that of most readers. For this reason, the effort to revisit the nightmarish landscape of those compounds places an enormous strain on the task of remembering well. The poet was not there; the majority of his readers were not there; but *there* is the place where the calculated energy of the Holocaust plummeted to its most sinister depth and depravity. For the purpose of remembrance, therefore, the history as well as the poetry urge us there; or as the fifth poem of the 'Figures' sequence aims to situate us: 'Here'. But what form(s) can deliver the needed intensity without presumption, and issue a summons to remember that prepares readers for the possibility of hope's *complex yes* towards which the subsequent sections aim (see 'Never', l. 14)? The poet's unexpected answer to this need and this summons is the sonnet.

   The peculiar advantage of the sonnet consists of its capacity to compress a range of ideas and impressions into a concentrated expression of thought and feeling. Its structure and regulated metre and rhyme demand a discipline of expression that underscores and supports the intensity of poetic effect. (Because of these advantages, it traditionally has been the form of choice for love poems, which itself serves up an irony in this context). As with the other poems in the *Gossamer* suite, however, how O'Siadhail handles this traditional form demonstrates its facility for the acts of attention and remembrance that he seeks to achieve. Accordingly, the first sonnet in the 'Figures' sequence, 'Summons', delivers a poignant blend of temporal and spatial referents and images, variegated rhyme and verbal texture, all woven into the insistent plea of a witness to *imagine* what can only surpass our comprehension but which must not escape our present concern. It performs what O'Siadhail has himself announced as poetry's distinct advantage for remembrance and historical reflection: its 'special way to cut through history with images'.[9]

   The poem begins and ends with a similar plea: 'Meditate that this came about. *Imagine*' (l. 1); '*A summons to* try to look, to try to see' (l. 13)[10]. Between this bracketing charge to the reader we find carefully choreographed shifts in perspective, verb tense, and points of view that coalesce around four visual images. The first is told in the present tense, evoking an impression of the living-dead:

   Pyjama ghosts tramp the shadow of a chimney.
   Shorn and nameless. Desolation's mad machine. (lines 2-3)

The word '*tramp*' in this context connotes a death march as these figures make their wraith-like appearance to our imagination, recalling Tony O'Malley's portrait *Concentration Camp* on the book's cover and the now familiar archival footage taken when these camps were liberated. The images are perhaps *too* familiar. The internal rhyme of '*Imagine*' (l. 1) with '*Desolation's*', the 'am'-'im' half-rhymes, the assonance of '*ghosts*', '*shadow*', and '*Desolation's*', and the alliterated '*shadow*'-'*shorn*' and '*mad machine*' verbally animate these figures. The poetics supporting the image serve to re-summon the dead who are made to live again in our imagination. Though at one time 'shorn and nameless', they still 'tramp the shadow of a chimney'. The reader, then, must consider that this happened ('*this came about*'), and how it could have happened, not as an accident of history but by '*Desolation's mad machine*'.

The next image conflates time past with time present, marking a complex shift in scenery and a poignant interweave of texts:

> For each who survived, every numbered
> Arm that tries to hold the wedding-guest ... (lines 5-6).

The moment echoes and reprises Coleridge's *Ancyent Marinere*,[11] the detainment of the wedding-guest by the wizened stranger who pleads with him to forestall entering that celebration in order to hear his tale of '*woeful agony*', of death and remorse. The allusion is provocative, suggesting that the poet and his readers stand in the same position as the wedding-guest, accosted now by a tattooed survivor – having to forsake the bright pleasantries of the present moment to enter into an abyss of disturbing memory. The transference is acute, for us as for Coleridge's protagonist who '*went, like one that hath been stunn'd ... A sadder and wiser man*'. The reader of 'Summons' is left to draw out the impression the allusion excites, ultimately to consent to what the poem explicitly endorses – to '*Try to see!*' (l. 4) – and through that arresting vision of the living-dead also to grow wise in remembrance.

The image of 'figures' as numbers, found elsewhere in the suite, also reappears, acquiring added emphasis because of the dehumanizing circumstances depicted. The poem develops this motif throughout with expanding proportions: in addition to '*numbered*' arms there are '*endless counts and selections*' (l. 4), '*A thousand urgent stories*' (l. 7), '*In each testimony a thousand more suppressed*' (l. 8), and finally, '*this infinite nightmare*' (l. 10). 'Each' and 'every' among the surviving witnesses and testimonies yield to the 'thousand urgent stories' of '*The muted dead*' (l. 14) as the poem gradually swells towards an 'infinite' horizon. The word play with numbers serves to signify the disproportion between the scant surviving evidence of these lives and the many more whose testimonies are 'suppressed', thus underscoring the difficulty of recovering to our remembrance those who remain silenced but who also '*demand their debt of memory*'.

The third and fourth images display the paradox of their present-absence or absent-presence:

> A Polish horizon glows with stifled cries:
> Who'll wake us from this infinite nightmare?
> Out of the cone of Vesuvius their lives rise
> To sky-write gaunt silences in the frozen air. (lines 9-12)

The coalescence of time and space, of the verbal with the visual, of sound and silence, of the visible with the invisible or barely visible, yields an emotional and cognitive density to the experiences of these silent witnesses. With the first image in this quatrain, we are summoned to see and hear simultaneously a Polish horizon *glowing* with their stifled *cries*, though we in fact can neither see nor hear. The scene conjured here is a scene of writing, but writing that is unwriting itself even as it seeks to enable the reader to somehow see through the paradoxical imagery in order to attain sympathetic awareness. Without the paradox the complexity would evaporate, and naively so. But without the effort to bear witness to the un-witnessed and un-testified, the 'debt of memory' would remain unpaid.

The further paradox of attempting to resolve what remains irresolvable accentuates the difficulty the poetry faces. Had the poet chosen to report his own experiences of contemplating the Holocaust he may have settled for paradox. But because the stakes exceed any such *self*-reflection, directing his readers ultimately to remembrance of the other, some form of resolution becomes morally obligatory. Why is this so? To heed Holocaust commentator and literary critic Lawrence Langer's commendations from the 'literature of atrocity' he upholds as exemplary, one might conclude that our moral obligation to Holocaust remembrance is best fulfilled in literary forms that defy all efforts at resolution. That is, such evidently irresolvable circumstances of nightmarish disorder are better addressed *with integrity* by unresolved, disordered poetic forms. (So when the poem 'Never' declares, '*we cannot sing dumb*' (l. 9), Langer might respond, 'Why sing at all?'). Hence, when Langer declares unequivocally that as an effect of the Holocaust, 'For the first time in history human beings found themselves confronted with a situation totally incommensurate with their capacity for hope', he rightly assesses how these events radically disorient and problematise familiar categories of resolution.[12] In my opinion, however, despite Langer's otherwise brilliant and insightful analysis, on this score he over-determines what constitutes an 'appropriate' response.

Micheal O'Siadhail's contribution to this genre involves taking up this implied gauntlet, and demonstrating how, for all of the risk, one can both honor the memory of victims and speak hope to – albeit in the shadows of – that experience. On the one hand, Langer's view has considerable merit when a literature of atrocity aims to evoke the perverse and acutely disorienting character of Holocaust experiences. On the other hand, remembrance as memorial, if it is to have any substance, must include in its aim to honor the memory of victims a reassertion of *the meaningfulness of their lives*. How else can we refer to their destruction as an 'atrocity' and a violation of their humanity at all?

The poem 'Summons' enacts this distinction in response to this summons of the human: the moral resolve to remember *them* – these *others* – finding expression in the formal, aesthetic resolve of the poetry. The deep patterning of the poem's verbal-musical texture provides a form of resolution without sentimentality or presumption, as rhythm and rhyme interact with images to elicit emotional proximity to the irrepressibly human experiences of the camps. We see, and hear, this in the third quatrain as '*stifled cries*' re-emerge in the phrase '*their lives rise*', and in the buoyantly alliterated end couplet,

> A summons to try to look, to try to see.
> A muted dead demand their debt of memory. (lines 13-14)

The unnamed, and not their murderous un-naming, are given their song, the poet's song of remembrance. The 'living-dead' introduced at the beginning of 'Summons' are now the 'dead living', memorialized in the imagination. That debt of memory abides, however, as living memory requires – here paid not as if it were an economic transaction or a form of absolution, but paid through the musical economy of poetry as a revitalizing witness to the enduring humanity of Holocaust victims.

As a result of this poetic redress of history performed as a recall of their humanity, the summons 'to try to look, to try to see' these others stands the reader in the place of witness as well. Against the tendency to distance ourselves from their experiences, hence to act as co-conspirators of forgetfulness, 'Summons' calls upon us to be co-rememberers. The music of the poem restores this capacity, and in so doing establishes a basis for a hope rooted in the living. As one of the final poems in the *Gossamer* suite proclaims ('Faces', 122), quoting the hopeful strain of the prophet Jeremiah in whose ' *darkest scroll*' we find '*a jazz of hope*' ('Stretching', 116):

> I'll change their shame to praise and renown in all
> *The earth.* ... Always each face and shoeless footfall
>
> A breathing memory behind the gossamer wall. ('Faces', lines 11-13)

11 | *The Gossamer Wall*: Poetry as Testimony and History

Rory Miller

The role, and even suitability, of poetry in narrating the history of the Holocaust was addressed most famously in 1949, when the German critic Theodor Adorno declared that 'After Auschwitz it is barbaric to write poetry.' Adorno was not simply questioning the suitability of using poetry to deal with the Holocaust, but was also arguing that in the wake of Nazi crimes it was unnatural and improper for an artistic form as vulnerable and beautiful as poetry ever to recover.

The issue of whether it is possible for language in general, and poetry in particular, to express the horror of the holocaust has been debated ever since. As Professor Susan Gubar has noted in her book *Poetry After Auschwitz: Remembering What One Never Knew*,[1] there are many pitfalls that poets, especially those who never directly experienced the Holocaust, face in choosing to bear witness to the tragedy. There is also the related issue of whether from an artistic perspective, as much as a moral one, poetry is a suitable form for dealing with the Holocaust. As Milton Hindus has put it:

> If even the expressions of survivors sometimes seemed to be little better than exploitative 'Kitsch' and those of others more sincere and genuine proved repetitive, diminishing and sentimental, was it possible for an American Jew to do any better? There was an abyss of cliché, propaganda and editorialism in the subject which even the wariest writer might have difficulty in avoiding. Was it possible, then, that the central event of Jewish history in almost two thousand years defied the imagination and had best be surrounded by silence?[2]

But despite such concerns poetry dealing with the Holocaust has been a prolific genre in the sixty years since the liberation of the concentration camps. Indeed, it is arguable that there has been such an irrepressible urge to bear witness through poetry precisely because of the moral enormity of the Nazi genocide – what Primo Levi has termed 'the demolition of man'.[3] As Marguerite Striar has written in her introduction to *Rage Before Pardon: Poets of the World Bearing Witness to the Holocaust*, 'most poets don't choose to write about the Holocaust. It chooses them.'[4]

This is primarily because poetry provides an outlet through which raw emotion can be expressed that is not necessarily available in other literary forms. One thinks in particular of the work of the late Paul Celan, who was a survivor of the destruction of the Jewish community of Czernowitz. For many Celan is the greatest poet of the Holocaust and as John

Felstiner shows in his study of the man – fittingly entitled *Poet, Survivor, Jew* – prior to taking his own life at the age of forty-nine, Celan used poetry to deal with the harrowing experience of seeing, among other things, his parents shot by the SS. In his Nobel Prize for Literature acceptance speech in 1995 Seamus Heaney addressed Celan's use of raw emotion in his Holocaust poetry. In particular, he acknowledged that he was 'in awe of the torsions' in Celan's poetry because it provides 'evidence that art can rise to the occasion and somehow be the corollary of Celan's stricken destiny as [a] Holocaust survivor'.[5]

Most Holocaust poetry, whether written by survivors like Celan, their descendants or those with no direct links to the tragedy, is primarily concerned with expressing such emotion. A good example is the work of William Heyen, who was born in Brooklyn, New York, in 1940 and whose 1991 poem 'Riddle'[6] is an excellent case in point. Throughout this piece Heyen asks 'Who Killed the Jews?' but this is a purely rhetorical device that allows him to indict all those involved, at all levels, in Hitler's Final Solution:

> David Nova swallowed gas,
> Hyman Abrahms was beaten and starved.
> Some men signed their papers,
> and some stood guard,
>
> and some herded them in,
> and some dropped the pellets,
> and some spread the ashes,
> and some hosed the walls,
>
> and some planted the wheat,
> and some poured the steel,
> and some cleared the rails,
> and some raised the cattle.
>
> Some smelled the smoke,
> some just heard the news.
> Were they Germans? Were they Nazis?
> Were they human? Who killed the Jews?

The same is true of Nobel Laureate Nelly Sachs,[7] a Jewess from Berlin, who emigrated from Germany to Sweden in 1940 to escape the Nazis and so was spared any direct experience of the full horror of the Holocaust. Nevertheless, she was driven to write about the tragedy as a way of providing a voice for her co-religionists in the country of her birth who could no longer speak. Anthony Hecht, another of the genre's leading poets, came into contact with the Holocaust when his US army unit helped liberate Flossenburg concentration camp, following which Hecht was given the job of interviewing inmates in order to collect evidence needed to prosecute the camp's commanders for war crimes. No less than Sachs, his experience haunted both his poetry and his life for decades to come and, years later, he admitted that 'The place, the suffering, the prisoners' accounts were beyond comprehension. For years after I would wake shrieking.'[8]

Numerous others like Ursula Duba, a German Gentile who was six years old when the war ended and Stephen Hertz, who in his ambitious work *Whatever You Can Carry: Poems of the Holocaust*[9] writes from the perspective of concentration camp inmates and the American soldiers who liberated them, as well as Nazi officials and German bystanders, have also used poetry to convey the horror of the Holocaust though they did not experience it at first hand as either bystander or victim.

But there is also a second kind of Holocaust poetry. This draws primarily on many of the same sources used in the conventional historical scholarship on the Nazi era – survivor testimony, official documents, memoirs etc. Like academic research it serves not only to record specific events that occurred during the Shoah but to extrapolate on them. This approach is seen most clearly in works like Charles Reznikoff's *Holocaust*, published in 1975 and written in twelve chapters each of which deals with a specific aspect of the tragedy – 'Deportation', 'Children', 'Marches' etc. It is based solely on two primary sources – *The Trials of the Major War Criminals at Nuremburg* and *The Eichmann Trial in Jerusalem* – from which the author draws on affidavits given by witnesses and on material in official documents that were submitted as evidence in both trials.[10]

As Dan Featherston has noted, this work has been dismissed as 'prose narrative' by some and has also been criticized precisely because it is 'devoid of metaphorical language and the rhetorical framework of interpretation'.[11] The renowned novelist Paul Auster, for example, has taken Reznikoff's work to task on the grounds that the Holocaust 'which is precisely the unknowable, the unthinkable, requires a treatment *beyond the facts* in order for us to be able to understand it – assuming that such a thing is even possible'.[12]

But as Robert Franciosi has convincingly argued, Reznikoff succeeds in bringing an emotional power to the bare facts of the transcribed testimonies on which he bases his work. To take just one example, Reznikoff's depiction of the experience of survivors who witnessed the massacre of families is profoundly moving, even if it eschews emotional language:

> Her father did not want to take off all of his clothes
> and stood in his underwear.
> His children begged him to take it off
> but he would not and was beaten.
> Then the Germans tore off his underwear
> and he was shot.
> They shot her mother, too,
> and her father's mother—
> she was eighty years old
> and held two children in her arms;
> and they shot her father's sister;
> she also had babies in her arms
> and was shot on the spot.

More recently and on a more modest level, Lois Olena, who was first moved to write Holocaust poetry while employed to transcribe Holocaust survivor interviews for the Gratz College Holocaust Oral History Archive in Philadelphia, has also successfully drawn on primary historical sources (in this case oral history) without sacrificing any intensity of feeling.

Following its publication in 2002 *The Gossamer Wall*, described succinctly by Sarah Kafatou in *Harvard Review* as 'a series of poem-sequences in witness to the Holocaust of the European Jews',[13] gained immediate recognition both in Ireland and across the world as an 'exceptional', 'extraordinary', 'fascinating', and 'beautiful' work. It was also short-listed for the 2003 Jewish Quarterly Wingate Literary Prize in the fiction section (where it received a special recommendation from the judges). As such it can be viewed as a heartfelt and emotional literary tribute to the victims of the Holocaust that follows on from the work of Celan, Sachs, Heyen and others.

But *The Gossamer Wall* is not only a remarkable collection of poetry: it is also a hugely important historical study based on deep research into the testimonies of Holocaust survivors and perpetrators, as well as numerous academic studies. Indeed, though in the acknowledgements section in *The Gossamer Wall* O'Siadhail lists what he terms 'the imaginative literature' on which he drew in the course of writing, much more space is given over to listing the historical works that he used – 'the numerous testimonies of survivors', as well as the historical works of leading scholars from Sir Martin Gilbert and Christopher R. Browning to Joachim Fest, to name but three of the most prominent. He also pays tribute to the 'crucial conversations' he had with survivors, scholars, and teachers of the Shoah at an international conference entitled *Remembering for the Future: The Holocaust in an Age of Genocide*.

It is certainly necessary to 'Remember for the Future' and in these terms the publication of *The Gossamer Wall* came at a crucial time. The survivor generation is dying off and the full horror of the Holocaust is becoming so vague that the label 'Nazi' and the accusation of 'Nazism' is now a common (and hugely debased) part of the political vernacular. Thus a Euro-barometer poll conducted in nine European countries and released on the eve of Holocaust Memorial Day 2004, found that 35.7 percent of respondents believed that Jews 'should stop playing the victim for the Holocaust'. Meanwhile, a BBC poll of 4,000 people taken in the United Kingdom in the same month showed that 45 percent of all Britons and 60 percent of those under 35 years of age had never heard of Auschwitz! [14]

This growing ignorance and indifference to the enormity of the Nazi Holocaust has in turn reduced the taboo that has been attached to anti-Jewish rhetoric and violence for much of the last half-century. In consequence, over the last few years there has been an upsurge in attacks against Jews, as well as against synagogues and Jewish schools and cemeteries, across Europe on a level unknown since the Nazi era.

It is in these depressing circumstances that *The Gossamer Wall* makes an important contribution to the history, not only of the Holocaust, but the Jewish experience over the centuries. From the first set of poems, which deal with the position of Jews in European society prior to the birth of Nazism, one not only sees the poetic beauty of this work, but also its historic scope and ambition. The real challenge of writing about European Jewish history in the medieval, early modern, and post-emancipatory eras is to convey the depth of anti-Jewish persecution at the hands of the Church and state and within society at large without adopting what Salo Baron, the doyen of Jewish studies, termed the 'lachrymose conception' of Jewish history – that the history of the Jews has been a succession of disasters and not much else.[15] This is a point of view eloquently restated more recently by Jewish intellectual Leon Wieseltier, who in his masterful work *Kaddish* argued that 'there is no more fundamental misunderstanding of Jewish history than its reduction to Jewish adversity'.[16]

Yet avoiding this negative tendency is not an easy task. Heinrich Heine, a product of German emancipation and a convert from Judaism, would, in his own poetry, refer to Judaism as 'the family curse that lasts a thousand years' (The New Jewish Hospital in Hamburg). Even the hugely knowledgeable Jewish historian Sir Lewis Namier argued that there was 'no modern Jewish history, only martyrology'. Thus what is really impressive about the poems in *The Gossamer Wall* dealing with the pre-Nazi era is O'Siadhail's ability to evoke the 'Scattering. Ghetto. Yellow Badge. Pogroms' ('Forebodings', 15) while still managing to remind the reader that the real tragedy of the historic persecution of Jewry was not solely the persecution itself, but the negative impact that this had on a Jewish world rich in history, culture, and learning, and eager to make a valuable contribution to the wider society from which it was excluded. In doing so O'Siadhail captures the profound frustration and helplessness of Jewry that led Moses Mendelssohn to cry 'they tie our hands and then reproach us for not using them'.[17]

These poems also raise a second aspect of historic Jewish persecution – the contradictory and nonsensical nature of the accusations and, in particular, the portrayal in the twentieth century of the Jew as both the 'Arch Bolshevik' and the 'scheming international Rothschild' (Wilderness, 20). Here again O'Siadhail provides an important historical lesson by highlighting the ludicrous nature of such claims, and again it is hugely timely that he does so.

These vile slanders against the Jewish people have been perpetuated most successfully in the anti-Semitic forgery *The Protocols of the Elders of Zion*, which claims to be the authentic record of the protocols of a meeting of a secret Jewish government – the Elders of Zion – on how international Jewry will achieve global domination.[18]

Since the late nineteenth century when a group of professional anti-Semites, mid-level functionaries, and tsarist secret policemen let it loose on the world, *The Protocols* has not only been used to stir up anti-Jewish feeling but has provided much of the intellectual justification for Russian pogroms, Nazi gas-chambers, and more recent attacks on Jews. *The Protocols* have been a staple in Eastern Europe over the last hundred years and are doing thriving business in the Arab world where blood libels and conspiracy theories that blame Jews for the world's ills are both prevalent and state-sponsored. They are now making a return to the mainstream debate in Western Europe. So O'Siadhail provides an invaluable service in demolishing the slanders on which they are based.

The charting of the descent into the darkness of the Nazi era is set out in simple language and the unique nature of the genocide against the Jews compared to previous crimes against humanity is deftly handled:

> And the one strain singled out for elimination
> This breed apart. A whole apparatus of hate
> Bent on wiping a people from Europe's face. ('Signatures', 22)

The cry 'Will no one see when the serpent rises?' ('Signals', 26) asks a question that has preoccupied scholars – why did the German population, and those in the nations under Nazi control, respond to Hitler's Final Solution in the way they did? (On this issue one particularly thinks of Browning's *Ordinary Men*, which is cited by O'Siadhail in his acknowledgements, as well as the more controversial *Hitler's Willing Executioners* by Daniel Goldhagen). It is answered here in uncompromising terms in an intricately crafted set of poems in which we meet those men and women who refused to see (and in many cases, embraced) this rising serpent of Nazism. We see the indifference ('Blind eyed Northeim doesn't want to know', 'Them', 42), the fear, the ignorance and the prejudice among the wider population. But in addressing the reasons for this 'dumb compliance' ('Power', 42) the author (very fittingly in a collection subtitled 'Poems in Witness to the Holocaust') is really addressing a much harder historical question and one that every serious student of the Holocaust must repeatedly ask himself – 'How would I have acted if I had been there?'

Though it may be consoling for us to believe that we would have been part of the small minority of Germans, Poles, Ukrainians and others who refused to sign up to a policy of 'Apathy. Denial. Accommodation' or the 'soft collusion of silence' ('Stand off', 46), the facts of the time paint an utterly different picture. Indeed, very rarely was there any correlation between one's education, learning, love of family, religious commitment, or artistic achievement and one's refusal to participate as an accomplice to, or even a perpetrator of, the ongoing atrocities. As George Steiner has reminded us, within the 'bureaucracy of torture and the ovens' there existed 'those who cultivated a knowledge of Goethe, a love of Rilke'.[19]

It has always been fascinating to see how the poetry of the Holocaust, especially compared to more conventional historical studies, has dealt with the perpetrators of this evil rather than its victim because the incomprehensible nature of the crimes make it both challenging and disturbing to attempt to get inside the minds of those who carried out such appalling acts. O'Siadhail deals with this challenge in a group of eight remarkable poems under the heading 'Battalion 101' – this was an actual unit of the German Order Police, which played a key role in the implementation of the Final Solution in Poland. O'Siadhail tells the story of the perpetrators of Battalion 101 – the 'everyday men' ('Battalion 101', 49) of the Nazi genocide. Only a tiny minority rebelled. The majority followed orders (no more no less), while some revelled in their newly gained power to snuff out life and succumbed to the monster 'Vesuvius within' ('Lieutenant Gnade', 57).

But close quarter killing on this scale is neither easy nor without psychological consequences (even when the victims are Jews) and a chilling transformation takes place with the industrialization of the extermination process:

> Measures taken to ease
> The burden. A system refined.
> A butchery out of sight and out of mind. ('Measures', 55)

Here the terse and business-like description of this major development in the technology of genocide, in language similar to that found in any workplace memorandum, is striking. O'Siadhail could just as easily be reporting the decision of a company to upgrade its computer system and in a few short lines we see how the job of destroying European Jewry quickly came to be viewed as a humdrum, though necessary, task.

O'Siadhail's approach to this is evocative of Reznikoff's *Holocaust*, which, in the style of court transcripts, is free of conclusions or judgments. For example, eschewing emotion, Reznikoff describes the fate of 'four women and a little girl about seven' found in their hiding place by two SS men who

> began to beat the women with whips.
> The women begged for their lives:
> they were young, they were ready to work.
> They were ordered to rise and run
> and the S.S. men drew their revolvers and shot all five;
> and then kept pushing the bodies with their feet
> to see if they were still alive
> and to make sure they were dead
> shot them again.

However, unlike the above lines from Reznikoff, many of O'Siadhail's descriptions of the terrible suffering of the victims are not only haunting but also full of emotion and beautifully constructed. None more so than when the author attempts to imagine just how the new arrivals in the camps felt at the exact point when they realized they were destined for immediate death. Was there, he asks, 'In every heart one moment when it knows?' ('There', 66) and 'Did they hold hands the moment they knew?' ('Faces', 122). There is no attempt to answer such questions. Perhaps this is how it should be. No one spared this fate can ever hope to capture fully the exact experience, but it is appropriate that these questions are raised because it is necessary that readers contemplate them.

An existence (not a life) of despair, dehumanization and ultimately death was the reward for those who survived the initial selection process. Again the choice of words to describe the state of these individuals – deliberately reduced to empty shells – is superb, while the chilling description of 'A tattooed number who'd once been someone' ('Here', 67) cannot be easily forgotten. Nor can the description of the Ravens – the inmates whose job it was to man the gas ovens. Again the choice of simple, non-judgemental language, combined with Biblical references to convey the incomprehensible predicament this group of prisoners faced is harrowing:

> Cain sucking his marrow from Abel's bone
> Pity these ravens for what driven ravens do
> Bitter complicity that Jew should oven Jew. ('Ravens', 72)

But all is not lost in the hell of the camps. Even in the face of such horror the author draws attention to the individual attempts of inmates to maintain normality by the keeping of a diary, the humming of a tune, the retelling of a story. In the camp environment all these otherwise trivial pursuits amounted to a refusal to abandon hope in humanity and were thus the ultimate acts of defiance. Here one is reminded of a recollection by the late American critic Irving Howe in his memoirs, *A Margin of Hope*, of a Polish Jewish acquaintance and Holocaust survivor, Yuri Orlev, who almost forty years later showed Howe a tattered notebook full of poems in Polish, which as a young boy in the concentration camp, he had traded for several days food rations.[20]

Of course some, like Orlev, did manage to survive the camps, and their experiences, as told here, will be familiar to anyone who has read the works of survivors like Primo Levi and Elie Wiesel (both of whom are acknowledged by O'Siadhail). But such familiarity does not lessen the impact of these poems and indeed my favourite piece in the entire collection is found here. In 'Dust-Veil' (108-112), one is forced to consider the ghoulish anti-Semitic attacks on survivors following their liberation from the camps. Such attacks are widely forgotten in contemporary discussions but were among the most traumatic experiences for survivors. Dr Zarah Warhaftig, writing in *Azure* magazine, recounted her own harrowing experience of this phenomenon.

> After the Holocaust I helped to organize the Tora Va'avoda conference in Cracow, Poland. Several young men and a young woman were on their way to this conference when a band of Polish Gentiles attacked them, killing a number of them. The girl was carrying papers attesting she was a Gentile, and her friends urged her to show her papers and save herself by telling the attackers she wasn't Jewish. She refused saying that during the Holocaust she had been forced to hide, but now she would no longer do this: She preferred to stand with her friends, whatever the price.[21]

The poem 'Dust-Veil' also starkly addresses a far more abstract form of suffering experienced by survivors – the pain of rejoining a society that has no comprehension of what they have gone through, or as O'Siadhail puts it: 'A world that lusts for life soon loses interest' (110).

As early as 1943, Abraham Sutzkever, a resident of Vilna Ghetto and a member of the Jewish underground, chillingly predicted the situation that survivors would face in the post-war era.

> And time will gnaw you mute
> Like a grasshopper caught in a fist
>
> They'll compare your memory to an ancient buried town
> And your alien eyes will tunnel down
> Like a mole, like a mole. (*How*, 1943)

Sutskever, perhaps more than any other individual, has shown the power of the poem to record the horror of the Holocaust. Who can fail to be terrified by lines such as:

> Have you seen, in fields of snow,
> frozen Jews, row on row?
> Blue marble forms lying,
> not breathing, not dying.
>
> Somewhere a flicker of a frozen soul –
> glint of fish in an icy swell. All
> brood. Speech and silence are one.
> Night snow encases the sun. (*Frozen Jews*, 1944)

O'Siadhail, unlike Sutskever, is an outsider – a non-survivor with no familial connections to the tragedy, who also happens to be a non-Jew. He also writes under personal circumstances very far removed from those found in the Polish ghetto in the 1940s. Nevertheless, O'Siadhail, precisely because he readily acknowledges throughout the work the unbridgeable divide that exists between those like Sutskever who directly experienced the Holocaust and those like himself who comment on that suffering from afar, has managed to create a work so ambitious in scope and so passionate and sincere in execution that the reader cannot fail to appreciate his intellectual and emotional commitment to the subject. He has given his artistic all not only to honour the memory of the victims but to record their suffering in an historical work of epic proportions. No one can do more than that. Moreover, he has succeeded in reminding us not only of the invaluable role of poetry in narrating the history of the Holocaust but also of the moral force of poetry, something which we too often forget. Very rarely has Adorno's warning about the barbarism of poetry after Auschwitz been further from the truth.

12 | *The Gossamer Wall*: 'We Can't Sing Dumb!'

David Cain

It is one of the most mysterious penalties of men that they should be forced to confide the most precious of their possessions to things so unstable and ever changing, alas, as *words*. – Curé of Ambricourt[1]

The terrible inadequacy of words always falling short of desire. The ungraspable joy, the uncommunicable sorrow. And even here there's another paradox. The drift and shortcomings of language which cause us to fail again and again are also what urge us to begin afresh, poem after poem, generation after generation. This inexhaustible hankering after the absent. The necessary absconding of the sacred. – Micheal O'Siadhail[2]

I. Propriety, Witness, Memory

The Gossamer Wall: Poems in Witness to the Holocaust. What of the propriety – or impropriety – of conjoining poetry and Shoah? Micheal O'Siadhail is there and aware: 'That any poem after Auschwitz is obscene?'[3] (*Any* poem–or *Poems in Witness to the Holocaust?*) Or what of the impropriety of *not* doing so – challenging poetry with Shoah, Shoah with poetry – if the concern is 'witness' and if, as O'Siadhail proposes, 'Memory is at the core of poetry both on a personal and on a societal plane'[4]:

It's best another generation remembers
Never to forget it could happen now.
No, not so much to rake the embers

But to recall how something not faced
Goes underground and then reappears
To haunt us. ... (*GW*, 12)

'Underground' – hidden below where the blow-up builds. Further, 'To forget breaks sacred promises to the gone' (*GW*, 13). 'Witness' and 'memory' go together and are in league with O'Siadhail's proposal: 'Poetry is a form of hospitality.'[5] Is poetry as hospitality vanquished in and by the Shoah? This is a question to which *The Gossamer Wall* seeks to respond. Response need not be answer. Central to the response of *The Gossamer Wall* is risk ('Risk' is the title of a poem, *GW*, 98-9). O'Siadhail risks entering in with no assurance of coming out. One assurance is that no coming out is possible without entering in.

The dedication of *The Gossamer Wall*:

For those who died,

for those who survived,

for those who told (*GW*, 5)

Witness and memory. The three assemblies of the dedication overlap: dying and telling – can dying be a form of telling, a cry of silence ('crying silence' [*GW*, 115], 'cries of silence' [*GW*, 118])? – and surviving and telling. (We must beware of pronouncing 'survival' too cleanly. There is surviving and there is ... surviving: 'Even the numbed and busy daylight cracks[6] / A survivor's mask' [*GW*, 88]).

> Still a moment when testimony and story meet
> Before the last attesting faces will retreat
> To [before, to give way to, to be replaced by] echo chambers of second-hand remembrance.... .[7]
> Is this the moment where testimony and story meet? (*GW*, 13)

II. Form

The Gossamer Wall is symmetrical architecture. Apart from the opening 'Cataclysm', the five divisions place the third division, 'Figures', in the centre. Surrounding the centre are two two-part sections which balance each other, 'Descent' with '*Northeim*' and '*Battalion 101*' on the way in (or down) and 'Refusals' with '*Spoors*' and '*Le Chambon*' on the way out (or is this too strong?). The contrast with 'Descent' ('Ascent' would be too strong) teaches us to read 'Refusals' affirmatively as refusals of descent. So 'Figures' is junction, chiasma, intersection, a crossing of the ways. '*Le Chambon*' contrasts '*Northeim*'; '*Spoors*' contrasts '*Battalion 101*'. Likewise, sections one and five ('Landscapes' and 'Prisoners of Hope') are in contrasting balance, a symmetry of tension.[8] From 'Meltdown of trust' (*GW*, 43) to 'undertow of trust' (*GW*, 95) to 'Fragile city of trust' (*GW*, 101) to 'A healing trust?' (*GW*, 123): the question mark matters.

The form of the poems is varied and complex. Poetic forms impose discipline which can occasion discovery. Would O'Siadhail have found 'Polish clay' had he not been seeking a word to rhyme with 'Pompeii' (*GW*, 64) or 'broken nightmares of days' apart from 'replays' (*GW*, 70)?

To the centre belongs the sonnet. 'Figures' (echoing 'Numbers', the first poem of 'Landscapes' [*GW*, 12-13]) consists of fourteen sonnets, fourteen lines each, octave and sestet together with strict rhyme patterns (ababcdcd efefgg or ababcdcd efgefg). Sonnets inhabit poems (see 'Haunted', with three sonnets alternating with three sets of rhyming couplets [aabbccddeeffgghh], *GW*, 88-90). Of course alliteration and assonance are operative:

> *Whipped* by one of those *skin*flint *winds*
> that *blows* in across such *exposed tableland*,
> a thin dark-*eyed woman shawled* in *snow* ... (*GW*, 93, italics added)

This stanza also contains instances of a ubiquitous internal or migratory, roaming rhyme[9] (those, blows, exposed, snow). O'Siadhail's entire project is animated by alternation of end-rhymes in various patterns and migratory rhyme. The migratory rhyme becomes nearly predictable in the third section of 'Power', where end-rhyme and next line beginning-rhyme yoke the lines together, gather momentum, and quicken out-of-control plunge, 'Descent':

> ... A house *scheme*
> the *regime* they'd *ousted tried* they *now*
> *allow*, thought they *stymied* it *before*
> *more* public works. The Shirts *know*
> how a *show* of action will for a *while*
> *beguile* the burghers. Lulled for a *time*
> *Northeim* believes what *Northeim* desires. (*GW*, 44, italics added)

Leonine and near rhyme – 'Time to *end* – an officer butts *in*' (*GW*, 84, italics added) and 'delayed' leonine rhyme –

> *Willingly, lovingly to accept our fate.*
> The ditch graves gape and wait. (*GW*, 84, italics in text [fate – gape – wait])

Each poem discovers and discloses sophisticated, subtle, skilled, rich, poetic patterns. Without calling attention to itself, form binds and tightens – and so intensifies – the poems. O'Siadhail's poetry is 'in-formed' – but not slavishly.

III. Language and Imagery

A true writer teaches one a language. The vocabulary of O'Siadhail calls forth: trust, knots, stitches, threads, bones, marrow, stones, jazz, dance, face, gaze, glance, glimpse, mask, veil, embrace, caress, broken, wheel, rim, hub, garden, orchard, spruce, worm, detour, roof, boundaries ... wall – and fragile. 'Fragile' seems one indispensable word in the poetic vocabulary-repertoire of O'Siadhail. 'Fragile' works in every direction – pertaining to what the poetry is about and to the poetry itself. Within the fragility of O'Siadhail's lines is a disciplined toughness, a circumspect and understated accord.

The adventurous, bold imagery will, of course, be instanced throughout what follows; but the 'black sun' shadows forth:

> The black sun shines.
> Quantum leap in some darker mystery of evil. (*GW*, 25)

In writing to the Roman historian Cornelius Tacitus (55?-after 117 C.E.) concerning the death of Pliny's uncle, Pliny the Younger (62-113 C.E.) offers some description of the eruption of Vesuvius:

> Mount Vesuvius was blazing in several places with spreading and towering flames, whose refulgent brightness the darkness of the night set in high relief. ... It was now day everywhere else, but there a deeper darkness prevailed than in the most obscure night; relieved, however, by many torches and divers illuminations.[10]

Does such imagery of light and darkness inform O'Siadhail's potent, ominous image of 'black sun' – 'The black sun shines in blacker satellites' (*GW*, 41), 'A marked man while the black sun shone' (*GW*, 42),

> A willed and grievous oblivion
> While the black sun shone (*GW*, 46)

> 'Men long grown before the black sun shone ...' (*GW*, 49)

> '*Under black sunlight the will to endure ...*' (*GW*, 81)

> 'Aroma of mistrust, distant fall-out of Vesuvius ...
> Deep in the memory gene a black sun ... (*GW*, 88)

'Black sunshine' (*GW*, 90), 'Imagine another black sun ...' (*GW*, 119) A 'black sun' is a dark, deceptive, lying light, an eerie light, as when a volcanic cloud eclipses the day: 'It was now day everywhere else, but there a deeper darkness prevailed than in the most obscure night ...' A 'black sun' is analogous to 'empty-eyed' and a 'hollow upbeat' of music in the camps:

> ... they play for their lives.
> Chosen by an exam, many who'd been *virtuose*
> Now grind a music complicit and empty-eyed;
> A band conductor from a famous Vienna café
> Parodies for all she's worth her life outside . ...

> Then *The Blue Danube* or even *The Merry Widow*
> For a commandant who loves waltzes. A violin
> Is singing against the grain its hollow upbeat. (*GW*, 71)

Understated horror becomes all the more horrible:

> Aesthetic of function. Delicate efficacy.
> The tall pleasing line of a chimney ... (*GW*, 27)

Macbeth offers commentary:

> *From this instant, there's nothing serious in mortality.*
> *All is but toys.* (*GW*, 28; *Macbeth*, II, i)

> 'A miracle', *der Führer* calls his success.
> Thousands torch-light Wilhelm Strasse.
> The opposition slips away into darkness ... (*GW*, 29)

'Into darkness,' yes – the darkness of what is, the darkness of what is to come.

> How nearly it didn't happen. Fortune's somersault,
> Blind worm of disaster,
> A blundering drama,
> Tragedy of this black knot somehow tied by default.

Sophocles watches.
The flaw. The downfall.
So little might have brought a juggernaut to a halt. (*GW*, 30)

O'Siadhail likes months and seasons. The calendar marks his poetry as a form of the particularity of name and place:[11]

The last hours of June 1934
At Bad Weisee (*GW*, 27) [,]

'... summer is a chance he can't miss' (*GW*, 50) [,]

... winter in.
Three months of yellow summer, nine of grey (*GW*, 94) [,]

... 1944,
August 20th, some days before the liberation
of Paris ... (*GW*, 104) [,]

At Minsk in '42 at least
Five thousand from the ghetto killed
To mark their feast. (*GW*, 111)

In other words,

Ashen calendar of bitter eruptions,
Almanac of grief. (*GW*, 111)

The stanzas are never far from music. Music will not go away.[12] Sensitively, exuberantly, O'Siadhail relates Jewish music, *céilí* bands, gypsy music, and blues (*GW*, 21). The poem belongs whole, but here is an indication of the musical celebration:

Freylekh, Bulgars, walzes and Klezmorim
Playing with such a confused abandon
Dances at once rumbustious and sad that seem

To summon up centuries of teeming ghetto life,
Weddings, bar mitzvahs, circumcision feasts
Hoisted out of the ordinary into some repetitive

Delight in sound ... (*GW*, 21)

Depths of survival. Klezmer or jazz or *céilí*,
A story squeezes at the edge clamours of music;
Out of darkest histories, profoundest gaiety. (*GW*, 117)

'Out of darkest histories, profoundest gaiety'? Too audacious? No. Description. Anything but prescription, recipe. Kent in *King Lear* asides one of the great lines in Shakespeare:

Nothing almost sees miracles
But misery. (*King Lear*, II, ii)

'Almost' makes all the difference. *The Gossamer Wall* is intense poetry striving – straining –
to find some honest way to celebration in the black sun of the pit.

O'Siadhail's poetry is not easy but, with care, accessible and rewarding – better,
heartening. This poet does teach us a language. In living with his poems, the poems become
richer, opening out evocatively on themselves, on one another – and on us.

IV. Context

Where do the concentric circles stop? They do not. We must stop. J. Hillis Miller writes
perceptively:

> The notion of intrinsic meaning is not incompatible with the idea that each poem draws into
> itself all those connections it has with its various contexts. It is often useful to have those
> connections identified, not only for their own sake, but for the light they may shed on
> meanings which are there in the words of the work. Such investigations may show how a
> certain text draws its life from similar passages in other works by the author, or from books
> read by the author,[13] or from the social and historical milieu in which it came into existence,
> or from the tradition to which it belongs.
>
> But where does the context of a poem stop?[14]

Let us stop by recognizing that O'Siadhail's daring *The Gossamer Wall: Poems in Witness to
the Holocaust* is not for him a new departure. Here is a courageous poet and a courageous
poetry: we might have seen it coming. *The Leap Year* asks,

> Still this twentieth century.
> What news item will we run today? What's the story
> To break?[15]

The breaking story, yes, but also the story which breaks, obliterates ... stories.[16] In *Belonging*,
there is 'Ghetto' (*HMJ*, 40; *P*, 46). In *Springnight*, 'Already the sun has outdated darkness
...';[17] and we come upon 'the gossamer's nervous growth ...' (*SN*, 9). Granted this is not a
wall. Yet there is 'the waiting-room wall' (*SN*, 27 and, perhaps more significant, 'Pinpoints
and overviews' [*SN*, 27]). In *The Image Wheel* is 'an old garden wall ...'[18] – and what of 'this
gauze of living' (*IW*, 35)? In *The Chosen Garden*, 'History' comes close.[19] Walls abound (*CG*,
84), and Dietrich Bonhoeffer is hanged (*CG*, 87). In *A Fragile City*, 'Hollows of famine
rumble the bowels of the earth'[20]; we are fearfully near eruption, which is elemental in *The
Gossamer Wall*. 'Gauze' again: 'our gauze / of meanings' (*FC*, 39). In 'Abel' appear 'whipping
boy and scapegoat' and 'Unbroken line of pogroms' (*FC*, 46). 'At Auschwitz Wolf hums
Brahms' rhapsody by heart' (*FC*, 69). In *Our Double Time*:

> Broken youths of plagues or war,
> Whole generations went *en masse*.[21]

At the end of 'Out of Eden,' the second part of *Our Double Time*, we encounter 'Our side and the other side. Have all the boundaries already started to blur?' There is 'the darkly-seen-through glass ...' (see I Corinthians 13:12). 'Some need to name the gone grows with years' (*ODT*, 54): this line introduces the next part, 'Namings', and also heralds *The Gossamer Wall*. 'Tapestry', the first poem in 'Namings', continues the theme—and 'tapestries of being':

> That they should simply vanish. Could that be?
> A great divide. Cessation. An absolute cut-off.
> Somehow they still encompass and transfigure me. (*ODT*, 57)

One of the 'Namings' is 'Etty Hillesum' (*ODT*, 62-65; see 75, 95), who is a principal presence in *The Gossamer Wall*. In 'Secrets of Assisi', we face 'the boundary wall ...' (*ODT*, 109) and lines offering yet another introduction:

> There in secret gardens voices of the gone
> Speak their lines in overtones of history,
> Harmonics of the past refiguring our story,
> As though the narrative selves of long ago
> Somehow in their wholeness seem to throw
> A shape on ours. (*ODT*, 109)

Shape:[22] 'Can how we remember shape what we become?' (*GW*, 118). Assuredly. Look out and beware

> The overlords and barons of print and screen,
> Oligarchies of news
> Shaping our images. (*GW*, 119)

The power of images to shape us is a large part of the peril and the promise of art. Of course, these familial volumes of poetry overlap, join, converse, and reference one another in so many other ways[23] on what becomes the way to *The Gossamer Wall*, where history is the wide, motivating context:

> As though things can be too big for us close-up
> and need the slow-down of both time and distance;
> a wider angle, the gradual *adagio* of truth. (*GW*, 14)

Historical panorama gropes for perspective: 'A new millennium. An ancient slate' (*GW*, 12).

> So is all history one secret narrative of power
> Broken in the brick and rubble of Babel's tower? (*GW*, 116; see Genesis 11: 1-9)

'Dust-veil' (in nine parts – part 5 a sonnet, five pages – the longest poem, *GW*, 108-112), volcanic and panoramic, is absorbed in updating the immediate (Battalion 101, etc., part 6) and in 'indating' the vast past from Jewish feasts to Aztec to the Shang dynasty, eruption of Iceland's insistent Hekla, and 'Roaming three millenniums ...' (*GW*, 108).

V. Particularity

The text is teeming with particularity of place – countries, camps, rivers, mountains, cities, towns (ancient and modern) – and person – biblical, literary, fictional, philosophical, religious, scientific, political, historical, musical. A slim volume: is room to be found for anything other than *names*? The throng and deluge here noted, perhaps not complete but so much more than representational, evidences something essential about the flavour, the clamour, the tumult, the specificity and individuality of the body, the flesh, of this text.[24] Not numbers but non-quantifiable *names*. Not flight from particularity and direct assault on universality but plunge into particularity is poetry's possibility of universality.

VI. Overture: '*Cataclysm*'

As already observed, five major divisions – 'Landscapes', 'Descent', 'Figures', 'Refusals', 'Prisoners of Hope' – structure the work. The first four are introduced evocatively with Yiddish verse, the last with Hebrew. Preceding these divisions in italics is '*Cataclysm*', a kind of overture. The musical association is right for O'Siadhail:

> 'Cataclysm'
>
> In each human moment as in the time of stone
> Such build-up before a lava fumes in the cone.
>
> Cumulative time, a gradual hidden crescendo,
> Those lids of the earth's crust shifting below.
>
> Rifts in a magma chamber, a vicious blow-up;
> Bombs and cinders spewed from an angry cup.
>
> Sleep Vesuvius that once covered up Pompeii
> With pumice-stone and ash. Sleep and allay
>
> What fears we must both remember and forget.
> Sleep Vesuvius. Within us all your molten threat.
>
> And yet. Another beginning. Another landscape.
> Can the sun still sweeten even the sourest grape?
>
> Shared scars of forgiveness, our fragile hopes;
> The fruits and vines tended on your lower slopes. (GW, 10)

So much is going on here – and 'all at once'. Poetry is inexhaustible. If it is not, it is not poetry. The inexhaustibilities of poetry are to be ... not exhausted. Let the challenge here be to indicate some of the inexhaustibilities of disciplined, controlled ambiguities, of the intertwining of image patterns, and to point back to the poems (any responsible treatment of this text tends to return us readers to the text itself) which are poems because they could not be otherwise. Shall we?

Three stanzas of volcano imagery 'crescendo' (the musical is not spared the demonic) to eruption. The analogy with human eruption is ventured: the Shoah as human volcanic eruption –

> *In each human moment as in the time of stone*
> *Such build-up ... [;]*

'*Within us all your molten threat.*' Two stanzas address Vesuvius.[25] Three times Vesuvius is bid to sleep.

> *Sleep and allay*
>
> *What fears we must both remember and forget.*

Is this line both ironic and not? '*Sleep*' – that we, too, may sleep? '*Allay*': lay to rest, pacify, appease, lessen the severity of, alleviate. Does this sound healthy – or cravenly? Yet remembering – witness and memory – is the cost of any possible honest living forward – 'we can't sing dumb!' (*GW*, 120); while a kind of forgetting could be the cost of '*Shared scars of forgiveness, our fragile hopes ... .*'

'And yet' turns the last two stanzas to '*Another beginning. Another landscape.*' 'Landscape' prepares us for the first section, 'Landscapes'. 'And yet'[26] frequents O'Siadhail's poetry and, as here, is often a turn in the direction of fragile hope:

> And yet
> Slow bleedings to be wise.
> Even in shadows of regret
> Am I grateful for what is? (*ODT*, 18)

So we arrive at 'Another landscape' yet still on the slopes of sleeping Vesuvius. Does sleeping threaten dreadful awakening? Other connections: what is '*each human moment*' in relation to '*the time of stone*'? Why describe volcanic eruption in terms of '*Bombs*' and '*an angry cup*'? Because 'bombs' suggest war and the (inhuman) human; and 'cup' suggests the human and that which one must drink, however bitter ('My father, if it be possible, let this cup pass from me; nevertheless, not as I will, but as thou wilt' [Matthew 26:39])? The analogy of volcanic eruption and human volcanic eruption is sustained. '*Angry cup*' and '*sourest grape*' cohere. The capacity of the 'sun' is questioned as is the case throughout. Cup, sun, grape, fruits, and vines combine to suggest wine. Why '*on your lower slopes*' – because this is where grapes would be tended and because lower slopes image appropriate humility? The movement of '*Cataclysm*' – from '*build-up*' to '*blow-up*', volcano and human beings, to sleeping Vesuvius, not without '*molten threat*', volcano and human, to '*fragile hopes*', precarious promise, volcano and human – foreshadows the movement of *The Gossamer Wall*.

> And yet there's no Richter scale of tragedy.
> How to measure suffering? (*GW*, 22)

A qualifying of the analogy: volcanic eruptions can be quantified; the human kind cannot.

VII. 'Landscapes'

'Landscapes' sets the scene, ranges the history – history haunts poetry – presents panorama and tormented agenda – and questions to keep. The poetry moves effectively from panorama to place and to person again and again ('Pinpoints and overviews'): poetry with a zoom lens.

In many poems, the titles are tucked deftly down into the lines – we can locate and explicate the titles in the poems; or, more probably, titles are taken from the texts once written: 'Hankerings' – 'Europe hankers ...' (*GW*, 16); 'Lull' – 'Sweet lulls of peace ...' (*GW*, 17). Let us follow some titles and see where they lead. 'Numbers' finds different kinds of numbers: 'Two millennia blurring Jew and Judas' and 'six million dead' (*GW*, 13). Then 'Remembrance', 'Forebodings', 'Hankerings', 'Lull', 'Reverberations', 'Wilderness' – wilderness, to be sure. In 'Remembrance', which is musical, geological, temporal, and spatial, we come to '... a tacit crying out for the forgiveness of the dead' (*GW*, 14). Forgiveness both ways: may the dead forgive us; may we forgive the dead. For what? For compelling *The Gossamer Wall*.

> Rumbles in bowels of myth. Again and again
> Eruptions, sulphurous gases of blames.
> An inwoven scapegoat down two millenniums. (*GW*, 15)

Again, the analogy of human and natural:

> Tragic fault line within us,
> Moody engines of prejudice underground (*GW*, 15)

– the volcano *within*, 'Vesuvius within' (*GW*, 57).

> What happened to ... ?
> That marvelling at being just as we are,
> Our lovely jumbled here-and-nowness,
> Particular, once-off, centered at the edge,
> This cussed and glorious human mess.[27] (*GW*, 16)

This – as mightily preferable to what 'Hankerings' hankers after: 'certain', 'hierarchical', 'order', 'Intolerance', 'axioms, timeless abstractions ...', 'laws', 'universal', 'Species, genus, our races and nations', 'all things steady',

> ... overviews, flawless stock,
> Unblurred theories, the pure nightmare
> Of ideal boundaries, *ein Land, ein Volk.*
> *Übermensch* of dark-willed Nietzsche.[28]
> Outcastes, outsiders, freaks, beware
> Our tick-tock reason's overreach. (*GW*, 16)[29]

In the 'White noise' of 'Lull',[30] colour and sound, seeing and hearing, converge in disquieting confusion as trust loses in a trust-distrust dialectic: 'A wobbling trust. Dangerous subsoil' (*GW*, 17). 'Gulfs of language, religion and scorn' – scorn because of gulfs, gulfs among different kinds of scorn: 'seething mistrusts' (*GW*, 18). 'Whatever the angle, same kinetics of mistrust' (*GW*, 20). Music and dance whirl in 'Signatures', adding to the build, to the intensity–

> ... almost like those *céilí*
> Bands melodeoning out their tunes
> Battered and entrancing, a kind of cyclical gaiety
>
> That goes on gathering its own quickened logic
> Of unbroken desire. Or do they recall
> Zigzag tensions and rhythms of Gypsy music? (*GW*, 21)

Numbers, again: 'Each of these millions, someone's remembered face' (*GW*, 21). This precious, caressed face defies numbers. Yes:

> Still trembling in our galaxy's outer spaces
> The crying silence of six million faces. (*GW*, 115)

But: 'Each someone's fondled face' (*GW*, 122). From panorama to person.

> Factories, trains and railroads now gearing up
> Machinery of oiled governance in a modern state (*GW*, 22)

– 'state' as nation and as condition, predicament. What a predicament.

VIII. 'Descent'

Having prepared his canvas, O'Siadhail paints his second division, 'Descent', in the repulsive specificities of '*Northeim*' and '*Battalion 101*'. We meet Wilhelm Spannaus:

> A brother had fought and perished in the world war.
> Another in academe. (*GW*, 34)

Perhaps a touch of humour may be permitted. But there is no humour in the conjunction of order and brokenness as Spannaus' train 'snakes across the heartland into Northeim' (*GW*, 34). We have met snakes before. This is an example of a move O'Siadhail makes effectively. He turns nouns into verbs and verbs into nouns or rather invites a word to be both noun and verb in the poetic richness of controlled ambiguity[31]:

> Strange vibes and currents in rocks
> Reptile sense before earthquakes;
> In hoar-frost the hibernating snakes
> Stir from a warm underground lair.
>
> Will no one see when the serpent rises? (*GW*, 26)

We meet Ernst Girmann, who 'seizes power' (*GW*, 37) in Northeim. 'Fever Chart' is spurred by 'Suddenly a fringe of zealots ...' (*GW*, 39). These words begin each stanza and intensify the terror. Again the trust dialectic: 'Wide-eyed trust' (*GW*, 41), 'Meltdown of trust' (*GW*, 43).

'The wall around the town repaired ...' (*GW*, 43): this is not the gossamer wall. 'Northeim' is a peopled poetic narrative of the fall of a town to The Party.

'Battalion 101' gets nasty.

> But who rounded them up in scattered villages
> sealed the trains or slew the lame and frail?
>
> Everyday men. The plain and run-of-the mill
> as Battalion 101 whose rank and file
> would shy at first from point-blank slaughter.

But then:

> Humdrum murder, dull and commonplace
> as weeks lull them into a norm of violence.
>
> ... Immunities of routine.
> Ordinary men hardening in their daily carnage. (*GW*, 49)

Or as Gower observes of the incest of Antiochus and his daughter:

> But custom what they did begin
> Was with long use account no sin.[32]

The dissonance of music and murder is mercilessly shot forth in rapid-fire lines ('A Polish Village', *GW*, 50-3) – 'as darkness falls' (*GW*, 52). Matter-of-factness understates matters of fact. Captain Hoffmann and Vice-Commander Wohlauf: the names are planted before they get their own poems.

IX. 'Figures'

'Figures' is division three, entering the death camps. Do we find here a deliberate irony of form and content? Sonnet form covers – by no means contains – calamitous content. The poems here strikingly parallel parts of Elie Wiesel's *Night*.

> A thousand urgent stories forever unheard;
> In each testimony a thousand more suppressed (*GW*, 63)

Wiesel affirms, 'God made man because he loves stories.'[33] *We* are stories, the stories we tell, live, are, and become. Early in *Night*, Wiesel writes:

> Night fell. There were twenty people gathered in our back yard. My father was telling them anecdotes and expounding his own views on the situation. He was a good story teller.
>
> Suddenly the gate opened and Stern – a former tradesman who had become a policeman – came in and took my father aside ... .
>
> The good story he had been in the middle of telling us was to remain unfinished.[34]

So many unfinished stories: 'A muted dead demand their debt of memory' (GW, 63). In 'Figures', the poem bearing the division name:

Boarding-school girls ... holding hands and unaware.[35]

... A neighbour's child so forlorn that she chooses
The other side [of the gossamer wall]. A waif shouldn't vanish alone.
Figures forever sealed in a molten Pompeii,[36]
Marrow spread as bone-dust in Polish clay. (GW, 64)

The alliteration cements the rhyme. As here, rhyme, when not sing-song, suddenly and joltingly can pull lines and meanings together into a felt fitness. The last lines of 'Chinks':

For some, for a while, bitter and sweet parallel
As rifts of light blink through the walls of hell. (GW, 75)

We begin to recognize – to realize – different kinds of walls.

In sonnet three, 'Arrivals', fearful thirst, 'Uncanny ordinariness' and SS men questioning arrivals: age, health, and '... pointing either here or there' (GW, 65). Next sonnet: 'There'. Next sonnet: 'Here'. The 'here or there' order is reversed. 'There' is death, and 'Here' is hell. 'There' is imaged as theatre. Human beings are 'batch', and: *Sonderkommando* ... hurriedly prepare the set for another show ...', 'this theatre of despatch ...', 'a well-rehearsed scene ...', 'changing room wall ...', 'Just affable ushers' (GW, 66).[37] Again, 'There' is death: 'In every heart one moment when it knows ...' (GW, 66) and 'Here' is not life but hell:

Here no future or no past ...
There's no why here ...
A tatooed number who'd once been someone. (GW, 67)

And 'Each somewhere someone's remembered face' (GW, 76). The face, the face. Poor Battalion 101: 'The trouble is these killings face to face' (GW, 55). The last line of 'Figures': 'The silent alone fathom the depth of silence' (GW, 76). The silent alone: alone – only the silent and the silent all by themselves.

In the camps: stories lost, instant separation, selection, theft:

... Just staring
Listless and vacant goners (GW, 68)

hunger, 'broken nightmares of days' dreamed in 'Night' (GW, 70), empty music, clandestine love a sure recipe for death, 'and yet' – gestures of care.

X. 'Refusals'

What is intimated in the last lines of 'Figures' is indicated in division four, 'Refusals'. The vocabulary of 'Refusals': 'Resolute' (GW, 82), 'refuses' (GW, p 82), 'Defiance. Of record. Charged remembrance ...' (GW, 85), 'resistance of word' (GW, 85), *'resist'* (GW, 86), 'Ruses of refusal' (GW, 86), 'Resistance' (GW, 86), 'protested' (GW, 87), 'Lone random flowerings of courage' (GW, 87), 'resistance' (GW, 93). There are two parts: *'Spoors'* and *'Le Chambon'*.

Does the pace of the poetry accelerate, crescendo, as O'Siadhail taps terms and images he has earlier introduced and nuanced? Economy of reference increases. '*Murmurs*' opens 'Spoors':

> *Under black sunlight the will to endure;*
> *A victim dares to overturn her soup bowl,*
> *Warsaw's ghetto defended sewer by sewer,*
> *Reckless White Rose of the siblings Scholl.*
>
> *What to do if Germans evacuate Amsterdam?*
> *Frank gossips to her diary in an annex room.*
> *In Bürgerbräukeller Elser primes his bomb;*
> *Wolski the gardener is hiding Ringelblum.*
>
> *At Birkenau, Salmonovitch shins a flag mast.*
> *'Nearly a hundred,' he replies when they ask*
> *His age. Six hundred boys beaten and gassed.*
> *A crematorium log buried in a thermos flask.*
>
> *Crackles of resistance. Cussed moves to stall [verb and noun]*
> *The beast. Cards flung from trains, spoors*
> *Of memory, whispers behind a gossamer wall.*
> *Static of refusal. A grit of risk and gestures.* (GW, 81)

The rhyme pattern is abab cdcd eeff ghgh. Parallel phrases, '*Crackles of resistance*' and '*Static of refusal*', contribute to a build. From '*reckless*' to '*risk and gestures*' – and gestures are risk – behind *a* gossamer wall. So there is more than one *gossamer* wall. '*Crackles*' of resistance come from another kind of fire.

'To Life!' (*lechayim*) sets a raw, fierce juxtaposition: cut bellies trampled on, spilled guts, and '*Praise him with the timbrel and dance*' (*GW*, 83; Psalm 150:4). We see 'Lone random flowerings of courage' (*GW*, 87). In 'Haunted',

> ... Something always missing.
> Undertones of grief lurk below a crust
> Of everyday. Half-smile of broken trust.

Controlled ambiguity: in 'below a crust', Vesuvius is not far away (eleven lines), though bread may be far away, and crust, a hardened surface layer or shell which may crack ('cracks' comes in six lines) and give way.

> Behind a flimsy partition ghost parents call,
> Siblings eavesdrop behind a gossamer wall.
> A doubleness only revenants understand.
> Wounded alone know the wounded land. (*GW*, 88)

We are set up and made up for this sudden, simple, straightforward, no-nonsense line: firm, full rhyme, economy of word and rhythm.

'Siblings' recalls the context from which the title, *The Gossamer Wall*, comes. In Anne Michaels's acclaimed novel, *Fugitive Pieces*, Jakob Beer is haunted – literally – by his beloved, beautiful, departed sister, Bella:

> Awake at night, I'd hear her breathing or singing next to me in the dark, half comforted, half terrified that my ear was pressed against the thin wall between the living and the dead, that the vibrating membrane between them was so fragile.[38] I felt her presence everywhere … Watching with curiosity and sympathy from her side of the gossamer wall.[39]

Our minds and memories do not obey boundaries between life and death. Any 'theodicy' is non-theodicy:

> Trucks of half-skeletons, the demand
> Of the rabbi's son, desolate Elihu:
> *Show your power. This is against you!*
> Nothing happens. No lightning rod.
> Sonnenshein [sunshine] shouts *There's no god*.
> Six million brothers Cain can kill [siblings].
> Black sunshine. Ratchetings of evil
> As chill winds blow across a bowl
> Of stars. A world rattles on its pole.
> Broken vessels of a god in hiding,
> Agony's grinding down, a sliding
> Back to sacred nothingness that hovers.
> Beckonings, maybe. No more. A lover's
> Invitation rumouring through the dark.
> Rustles of absence in a silent ark. (*GW*, 90, rhyming couplets)

Desolate Elihu ('Elihu' means 'God himself') is right. The Shoah is (ultimate?) affront to any God in any way resembling a biblical God. 'Nothing happens' – and empty words pile up: desolate, nothing, no, no, black, chill, rattles, broken, hiding, grinding down, sliding back, nothingness, dark, absence, silent. When Sunshine shouts *There's no god*, the sunshine is black sunshine, different from but akin to that accomplished by Vesuvius. Why '*god*' with a lower case 'g'? To keep open, unlimited, comprehensive? Wiesel reflects on why the first murder in the Bible is of brother killing brother and suggests, 'Whoever kills, kills his brother.'[40] 'Ratchetings of evil'[41]: evil is locked in place, allowing one no alternative but to press on, to press on in what is suddenly a cosmic context. Chill winds blow, a bowl of stars; a world rattles on its pole. This sounds a bit precarious. Chill winds and rattling unite. 'Broken [broken, broken, broken] vessels [not only the bowl but the world] of a god in hiding …'.[42] But

> a sliding
> Back to sacred nothingness that hovers.

Ratchets do not slide back. How can a nothingness hover? Is this what makes it 'sacred'? ('This inexhaustible hankering after the absent. The necessary absconding of the sacred.') Hovering, 'Beckonings, maybe. No more' – but hovering and beckonings are more than nothingness. All at once comes something like

> A lover's
> Invitation

and 'rumouring through the dark' – not 'rumoured' but 'rumouring.' Even through the dark, this lover's invitation is not passive but active. 'Rustles of absence in a silent ark': the ark is silent – a god in hiding; but there are *rustles* of absence. Rustles are not silent. Can absence rustle? Perhaps in the same way that sacred nothingness hovers. In other words, we have spoors of the shyest hint of non-idolatrous hope. The ratchet stands guard.

'*Le Chambon*' is 'sentried to the south and west by spent volcanoes' (*GW*. p. 93). 'Spent' is good news. More than poetry offers hospitality: '*Naturellement*, come in, come in' (*GW*, 93). Trust is thematic: 'quiet trust' (*GW*, 94), 'undertow of trust' (*GW*, 95), 'an underground trust' (*GW*, 96). In 'Risk', Le Chambon is 'alive in the jazz of its chosen danger' (*GW*, 99). Jazz is life, challenge, promise. 'Fragile city of trust ...' (*GW*, 101): concentric circles. In 'Risk' are 'still waters ...', 'stirred. Swirls in a brackish pond ...', 'an eddying centre ...', 'ripples and widens ...', 'outwards ...', 'Some centrifugal love' (*GW*, 98-99) – a double image pattern of opening out and closing in: '... why then did they desist from closing in?' (*GW*, 104). From waters to doors: the first poem in '*Le Chambon*' is 'Hinge', all about an open door. More than doors swing:

> Swinging on a hinge of memory
> The door opens (*GW*, 93)

'Everything aware and ajar' (*GW*, 94). Stay with the image: 'A door ajar' (*GW*, 95), 'I couldn't close a door against a stranger's face' (ah, 'face'),

> backdoors that open
> onto woods (*GW*, 98) [,]

– 'doors hurriedly unlocked' (*GW*, 100), 'would we've been purer if we'd shut our door?' (*GW*, 102).

XI. 'Prisoners of Hope'

Division five is 'Prisoners of Hope', the title taken from the Hebrew of Judah Halevi,

> Is there any redeemer like you?
> Or any prisoner of hope like me? (*GW*, 105)

To be a prisoner of hope is to be without alternative to hope; yet hope is alternative. Hope is freeing. Hope *can release* its prisoners. 'Dust-veil' in nine parts ranges across millennia and throughout the world, juxtaposing imagery of volcanic eruption and dizzying history with Sukkoth, Lots, Esther, and Jewish identity: 'The battered wife of a God she can't forsake ...' (*GW*, 108). Here is a hint of retrospective – Northeim, etc. – caught as we are in the ratchet. But:

> To endure to tell the world but do they care?
> ... A world that lusts for life soon loses interest.

... They didn't understand, they didn't want to know.
... Who understands or wants to know? (*GW*, 110)

This question imposes itself and cannot be avoided if '*In remembrance resides the secret of our redemption*' (*GW*, 112). The following poem, 'Sign', returns to Jewish identity and 'Lonely Yahweh ...', 'Other. Among and not of [as in 'in the world, but ... not of the world'[43]]':

Glatstein at fifty odd
Quarrels with a wounded God.
We, your radiant vessel,
Palpable sign [this poem is titled 'Sign'] *of your miracle.* (*GW*, 113)

What is this 'miracle'? *We*. We real creatures, who can really be related to by and so relate to a curious creator – and quarrel with a wounded God or, in the weighty words of Kenneth Cragg, with 'a God who has gone out on a limb'.[44] 'A wounded God' implicates Christianity.

Is this what haters hate?
The chosen choosing to separate.
Kedushah. Apart and vagabond.
Singled out. Bearers of beyond. (*GW*, 113)

'Beyond' as burden – but more: 'beyond' as blessing. 'Bearers' as witness. ('The necessary absconding of the sacred': why 'necessary'? To give us room, to lure us on.)

In 'Soon':

Soon now their testimony and history coalesce.
Last survivors fade and witnesses to witnesses

Broker their first-hand words. Distilled memory.
Slowly, we begin to reshape our shaping story.

... Now our second-hand
Perspective, a narrative struggling to understand.

Victims, perpetrators, bystanders who'd known
Still cast questioning shadows across our own. (*GW*, 123)

Because '[w]ounded alone know the wounded land' (*GW*, 88), significantly and sensitively, O'Siadhail allows a simple hint of sanity to come from another voice, the voice of one who was *there*:

... how we can know
The words to put in the mouth of another ... . (*GW*, 107)

That one is Abraham Sutzkever.[45] In 'Paradise', '*The sea is the sea*.[46] *A chimney's just a chimney*' (*GW*, 114; *SS*, 352). What? A 'real world' once again [again?]? Praise the Lord!

> *I love the birth of light, the pure fantastic*
> *Of the naked and the real. Without bombastic.* (*GW*, 114; SS, 352)

The real is fantastic. The voice introduces '*the Wailing Wall*' (*GW*, 114; *SS*, 355). The relationship to a gossamer wall must be merger.

> Maybe a half eternity of God's restless time,[47]
> How often to trust to heal such broken rhyme … . (*GW*, 114)

'[A] broken rhyme', 'such broken rhyme': rhyme can be nothing other than broken in the midst of broken, broken, broken.

> Still trembling in our galaxy's outer space
> The crying silence of six million faces (*GW*, 115)

– the gossamer wall. 'In Jeremiah's darkest scroll a jazz of hope …' (*GW*, 116): in the poetic world of Micheal O'Siadhail, jazz is, again, promise, and, if promise, hope – hope for Jeremiah and even for us.

'A promise to remember, a promise of never again' (*GW*, 117) is prominent in the last poems. 'As never before we promise never again' (*GW*, 119). 'We feast to keep our promise of never again' (*GW*, 120).

> Never, never again. Pleading remembrance
> Whispers through the gossamer wall … . (*GW*, 121)

In the poem 'Never':

> A black sun only shines out of a vacuum.
> Cold narrowings and idols of blood and soil.
> And all the more now, we can't sing dumb! (*GW*, 120)

Dumb and dumb – speechless and forgetful: to sing requires both voice and remembrance.[48]

In those 'millions', O'Siadhail refuses to forfeit 'Each someone's fondled face …' – 'A breathing memory behind the gossamer wall' (*GW*, 122). Can memory breathe? The breathing is an important part of the reason the wall is gossamer. The reason for breathing is that the wall is gossamer. 'And still they breathe behind a gossamer wall' (*GW*, 124).

XII. Wall – and Mirror

Five sections, a kind of horizontal hourglass into the heart of the horror and, we timidly yearn, out the other side. Not quite. One does not quite come 'out' again. As 'White noise' returns, one's hope is more like the hope to enter into '… detours of repaired advance'. But there is that jazz. We cannot sing dumb, *but sing we will*. Suddenly, stubbornly, spiritedly,

> those gradients of love and let-go always undefined.

> His ardour still never sure where to draw the line;
> perpetual apprentice in the paw and pitch of things (*GW*, 97)

– 'subversive ragtime', 'raucous glory and the whole jazz of things', 'a music's brimming let-go' (*GW*, 120).

C.S. Lewis is referring to painting when he observes, '... there are a few who feed on a great picture for years'.[49] The same is true of poetry. The more one feeds on and lives here in *The Gossamer Wall*, the more the connections connect, the resonances resonate, the more the force and fire and passion of the poetry – and of the poet – penetrate. Finally, this poetry affords its own commentary, assessing, critiquing, qualifying, and affirming itself.

We recognize the remarkable, intense investment Micheal O'Siadhail has made to enter into this world, this anti-world, this world-which-should-never-have-been. The poet writes:

> *The Gossamer Wall* is a distillation over several years of various aspects of the Shoah and it is hoped that it will encourage readers back to the primary sources, in particular to the first-hand accounts of witnesses in which the poems are grounded, but also to historical or scholarly studies and the imaginative literature which undergird them. (*GW*, 127)

The Gossamer Wall: a 'wall' which is wanting to become a mirror in which we fear and flinch to see ourselves. 'Witness' is a complex, curious, multivalent concept. Witnessing can be creative. Witnessing remembers. In addition, witnessing may be to own – to confess – the dangers of our creaturely freedom as apparent price for the possibility of our creaturely integrity and dignity. Dmitri Karamazov confesses to his brother Alyosha, 'Yes, man is broad, too broad, indeed. I'd have him narrower.'[50] The price is extravagant.

What defeats a black sun?

> A light too broad for any black sun to shine
> Scope of conversations, brilliance of what is ... (*GW*, 124)

> ... a world
> Too deep and copious for black suns to shine (*GW*, 117)

> A black sun only shines out of a vacuum.
> Cold narrowings and idols of blood and soil.
> And all the more now, we can't sing dumb!

> A conversation so rich it knows it never arrives
> Or forecloses; in a buzz and cross-ruff of polity
> The restless subversive ragtime of what thrives.

> Endless dialogues. The criss-cross of flourishings.
> Again and over again our complex yes ... .
> The sudden riffs of surprise beyond our ken;
> Out of control, a music's brimming let-go.
> We feast to keep our promise of never again. (*GW*, 120)

Jazz sprains order but needs order in order to sprain order. David Ford and Daniel Hardy affirm '... the joy which flourishes where order gives play to non-order, and where the "jazz factor" can inspire a newly improvised future. Of course the "jazz" is irrepressible ... .'[51]

Micheal O'Siadhail witnesses:

> Next year in Jerusalem! Parting toast and prayer [prayer follows toast].
> And still they breathe behind a gossamer wall. (*GW*, 124)

May these hard (yet fragile) and well-wrought poems be mirror of hope – and air.

13 | A European Poet

Mary O'Donnell

> 'O my white-burdened Europe, across so many maps greed zigzags' – Micheal O'Siadhail, *Inheriting Europe*.

The word 'European' conjures something special and distinct today, comes conceptually kitted out with a vast and deep coffer of achievement, experience, and the sophistication which diversity of language and temperament confers. The languages are old and have gone through many transformations. We know the links. We remember Latin and Greek even if we do not speak them. There is this awareness of linguistic inheritance and it has brought in its wake a certain pride, especially for those who work with words.

Arguments about inheritance and allegiance, about greater philosophical complexity, about the one-sided opulence of colonialism, about religion, not to mention what European scientific endeavour has traditionally reflected about the aspirations of the continental populace, as well as a historically deep-rooted and comparatively *well-disseminated* literature, are usually what drives any consideration of how we inhabit the greater group, the larger space within which our regional lands and tribes exist.

If these are background concerns, by the same token, do the accompanying qualities – arguably those of striving, competition, a belief in the importance of and a passion for humanities and science-based discovery – lead us towards a definition of literature specifically 'European'? And does a writer who is European automatically cease to be 'Irish', 'English', or 'Norwegian'? Is the *Ur* group diminished by cultural associations that are seen to move above and beyond that group?

The answer to the penultimate question is that the question of one's European-ness is certainly debatable if one lives on an island off a greater island, if geography leaves one physically at a remove from the sprawl of the continental land mass. It appears to have been something of an anxiety for some commentators in recent years, who have gone to great critical lengths to declare that this or that Irish novelist is 'European' in his concerns, as if this somehow conferred greater authority and prestige on the work.

But undoubtedly there are writers whose constituency cannot be defined by the local concerns of Ireland (even if they are as epic as Patrick Kavanagh's ideal), nor by the myth-pool of our own culture, nor indeed by the appetite for immediate response to Irish social agendas which, at their best, reflect the sense of fracture felt by many contemporary Irish poets.

Today, the Ireland inhabited by Micheal O'Siadhail is a very different place from that portrayed in the works of Yeats, Joyce, Kavanagh, Lavin, Kate O'Brien, and Beckett. He became a writer during the 1970s, during the erosion of what was often viewed as a time of oppression and cultural unease. That was, significantly, also the time during which any poet in Ireland was usually viewed as a mystical interpreter; the poet was the highwayman of the subconscious, the silken seducer of the imagination who knew the routes and occult byways that allowed ordinary mortals free access to the subjective self in all its mysteries and revelations. This is the world O'Siadhail moved into as a poet, not the other, shame-filled one of unconscionable narrowness. His writing, almost from the start, developed within a newly minted field of idealized national autonomy, something which may have allowed him (unconsciously or not) to feel equally at home in Ireland or in Europe. That autonomy was not something readily available to or embraced by the majority of his contemporaries however. The poets, no less than their fellow Irish, limped into the light very gradually, emerging from the long dawn of an Irish Republic which was, in its early years, a severe parent to its children. The absent parent – the ex-colonial one – left a vast aperture in the social consciousness of Ireland that took decades to begin to seal and heal. So the poetic themes were often (among the men at least) Ireland, what it is to be Irish, self-affirming landscape poems, strong on lyricism, highly conservative in style when they emulated the forms of the greater island beside us, Irish poems written in English, yet sometimes nodding in the direction of a mixed inheritance; aware of the rhythms and metres of the bardic poets, attuned unconsciously to the voice patterns of native sounds which miraculously leaked through into Hiberno-English. There was anger in the poetry, often muted, more often fiery, as in the work of some Irish language poets, whose work has been translated into any language but English – a signalling of attitude, a pseudo-political stamping of feet.

Folklore was explored by some who used it as a vehicle to drive forward a sense of poetry as conscious of history and positioning; others 'turned away' from English, most notably Michael Hartnett. Still others straddled both fields of expression, like Eoghan O Tuairisc and Rita Kelly. To write in the Irish language conferred a purity on the practitioner, a valid one at that, but one which could be argued to circumscribe the attempts made by other writers to define themselves and their preoccupations as Irish poets.

In Ireland no less than in England, the blanking out of European – or 'foreign' – poetry reflected a resistance to Modernism, which was American-led and yet closely tied to literature from Europe. Pound and Eliot, for example, were free to pick and choose from world literature. They did not possess the long avenue of achieved verse that England had, which stretched back to Chaucer; nor did they have a feel for what the Irish had absorbed residually and by the miracle of language resistance: our own Gaelic poetry and its particular metres and rhythms.

Eliot, writing of Yeats, wrote: 'The kind of poetry that I needed, to teach me the use of my own voice, did not exist in English at all; it was only to be found in French.' In the same way, Pound found his own strength initially in translation, with *Homage to Sextus Propertius*. Meanwhile Beckett took things even further by abandoning his original language, writing in French and then translating himself back into English in one of the most original gestures of the twentieth century.

These writers felt free to pick their way, like serious and intent collectors, through the strands and threads of foreign literatures and histories, through politics and movements and philosophies. This is what lifted them hugely from their local culture of literature, so that although they may be termed 'American' or 'Irish', the drive for renewal meant that they undertook something that broke through the crust of tradition and made of them serious and largely hype-free writers. The absence of hype is something which similarly characterizes the work of Micheal O'Siadhail.

But before moving to speculate on the other, particular qualities that make O'Siadhail an Irishman who is European by sensibility and achievement, I want to consider other Irelands inhabited by our poets, the particular conventions available to poets, subjects touchable and untouchable and the No Man's Land of those who choose to stand apart from the tribe. We have had a Northern school of poetry, taking MacNeice as its progenitor, and Thomas Kinsella's opposition to this when he refers to it as 'largely a journalistic entity' in the introduction to his *The New Oxford Book of Irish Poems*. In the editorial in the Irish Issue of *The Poetry Review*, Kinsella is criticized for this opposition, which the editor regards as 'extreme'.[1]

But also part of that Northern tradition are Mahon and Muldoon. And the modern face of the North, which includes Carson and McGuckian, and other Northern born poets like Sinead Morrissey and Kerry Hardie, cause the traditional sense of division to blur. The edges of what is 'North' and what 'South' have frayed, leaving a great wet hank of poetry fabric to soak and trickle within various inherited juices. The ground of true opposition, has, I believe, shifted gradually in the past decade or so.

A parallel tradition can be identified as emanating from Patrick Kavanagh. Interestingly, Heaney began not with MacNeice but with the Ulster poet Kavanagh, yet Heaney's legacy has been, among other things, to 'Southernize' his experience of the North, to illuminate a local corner in the north of a divided island and make it meticulously universal.

During the 1980s the question of 'women poets' was much to the fore of contemporary debate, the term itself implying a sub-genre. Thus a stream of women entered the world of the printed volume of poetry. It was new, exciting, and it was still a good fifteen years behind what had been happening in the United States regarding the re-igniting and recognition of female ambition.

At the same time, new anthologies emerged with definitions and re-definitions of Irish poetry – from Penguin, Faber, Oxford, and, most traumatically in one sense (in that it essentially disfigured the existing forms and contexts of Irish literature through incomplete representation), from Field Day, initially a three-volumed gift of an anthology marred by a startling lack of recognition of the energy of contemporary writing, especially from women. That a group of academics and writers eventually had to produce a fourth, all women, anthology, is itself a marker for those times, times in which the novelist Roddy Doyle was heard to jest on radio 'sure any woman who wrote a postcard is in it'.

But that too, just like the Irish-to-English translation debates, just like the North-South tension, just like the great discussions attached to the publication of John Montague's poems (which for his readers forged a profound psychological connection to our own history), has melded into something else: a question, perhaps, of poetry carrying on in its mysterious way in a country which is now radically different from that which we lived in before.

What has changed, and how did Micheal O'Siadhail's work fare in terms of reception on his home turf throughout that period? Who heard him speak? In the case of the latter enquiry it is noteworthy, for example, that in the main poetry publishing organ, *Poetry Ireland Review*, no article nor assessing essay has ever appeared on his work, although he wrote two pieces himself. This is remarkable for a national journal which regularly undertakes either an interview or an in-depth extended essay on the working poets of our day. On the other hand, his work came to the attention of Nobuaki Tochigi,[2] Shigeo Shimizu[3] (both in Japan), and Audrey O'Toole Pfeil[4] (in Germany), to name but a few. His work has received consistently solid critical consideration in our local outlets, including *The Sunday Tribune*, *Books Ireland*, *The Irish Book Review*, *The Irish Times*, *The Enchanted Way*. Further afield the *Times Literary Supplement*, *Poetry Quarterly Review*, *The Guardian*, *Harvard Review*, CBC Radio 1 and John Felstiner at Stanford University have attended to this unique voice for our times and for times ahead. The short story writer Eilis Ni Dhuibhne, writing for *The Sunday Tribune* in 1998, notes that his voice '*is unusual among Irish poets. Tending to eschew the local and anecdotal, his work could be placed in a philosophical European tradition*'.

A European sensibility has always characterized much of O'Siadhail's work, in part because of his facility for language itself. In an essay he wrote for *Poetry Ireland*,[5] he refers to his training in linguistics:

> I'm glad that in my student days I was trained in linguistics. It has been such an enablement and at so many levels. It's not just the concentrated clarity which such a scientific rigour imposes, although I'm grateful for that. It provided me with a model of a living organism, adapting, rearranging, growing, shedding dead skin, all the interwoven patterns of a continuity and innovation. It stands me in good stead as a paradigm, no matter what field I explore in the long quest. (No wonder language has been at the core of many debates in our time, from philosophy to literary theory.) *It is such a gift to have the roots and semantic entanglements so wittingly in the foreground as I work … .* (my italics)

Something of a polyglot, he speaks both Irish and Norwegian as second languages, knows both Danish and German and is undoubtedly at home with French, Latin and Greek. This sense of linguistic adding-on certainly pervades O'Siadhail's work. If one speaks a language, it is automatically easier to understand the thought patterns of a people, in other words to 'read' the residues of the past and observe how they interact with the present.

But of course O'Siadhail is not preoccupied with 'thought patterns' in that distant, academic sense. What his facility with language does create is a portal into aspects of consciousness which have seethed, shifted and petrified over the centuries. The themes he explores are the constant ones: love, death, change, responsibility to the self, the interrogation of the self on its journey through life; the tools with which the exploration is undertaken are language, history, philosophy, and music. The source of tool production is Europe, the final polish individual and Irish. The effect created is of a poet of enormous intellectual inquisitiveness, emotional openness, reasoned debate, the whole dashed through with surges of eroticism, joy, and suffering.

*

O'Siadhail is both a public and a private poet, as the collection *A Fragile City* demonstrates. He has held a number of key academic posts, is a former member of the Arts Council of Ireland, as well as being friend, lover, and husband.

In this volume he considers the crossing over points between public and private, in which neighbour meets neighbour and finds him the same but different, in which nurses minister publicly to a privately ailing hospitalized body, and the body again finds ease and passing comfort in a night hostel for the homeless. Here, the poet considers the role of compassion – if it plays one – in the cycle of famines that ravage the African continent ('Theft'). Public and private intersect and encounter one another, the poet sifting through the residues in each, as if for points of common coherence. Coherence is absent though, or it emerges minimally and in a different form to that of reasoned logic, as the poet considers the face and eyes of a starving child with 'a shrivelled crowfooted face':

> ... There's no wool
> To pull over these eyes. Look long. Look deeper.
> Cycles of dominance; a hemisphere's rise and fall.
> She stares and stares. Am I my sister's keeper?

The collection is divided into four sections: 'Filtered Light', 'Veils and Masks', 'Boundaries', and 'Feast', each illuminating an aspect of the tension between public and private. The light from every visionary moment is 'filtered' into the poet's consciousness, be it the light of civil rights movements in the Sixties ('Flare'), the dialectic between individual and society – masses versus system – or indeed the opaque light from a formal meeting which sparks off a memory of boyhood and a bullying incident. An awareness of the cosmopolitan adventure characterizes many of these poems, deepening and darkening in the first three sections of the book until the release of 'Feast'.

It is worth taking a look at philosopher Emmanuel Levinas, some of whose ideas are alluded to in *A Fragile City*. Levinas was born in 1906 in Lithuania, survived the Russian revolution and travelled to France where he was to spend most of his life while moving back and forth to Germany to pursue his studies with Husserl and Heidegger. Much of his philosophy is directly related to his experiences during World War II, the death of his family in the Holocaust, and his own experiences as a prisoner of war in Germany.

Levinas had two major texts, *Totality and Infinity* (1961) and *Beyond Essence* (1974). Central to the latter is his study of our relationship to the Other, which is the foundation – he said – of developing subjectivity. He explains that the ethical requirement that we are responsible to or for the Other disturbs subjectivity. So, whereas Heidegger (one of his great influences, though he was to part ways with his thinking during the war) thought of death in terms of 'my death', for Levinas death is always the Other's death, the result being that human consciousness is determined by the way in which we are haunted by the Other's death and the possibility of that death.

O'Siadhail's encounters in *A Fragile City* can be seen to interrogate repeatedly this question of the Other, and to reject the ontological (as ontology, philosophy (and poetry) is narcissistic, seeking pleasure by incorporating the Other into the Same). But O'Siadhail – no less than Levinas – is not a seeker of the Same. Repeatedly, these poems demonstrate the ethical recognition of the Other and a turning away from the primacy of the self (or Same). According to Levinas, the Other is a 'relation without relation'.[6] The Other is never reduced to the Same, thus remains unknowable, outside of the totality of the Same. Freedom, for Levinas and O'Siadhail, is a signature existential concept. Indeed Levinas edited a collection of essays on Judaism the title of which is *Difficult Freedom*. If readers of O'Siadhail grasp the ethics of freedom which lie at the heart of the poems in *A Fragile City*, the journey with him as poet-thinker is an effortless one of discovery of the Other – largely at odds with much Western thinking, which tends to place Self at the centre of everything. Despite, or perhaps because of the foregoing, O'Siadhail's tone is sometimes effusive, effervescent even, as in the poem 'Embrace'. Here, he greets evening guests, welcoming them to his home, and captures the initial moments of jostling welcome and awkwardness of many social gatherings, especially among men, as he makes explicit:

> I want to fling my limbs open and embrace.
> A clumsy left hand glances a shoulder blade
> and I know at once he's feeling some hand laid
> to measure a deal's anxiety, nervous give-aways.
> A hug is a dagger too close, a dealer's grope.
> Something tightens at my touch and buttons up.

Then, moving on, he asks of the men: *What have we done to ourselves?*, comparing them to women, who *caress and touch with ease*.

But it is, in the end, a step more complex than that old argument of the contrast between male and female behaviour as he confronts a joint responsibility, an unspoken ethical contract perhaps, between man and woman:

> A coin's faces, each a keeper for the other.
> Woman and man, somehow we're in this together.

Whether man or woman is read as Other, the point is that in communication one is, quoting Levinas, 'found beside the Other, not confronted with him, not in the rectitude of the in-front-of-him'. Thus he, O'Siadhail, is responsible for the Other without waiting for reciprocity, being subject to the Other precisely *because* the relation between the Other and him is *not* reciprocal, despite the niceties and gloss of social encounter.

Throughout 'Veils and Masks' the human face is frequently encountered, and often the eyes in that face, referred to in 'Woman me as I am manning you'. From the poem 'La Différence', an advocation, a command to open to the twinnedness of experience, that doubling over that creates possibility and repels petrification. In this section, 'Clash', O'Siadhail explores a moment's misunderstanding. This time, language is circumscribed by the offended party in the poem, and silence does its festering work instead of language:

> 'If only you'd told me.' Instead you fester,
> harbour a wordlessness that keeps trying to say
> 'to have to say is to fail'. My best filibuster
> empties into silence.

Ever-conscious of what he calls the *cargo of my gender*, ('In the End') he repeats what was already alluded to in 'Embrace', that sense of mutual responsibility, as in *Your freedom is our freedom*.

O'Siadhail's way of re-ravelling the undone sometimes emerges in the habit of gazing and absorbing. In the poem 'Noon' he writes that *Archaeologies of thought define me*, and recognizes his 'encoded eye' with habits of absorption which go beyond the purely visual. We are influenced by the sediments of living, it is suggested, and experience accumulates even outside direct human experience in that day-to-day tactile sense. There is the unspoken. There is the sub-conscious. There is what we sense in memory even if we have not lived it. In the context of both O'Siadhail and Levinas, surely experience is itself the Other?:

some beckoning aim, a hovering remembrance.
My spirit is watching over the waters.

In 'Meditations' he pays tribute to Niels Bohr, Alain Aspect, and perhaps the most remembered and debated of these great physicists, Werner Heisenberg. O'Siadhail allies himself with other Europeans whose work has been to explore, to 'cry for meaning' through science, whether working with the tool of the electron or light quantums or the unfixable particle. Yet in the final section of *A Fragile City*, the word 'Feast' provides a hint of what is ahead. Having quoted George Herbert (*You must sit down, sayes Love, and taste my meat: So I did sit and eat*), the reader is ushered swiftly into an arena of abundance, an awaiting cornucopia which displays the delights of friendship, senses primed by weather-change and the prospect of things ahead. Words like 'fiesta', 'basket', 'Joy', 'laughter', 'Celebration', 'feasting', delight', 'dance', 'scent', 'playfulness', 'whirl', rhythm', 'gladness' texture a section which is not merely about feasting, celebration, love-making, and dance. Here, ironically, is where he most encounters the legacy of European history, some of it tragic in the great operatic sense of dooms survived. Our entry point to this mood which is the accompanying 'twin' of O'Siadhail's feast, is the poem 'Wireless'. In a way, this poem marks familiar territory for readers who will have recognized the setting at least, if not the implementation of the poem, in a work of Heaney's. Even without writing a poem, what Irish person of a certain generation has not twizzled the tuning needle and probed their way over Europe?:

Berlin, Stockholm, Paris, Hilversum, Prague.

Traces of static. An opulence breaking in.
I've grown to love the grit of interference.
Sizz and hubbub. So many cities of conversation.

In this longing to reach, as he describes it,

for timeless skies if only to gall
again into the deeper moments of what's ours

he picks up what I can only call soul-echoes, the traces of an Other with which he is co-responsible: *This feast at which I'm both host and guest.*

But the feast continues and O'Siadhail identifies Plato and Anaxagoras as brother explorers, though the feast unfolded in a different style at Auschwitz ('Invitation'), where *Wolf hums Brahms' Rhapsody by heart.* In 'Celebration' he gives the nature of time a Bergsonian twist, allowing for the possibility that time may be a turn or a spiral, a moving rather than a static and linear concept.

What one is aware of, before he returns to a poem like 'Delight', is that O'Siadhail draws on European history, of which he is the open-armed inheritor, miraculously un-skewered by nationality, nor Americanized (the American journey is a different trove which does not really impinge here) in the style of some of his compatriots.[7] Even before it was regarded as important to translate the work of European poets into English and thus make the significant voices available to Anglophone readers, O'Siadhail was at the forefront of awareness of who was writing and thinking and just what the value of a European inheritance is to Irish consciousness. Whether it is to the artists (Gauguin, Matisse, and Renoir), the musicians, the philosophers, the spiritual thinkers, the survivors of war, he has continued to draw on what I term the suffering change and steadfastness of Europe and made of it a substantial poetic. The effect of this consequently changes the face of Irish poetry, carving a revitalized new fault line in a frequently topic-driven landscape where a few obvious master and mistress-practitioners have bent their considerable energies into definitions and redefinitions of what it is to be 'Irish'. O'Siadhail, I would argue, is Irish without the hype – casually so, freeing himself up to the greater work of authentically searching for meaning through art.

*

The collection *Our Double Time* (1998), is redolent of twinned-ness, doubles, Doppelgängers, and open and secret truths. Friends are addressed; voices, poets and thinkers are written into, where sometimes he inhabits the memory of one who made a mark on the fabric of history (the Jewish Etty Hillesum, for example, and '*A life stretching beyond itself*'). Time is always doubled, this collection announces: where there is tradition, there is also its opposite, ripping up the ground in the spirit of renewal; where there is birth there is also death; with love comes other moods, the reserve and distance of the unspoken, where speech is unnecessary and language is circumvented by the spirit of a moment.

An attraction to the colourful spatter of summery Europe, Italianate, lavendered, is explored in 'Secrets of Assisi' where

> There in secret gardens voices of the gone
> Speak their lines in overtones of history,
> Harmonics of the past refiguring our story,
> as though the narrative selves of long ago
> Somehow in their wholeness seem to throw
> A shape on ours.

O'Siadhail the explorer needs to confirm what he already knows about 'our story', in affirmations in the imagined voices of those who are gone. So he examines the oppositions of history – the history of different places and how these reflect back on the history of self, which is, for most of us, a history of secrets.

In the poem's second section, the speaker himself becomes an instrument with which to make music, to sound out feeling:

> At San Damiano once on the shaded bench,
> Maybe you heard a quiver in my voice's reed
> As I recited a troubadour's love-song in French?
> The closer we are, the more secrets we need.

This is the reserve of spiritual eroticism that asks to be broken

> into more than I understood.
> Tue so le laude la Gloria e la honore
> O Lord, most high, all-powerful and good!
> Beautiful and radiant *cun grande splendour*.

In 'Tongues', all the languages are drawn together in iambic pentameter – one line in Italian, its translation in English, and so on through Icelandic, Norwegian, Irish, and

German. 'Tongues' runs to twenty lines. It is short but by no means lyrical, and the single-word title itself is coded with suggestions of speech in full flow, the liberated utterances of many languages unified in hot tongues of which O'Siadhail enquires if each of his voices is '*a mother/Nurturing me in the secret grammars of another?*' The making of the poem is an act of gratitude to language itself, which may be seen as the touchstone of feeling, the mediator of whatever is warm, joyous, and singing as lover encounters lover and he urges '*If you're mine be mine each inch of your heart for me.*'

The statement applies to speech and language as much as to the human encounter. Both are laden with histories, both arrive in our unfolding lives with a rich cargo of experience misremembered, re-remembered, sometimes 'gone' (a word O'Siadhail is fond of using to convey the going under of whole populations, as through tyranny and oppression). If language – and passion – are encountered as '*gurgled sounds, singing flames of tongues*', so too is the golden promise he speaks of to be encountered as speech finally rendered into silence. Speech, language, the thing through which love is so often manifested, is refined eventually into silence, like breathing through a breaking dawn and finding acceptance of what is, the full load of it savoured in a sense of the double which emerges from the weight of history and acts like a hook to ensnare the intimate present.

That we are dealing with a lover, in the archetypal sense, is beyond doubt. O'Siadhail knows his secret histories – Abelard and Heloïse, Etty Hillesum, Dante and Rilke. Their voices sail across the centuries and decades and to come ashore in the poems, to be named there, as in the section 'Namings'. He also includes Ireland in a series of voices and soundings from Europe. His 'Matins for You' does not shrink from the sheer joy of observing a wife, a lover, as she tumbles through the process of showering, drying, getting dressed. This is a lover's eye view of the delights of intimate presence

> Sit on the bed-end and pull a stocking on,
> Slip that frock over your head
> Let it slither a little, ride your hips, then spread
> Its folds and tumbles, flopping past those thighs
> To swish against your ankles. I'm still all eyes.

But the layers of physical presence are anchored, as ever, to the *wells of aloneness* which

> ... seem almost to imbue
> Your silence with the long wistful rubato
> Of a Chopin nocturne or is it a *sean-nós* tremolo?

The aloneness and beauty of his 'sitter' is observed, yet he is no voyeur so much as a man perplexed gradually by two views of the world: the incarnate presence of billowing life, and the invisible other, the undertow suggestive of possibility, realization, the glimpse of the impossible: *A muse the more a muse in being a muse.*

O'Siadhail turns to Rainer Maria Rilke on a number of occasions, most notably in the poem 'Rilke', a clear demonstration, if one were needed, of his sense of identification with one of Germany's greatest lyrical poets. Attitudes towards Rilke in the English speaking world have varied greatly. As Derek Mahon has remarked:

> To the young Pasternak, and above all to Marina Tsvetaeva, he was the master ... Others, like
> Brecht, irritated by his cultivation of aristocratic patrons, his rarefied life-style and apparent
> obliviousness to the harsher aspects of modern life, dismissed him ... [8]

Both O'Siadhail and Rilke share an elevated, sometimes incantatory tone. There is always
a sense of the invisible other, a broken line to be crossed through the osmosis of experience, a
tendency to proclaim and exclaim, to praise the fact of being alive. If one were to attempt to
reduce both – and I am aware of the leap here – to a simple statement, the basic intention of
much of the poetry might run something like this: *I live yet remember: here is my home, let
me praise it and find transformation!*

Rilke's greatness, elusive in definition, might be said to rest on the transcendentalism of
the best of his work, particularly in the *Ninth Elegy* and undoubtedly in the *Sonnets to
Orpheus*. But one senses the appeal of the life of Rilke, parallels read into by O'Siadhail when
he remarks:

> Me and Madam Jazz, you with your wild Orpheus;
> Those landscapes where music, always the alien,
> Expands our heart-space and still outgrows us.
>
> Your hand fits mine ...
>
> Anything we know learned from ripened women:
> The warmth of Lou Andreas-Salomé's praise;
> Magnifying silences, minds so open and human.

Within Irish culture one has to consider if, like Rilke, O'Siadhail has sometimes been
viewed as somewhat rarefied, as if oblivious to the 'harsher realities' of our society. But he
himself has a very clear view on this:

> ... there is a certain mood abroad which demands a societal perspective, given the nature of
> things, there is the risk that the immediate appeal of an openly political poetry could wrongly
> consign what I would call 'the poetry of the hidden consciousness' to the category of 'easy
> emotionalism'.[9]

Further on in the same essay, he remarks:

> So far, in an attempt to place a poetry, which may seem at first glance to be utterly apolitical, I
> have alluded to poetry's workings in 'the prepolitical hinterground' (Havel) at the imaginative
> junction of a memory and a future and to its political implications for language. But perhaps
> all this has wider significance? *Is it too daring to speak of poetry as a cry for meaning?* (my
> italics). It is as if, suddenly in the flow of the world, we are jolted into remembering an all-
> consuming desire for fullness, a desire we had almost forgotten.

Of course it is never too daring to speak of poetry as a cry for meaning! But in Ireland and
England the thematic fundament of poetry has undergone many a hiatus since the nineteen
sixties. Much of it in Ireland has involved a sometimes niggardly over-scrutiny of the
problematics of Northern and Southern identity, of journeys into places and origins in the
hope of finding a comfortable fit for ourselves as we grapple with the new, economy-

dominated Ireland. It is not though – frequently enough – a poetry of ideas, so much as a poetry of comfortable, prettified images that confirm how things are without stretching to consider the whole journey of what things might *become*, and how the present creates every future.

'Meaning' as a term carries certain *mitteleuropäische* associations from which Anglophone poets stand somewhat at a remove, finding it a circular and philosophical term whose origins are suspected of Teutonicism and of being laden with an inwardly spiralling cargo that has seemed surplus to requirements. O'Siadhail is absolutely correct to speak of poetry as a cry for meaning. But the journey has been argued differently for many Irish poets, who until relatively recently found themselves embroiled and perhaps more at home in the earthwork of folklore and in the opening up of formerly unploughed topical ground (sexualities, biology, life-phases, world travel excluding Europe!). O'Siadhail eschews topicality more than any other living Irish poet. For topicality, read 'hype' and 'media-friendly'. If topicality holds no interest for him then there follows an enormous liberation into the one quest that obviously suits his temperament: for meaning, which is something entirely different, for examining the curiosities of his own life and its relation to a world that agitates and excites him. The result is a range of enquiry at his disposal full of ideas, dialogues, dialectics, philosophies, all underpinned by fidelity to the question of emotional precision. The irony for this writer is that O'Siadhail's inner temperament may be at variance with the temper of the times in his homeland, though not in the least with that in the best European poetry.

*

As regards *The Gossamer Wall*, only a European sensibility could produce a work in poetry that balances stamina, conviction, and documentation. If he were not to write another word, this collection alone attests to O'Siadhail's active participation in the story that *is* Europe. Furthermore, by being a 'European' poet, it is not so much a question of separation from Irishness, as a recognition of the oneness of voice to be found among many different writers and thinkers over several centuries. The tune and theme is similarly orchestrated, one could argue – cultural oppression, language, war, with love and death played out within them – but the motets are local. Nonetheless, it is not about being *either* European *or* Irish, but about absorbing these motets and discovering them to be symphonic and vast. We can call *this* tendency 'European', born of the 'white-burdened Europe' where 'across so many maps greed zigzags'.

In historical psychological terms, the concept of greed has stiffened the spine of European thought and enterprise. Expansion, conquering this territory and that, political and revolutionary interventions that changed people's thinking in the wake of the French Revolution, went hand in hand with the writing, the philosophy, the music, and even the spiritual thought. To take one example: as Germany's small statelets gradually evaporated and the country moved towards unity and expansion under Bismarck, moving east into Poland and emerging as Prussia, so to did the literature of that country follow suit. It is no accident that the European novel, as we still know it today, shifted in structure and narrative style most markedly during this period. When Russia, Prussia, and France were most engrossed in nationalist thinking but also in expansion, so too did the great bourgeois/adultery novels of Europe emerge,[10] and so too a poetry which placed the individual in conflict with the new geographies of nation and spirit. Gradually, some would argue, the end result of expansionism was the Second World War, with its lethal and still enduring paralysis, the Holocaust.[11]

When O'Siadhail addresses the Holocaust in *The Gossamer Wall* we can take it for granted that he is going to explore a challenging historico-political situation. In the poem 'Reverberations' which anticipates what is to come in terms of violence, he retraces the journeys of armies and people from Napoleon to the Third Reich, but specifically the journeys of Jews:

> But in vasts of White Russia, Poland,
> Ukraine, Lithuania, Yiddish enclaves;
> Always an outcast to Orthodox Slavs,
> Catholic Poles, Lutheran *Volksdeutsch*
>
> Gulfs of language, religion and scorn.
> Europe of nationhoods and borders,
> Older jaundices, seething mistrusts;
> The enclaved with nowhere now to turn.

It is a fractured history, he suggests, that primes the ruthless campaign to draw in all the Jews of Europe and annihilate them. The effects are seismic, it is inferred, as 'mother earth bucks and quavers'. Interestingly, throughout this collection Shakespeare's *Macbeth* is the exemplar of tyranny. In 'Lull', which charts the silently growing German yearning for restored national pride, Macbeth's invocation to the powers of darkness is quoted, as well as two other excerpts from the Elizabethan language of prophecy:

> All hail Volk, Übermensch und Lebensraum!
> Let not light see my black and dark desires
>
> Spasm of precursors. Invisible shivers.
> Lamentings heard I' the'air, strange screams of death ...
>
> And prophesying with accents terrible of dire combustion.

The tragedy of the Holocaust, it may be inferred throughout this collection, is both 'singular and one'; what tears a people asunder in one place – whether in Ireland North or South, Germany, Poland, France, or Spain – creates reverberations which destabilize interior and exterior fault lines, and are experienced by one and all. That is the rule of human presence in Europe, whether it is tragic or whether it is in some manner wholesome and constructive. O'Siadhail's commentaries bear some resemblance at times – in content, rather than technically – to the Norwegian poet Stein Mehren, the intensity of whose recall of that period is encountered face-on in 'Sirens in December',[12] where

> Life and death
> are bound as deep as beaten iron.

Later in this poem, he encounters

> ... the dark room of memories, he whose father

came from the wrong side of the war, was that why
we made him eat a live rat
I am sitting in the air-raid shelter
Of forgetting
face to face, with myself
like pictures there below the ice, in dark flowing water.

The fourteen sonnets in 'Figures' capture life in the camps from arrival to dispatch, drawing a series of powerful thumbprint poems, each characterized by its attention to the individual experience. Here we encounter dishevelled, exhausted children, freshly off the train, boarding-school girls still wearing hats with blue ribbons, desperate mothers forced away from their children, the quick scurry of the camp subordinates to clear away traces of the previous batch of victims, then on to disinfection, tattooing, middle-of-the-night roll-calls in the freezing air, the ongoing starvation, the ensemble concerts in summer where

A band conductor from a famous Vienna café
Parodies for all she's worth her life outside ...
Then The Blue Danube or even The Merry Widow
For a commandant who loves waltzes ...

Here, Europe's scape-goated are united – Jew, political protester, gypsy, homosexual, and thief. This, O'Siadhail seems to be saying, is where we end up when 'white' Europe rewrites the rules and the Macbeths and Hitlers are not counterbalanced. It is where we end up when we are passive, in our lives and in our poetry. The heroism of survivors and fallen alike is described here, as the German plot to undo the Jews pervades Europe, through Austria, Poland, to the Netherlands. Individual lives are remembered in a poetic listing as emotionally wrenching as a purely historical equivalent such as Martin Gilbert's 'The Holocaust'.[13] The difference here is that poetry may attain a separate and perhaps more enduring level of penetration to that contained in a work of documentary prose. Poetry such as this can imagine the after-effects of the camps as survivors attempt to re-establish the threads normality. But flashbacks occur:

The dentist's drill smells of burning bone,
In a car behind a bus the choking fumes,
A crane's gibbet dangles inmates to atone
Escapes, a cinema queue for shower rooms.

Throughout, O'Siadhail explores what he terms 'the delicate balance between the dark and light' as other voices, some of whom we know from their writings, also emerge: Primo Levi, Jean Améry, Paul Celan. Levi, as we know, chose to take his own life, having trusted beyond trust, being maimed beyond healing.

It is a tale of betrayals – throughout Europe, including divided France – told in poetry, touching on geographical schisms as well as the inter-human one. In 'Dust-veil' the reflection on the fall-out of the atrocities of the Holocaust is framed by a consideration of the subterranean ash still interred beneath the ice between Uist and Shetland. This may have produced climate change that altered the entire northern hemisphere, spreading as far east as China. O'Siadhail reaches back as far as three millennia ago, linking this event to the journeys, the wanderings, the exiles and longings for a home place that have marked so many ethnic groups from Egypt by the Nile:

> … . Babylon, Nineveh the same script
> Of exile and bondage and wilderness sojourns
> Crying towards Jerusalem. Caravan of returns.
> The battered wife of a God she can't forsake,
> Even an enemy's bruisings a lover's keepsake.

It is an interesting, not to say a daring theory, to suggest a link between a volcanic upheaval in the very distant past and the uneasy wanderings of the physically disenfranchised, the uprooted, to suggest that the idea of movement into alien territory may have its origins in the physical upheaval of the earth's crust ('*Fall-outs of tephra still blow beyond our grasp*').

As I suggested at the beginning of this essay, poets are still to this day frequently challenged on the question of making their subject-matter 'relevant', to present work which is socially meaningful and to which the society out of which they write may respond. Not that society does actually respond very much to what poets write, but given the benefit of the doubt, it is argued that poets should produce something the equivalent of representational art. This is, of course, to misunderstand and interfere with the whole poetic process. In no manner could the collection *The Gossamer Wall* be described as 'relevant' in the socially prescribed sense. Thankfully, it rises beyond the actual representation of the Holocaust to become an encounter in poetic terms with the course of European history and its relationship to the human heart. O'Siadhail's range of poetic tools as well as the erudition which informs them – in other words a knowledge of the world combined with the technical skill to use it – elevate this work to a very different plateau of achievement. There is nothing like it in the English language in terms of its daring and ambition.

*

As regards O'Siadhail the 'European', like so many labels, that too is one, but for the purposes of supporting a thesis on the range of his thought and work, it is perhaps a necessary one. But he does not stop at the idea of Europe. His most recent volume, *Globe*, continues the exploration of the geographies of idea and identity through a series of poems which interrogate the present – with all its knick-knacks and contemporary toys – and our sense of ourselves as a global people whose daily encounter with the shift of tone, use, and emphasis differs in one respect only from similar encounters faced by previous generations. The one difference is: speed. Instantaneity. In 'Mobile',

> Each node of belonging homed by satellite
> Travels the dark fibres of a breakfast update
>
> To touch digital nerves of daily memory.

Everything is copied, worldwide, and the mood and sensation of any other culture can be instantly conveyed, whether one is a cab-driver in Northern Germany listening to the revered Egyptian *chanteuse* Oum Kulthum, or whether phoning home to Ireland from the Great Wall of China (as this writer once did). The 'chosen garden' of childhood, secure in its hurtling sputnik (the ultimate progress of its day), has given way to an 'everywhere' that is also 'everyplace', as John Donne knew. The connections of the world are explored throughout *Globe*, in underground systems, in the concept of flight from the past and touching down in the 'lift-off of our past': for O'Siadhail, we hear the convention of notes, accepted sound (as in sound-bites?), and miss the point of the greater 'arch of sound', still-resonant ancient syntax where 'our ghosts still nod at us'. Intensely preoccupied with perspective, we are led, through this poetry, on a journey which insists that we as readers *look and examine* from a variety of angles. Distance is no object, be it middle, wide angle, or close-up as the poet hones in on the shifting world which, one senses, displaces him even within his renewed chosen garden of adulthood.

The adventure of exploration continues in *Globe* as he looks to past masters of discovery and interrogation, among them Johann Mendel, botanist, whose discoveries regarding the workings of genetic codes were brushed aside during his life in his own 'chosen garden'. Emmanuel Levinas the philosopher is acknowledged in 'Après Vous Monsieur!' and again we encounter a history of thought in European voices – Sartre, de Beauvoir, Derrida and even Heidegger. The theme of the Other in Levinas's philosophy is alluded to one final time in this poem:

> *Autrui*, the other's face that seeks
> me out, a presence already a trace
> of what's concealed but speaks:
> I am the one thou shalt not kill!
> Traveller, traveller, where have you been?
> Après vous Monsieur, Madame!
> An outsider turns his insistent face.
> Stranger, come in.

Patrick Kavanagh, Picasso, Kafka, Shakespeare, Jean Vanier, and Norwegian novelist Sigrid Undset, Mandela, Ghandhi and Máirtín O Caidhean are, it is inferred, part of the Knot-tying which is the title of this section. The knot is, as Chaucer is quoted, '*why every tale is toold*'. Something is there, among us, agitating heart and mind, a tight, woven knot of human agitation which requires some loosening in the chosen garden of experience.

Borders are crossed, choices made,

> No moss gathering, *Swaraj*, Ourselves Alone.
> Together to shuttle a planet's shrunken girth,
> Border-crosser, globe-trotter, rolling stone,
> All *grenzgänger* now we dwarf our earth.

This is the conundrum at the heart of O'Siadhail's work: that the world has shrunk in terms of time-space, but paradoxically our grasp of planetary matters has conceptually and in terms of informatics expanded in a manner hitherto unimaginable even half a generation ago. This is not to suggest an Old Fogey lurking within these poems, but rather that in an attempt to grapple with the 'cry for meaning', the poet has had to recalibrate his sense of the world, has even recalibrated the axis points of the European relationship with the rest of the planet. As the external world becomes more and more virtual, poetry is challenged in new ways that overturn the old romance of the idea of what it is to be a poet. At the same time these are the exact qualities which prove themselves most worthy for the voyage into the future. Thinkers, scientists, musicians, and poets are still necessary, even to the virtual ship, and even as we become virtual pilots of our own destiny on this rapidly shrinking planet, the off-chance, the unexplainable, the unexpected remains to bring us forth 'out of history's tangled knots and loops' ('Only End'). Jazz, as ever for O'Siadhail, belongs to the category of the off-chance:

> Growling, wailing, singing Madam
> In anguish and joys ...
> Somehow original and still reborn
> Swooping back to mend,
> Resolving just to clash again.
>
> On song and off-beam,
> Hanging loose, hanging tough,
> Offbeat, off the cuff,
> Made, broken and remade in love ... .

In the end, the most durable, the most meaningful themes must be understated. O'Siadhail's is not a poetry of brash display; it does not celebrate for the sake of exclaiming. What it all leads to, it is suggested, is that if history teaches us anything the resultant lesson is a simple one. He has learned what he has learned from the masters of his experience, whether these are music and that great off-beat mistress Madam Jazz, from the playfulness and trials of love, from the historically suffered (war; the Holocaust; the oppression of ideals and of knowledge) which still deploys extended nodes of pain into our experience of the present, from observing and partaking in the particular and not the general. This is the work of particularity. It is studied; it is a vast and shimmering reflection of the individual in the world and how this poet-individual has learned to proceed. Like the Norwegian novelist Sigret Undset, to whom a poem is dedicated in *Globe*, like Stein Mehren, like the philosopher Emmanuel Levinas, he is the son of a Europe in crisis and he is very conscious of it.

A final voice with whom O'Siadhail shares preoccupations – from the life of the public man to the role of the individual in the world, and on to an exploration of identity and the idea of 'home' as in 'Europe' – is the great Estonian poet Jaan Kaplinski. Kaplinski writes:

> I have gathered and brought home stones from everywhere. From Saaremaa. From Armenia. From Ireland. From British Columbia ... . In Armenia I even wrote a poem, the only poem in Russian I have ever written ... when I had to propose a toast, I proposed it to the Armenian rock. Rock becomes sand, sand becomes soil, and out of soil grow the food and wine that has made Armenians Armenian. A writer from Leninakan promised he would try to publish my poem in an Armenian translation. I don't know whether he did, I don't even know what became of him and the other people I met in that town, after the big earthquake hit Armenia and the city of Leninakan turned into aheap of rubble like my native city in an old lament written, after the Nordic war, in my native dialect.[14]

This is the studied voice of a poet in continuous crisis about the state of the place or places his life runs through. Because life itself runs through places, and names them for one reason or another. In that naming spring the essences of our greed. Naming means false 'ownership' and the work of Kaplinski and O'Siadhail, instead of being preoccupied with considerations of bogs, landscapes and other lost zones of the local interior, is insistent on looking beyond borders in the search for resolution.

O'Siadhail writes, 'The only end of jazz is jazz.' This may imply that the end awaiting us is already contained in the beginnings of our experience. The lessons of history are simply that. Lessons from which we learn little beyond the recognition – if we are fortunate – that whether it is 'white-burdened Europe' or the entire planet, the search for meaning will characterize our lives. Candide-like we move processionally to till new earth, either literally or metaphorically. We choose our garden and listen to our music, we love and hate, but the context in which process occurs is subject to change. That is the only constant. Change despite all, despite our ridiculous tendency to exclaim at it.

In the end, Micheal O'Siadhail stands as Irishman, Irish and European poet, open to the burdens of our white centuries, willing to test the argument of existence for its effects on the geographies of the human heart.

14 | Translating O'Siadhail

Audrey Pfeil

> But remember that words are signals ... . – Hugh, in Brian Friel's *Translations*

I have often felt that a sentence, when repeated, loses something of its original vigour. In the context of translation, particularly the translation of poetry, this feeling becomes a conviction. So when asked to translate a selection of Micheal O'Siadhail's poems into German, all my defences were up: it would be impossible to do justice to the original; the translation would be subjective, a new creation inferior to the writer's work. As Germans say: 'Lass die Finger davon! (Don't touch it!)' The snag was that the request came from a friend, the poet himself. I had attended his poetry workshop in Listowel some years previously. Then in 1996, Irish Literature was the central theme at the Frankfurt Book Fair and several Irish writers, including Micheal, were asked to take part. My husband Walter and I invited him to visit us at our home in the Black Forest prior to the Fair. We translated a few of his poems into German, thinking it might be helpful for his readings in Frankfurt. There would certainly be people in his audience with a limited command of English. Little did we realize what this would lead to! Like many undertakings in our lives, we stumbled into this one.

And so we silenced our misgivings, defying the frequently asserted half-truth that 'poetry cannot be translated'. With permission from Bloodaxe Books, I set about translating a number of poems from two of their publications, *A Fragile City* and *Hail, Madam Jazz!* As a Dubliner with a background in language studies and some experience in writing poetry, I was at home in the original language. As a teacher working in Germany and married to a German philologist, I was well versed in the target language. So all the building materials were at hand. The question was, what would remain when the scaffolding was pulled down? The venture became an adventure. Three years later, the book *Aus Heiterem Himmel (Out of the Blue)*, a bilingual presentation of a selection of Micheal's poems, was published in Germany.

In those three years I experienced the teasing challenge of searching for just the right word or phrase, wrestling with choices (often between equally good alternatives), and agonizing over sacrifices to be made for the sake of rhythm. My husband's contribution was invaluable. Since his profession absorbed him from Monday to Friday, he would spend the weekends listening to and assessing the work I had done during the week. We would read aloud to each other, first the original English and then my German translation, constantly making changes, each change bringing us closer to Micheal's text. We were clear about our priority: strict fidelity to content. This was more difficult than one would imagine. It is not easy and sometimes not possible to retain the content, form, images, and rhythm of a poem when using the target idiom. For instance, we first decided to use rhyme where it occurred in the original but this constraint often resulted in forfeiting meaning and sounded contrived. With the poet's approval, we abandoned the effort and found the translation flowed better and was more authentic. The loss incurred was the lesser of two evils. A real problem was that words tend to be longer in German. So, for example, *byways* becomes *Nebenstraßen*, with double the number of syllables. Moreover, English is often more concise. Finding the equivalent German expression that could be contained within the length of a line was challenging. Occasionally the words were quite in tune with the English and seemed to suggest themselves:

I bring my basketful to serve	Ich bringe meinen vollen Korb
Our table. Everything mine is yours.	An unsern Tisch. Alles Meinige ist Dein.
Everything. Without reserve.	Alles. Ohne Vorbehalt.

Yet even here we had to forfeit the verb 'to serve' which would have required three German words in the context. It was sometimes tantalizing having to abandon a particularly appropriate translation because the syllables, as emphasized in German, jarred rhythmically. At other times we were overjoyed to hit on just the perfect word spontaneously, as with *caress* in:

A caress on the face of the earth.	Liebkosung auf der Erde Angesicht.

Often a slight shift in emphasis was unavoidable, for example:

The cherishings and waterings of intimacy	Vertrautheit, getränkt und gehegt
For a feast or drought.	Für Dürre und Fest.

Here 'intimacy' takes precedence and 'cherishings and waterings' become adjectival, while the positions of 'drought' and 'feast' are exchanged, once again in the interest of rhythm and cadence. Our concern was to ensure that a shift in emphasis did not result in a shift in meaning. Occasionally we would get completely bogged down, too involved, and too close to the subject to see clearly, incapable of forming any judgment. We would start questioning everything: could it be that the first drafts of translation had in fact been better than the results of the endless, tortuous tamperings? When this stage was reached there was nothing for it but to take our rucksacks and go off hiking in the forest. This worked wonders – every time. We would acquire the necessary distance and find on our return that all was right with the world again. The task could be resumed. When caught between choices, I could always communicate with the poet by e-mail. Since he speaks German he could clearly state his preference. Without this support, we might have given up for fear of distortion.

I referred to the undertaking as an adventure and it was just that in terms of magic and discovery. When you spend several hours a day in the mind of a poet, your mood becomes affected. From this point of view Micheal's poems were an enormous enrichment. We were dealing with an intellectual in touch with his feelings, one who knows the 'still, sad music of humanity' but is sufficiently rooted to preserve his *joie de vivre*. I found myself wondering what it might be like to spend three years wallowing in the dustbin / sand-grave / jutesack world in which Beckett's characters suffer existence. I would probably have ended up hanging from Vladimir's tree! Something of Micheal's generosity of spirit rubbed off on us as we dwelt on his poems and for this we are grateful. The time and energy spent were more than rewarded by the stimulation we received, not to mention the aesthetic joy of the language itself, rich and multilayered. We revelled in the sensuousness of lines such as:

Silk I love: fall and flow and cocoon,	Seide liebe ich: fallend und fließend, Kokon,
the worm's sheen, desire clinging and loose.	Glanz des Wurms, Verlangen, schmiegsam
	und lose.

His evocative imagery – visual, auditory and tactile – never ceased to fascinate us, as in the verse where the poet is seen observing life from his table in a London café:

Outside the door, the buses shriek,	Draußen vor der Tür kreischen die Busse,
rush and judder; a city's jamboree,	Eile und Ruckeln; Rummel einer Stadt,
hope and haphazard, limitless	Hoffnung und Zufall, unbegrenzte
chances, choices wait. Sitting	Möglichkeiten, Entscheidungen warten.
here I know I've felt the throb	Ich sitze hier und weiß, daß ich gespürt
of Jerusalem or Rome or any city	das Pulsieren der Stadt Jerusalem und Rom
yet to come, where there's a café	und jeder künftigen Stadt, wo es ein Café gibt,
and we, citizens all, break bread.	und wir, Bürger alle, brechen Brot.

This poem, as all of Micheal's work, is the product of a philosophical mind. Constant exposure to language of this calibre was both a pleasure and a privilege. It generated energy, giving fresh motivation whenever it tended to lag.

Normally a text is translated by one person so that all the wrestling and juggling with words, the conflict, the doubt, take place in the one mind. But there were two of us, close enough to show exasperation. Our teamwork was not always harmonious. At times we were at loggerheads over conflicting responses to sense or sound, both digging in our heels, not conceding an inch. A matter of principle. A matter of perception, male and female. Or was it the difference in mentality, the German, the Irish? In Brian Friel's play *Translations*, the Englishman Lieutenant Yolland arrives in an Irish-speaking community and becomes aware of 'experience being of a totally different order'. Walter and I know what Yolland is talking about. At any rate, our translator troubles never reached the stage of marital crisis! We would solve our differences by taking our case to the 'Court of Appeal', i.e., to Micheal, who would pronounce the final judgment. This we could both accept. Then again, the fact that we worked in tandem – one a native speaker of German, the other of English – was a huge advantage. No matter how proficient one is in a foreign language, one can still miss a nuance, a code known only to the insider. This accounts for the mistakes one sometimes comes across in otherwise good translations. As Hugh says to Yolland: 'I will provide you with the available words and the available grammar. But will that help you to interpret between privacies?' Our antennae were sensitive to such signals, the trusted intimacies of a native language.

Finally the translations were finished. The timing was auspicious because just then we heard that ILE (Ireland Literature Exchange) was promoting the publication of Irish writers in translation. We wrote to their office in Dublin enclosing the manuscript and describing our project. To our delight, they agreed to support the project financially. We then set about the daunting task of finding a publisher. The breakthrough came with a tip from a German poet. He told us about Heiderhoff Verlag which specialized in introducing German readers to poets from other countries, publishing them bilingually. We sent off our manuscript and held our breath. Eventually the response came. Heiderhoff was impressed by Micheal's work and would be happy to publish. In our dealings with the publisher during the following months there were many setbacks and irritations. But we were sustained by the knowledge that each book published by Heiderhoff is extremely well produced, a delight to handle, a thing of beauty. In fact the owner, Frau Roswitha Heiderhoff, received a coveted German award for excellence in this area. Finding a title for the book was easy. Since the most important encounter in Micheal's life was that with his wife Bríd, we chose the sonnet dedicated to that first meeting: *Out of the Blue / Aus heiterem Himmel*. This poem also touches on some of the themes frequent in Micheal's poetry: trust and vulnerability in a love relationship; music (especially jazz) as a symbol of life with its fluctuating frontiers, improvisation, openness to surprise. The sonnet shows a man lost in childlike amazement before the wealth and wonder of life, a posture characteristic of the poet. For all of these reasons *Out of the Blue* seemed the obvious choice for the title.

The final stage in the adventure was the organization of readings in Germany. Venues were found in three of the Federal States, Baden-Württemberg, North Rhine-Westphalia, and Bavaria. Micheal came over and, as always, his readings were a celebration – of the word, of poetry, of life. Since it is difficult to absorb a poem in a foreign language on a first hearing, we decided that each poem would be read in German (by my husband or me) and then immediately in English (by Micheal). This worked very well and precluded any pseudo-intellectual games of pretence. Not all poets have a voice suited to public reading. Micheal has it *par excellence*. No one could read his poems as well as he does. His rich timbre, clear diction, and utterly sincere tone are the perfect vehicle for getting them across. In every reading he pays homage to poetry, giving great care to the preparation even down to planning details, such as the position of the rostrum or lighting. Judging by the atmosphere at the readings and later by the feedback, Micheal's audiences were moved and inspired. One listener, Frau Christina Saucke, a woman who for years has been involved in organizing readings for German writers, was profoundly impressed by his performance and commented: 'We can learn from the Irish how to give a poetry reading.' The perfect framework for the readings was provided by a cellist who opened and closed the evening with extracts from the Cello Suites of Johann Sebastian Bach, calling to mind Yehudi Menuhin's belief that 'Bach is the beginning and Bach is the end.' The last of the readings in Baden-Württemberg took place in the town of Rottweil so that Micheal quipped as we got into the car for the final journey home: 'Now I know what it's like to be a Rottweiler!'

For my husband and me, the experience had come full circle. It was by no means at an end. The poems are engraved on our minds forever. Often, during our many walks along forest trails, we find ourselves quoting lines. But what we gained most from our involvement was the gift of friendship – with Bríd and Micheal O'Siadhail. Just what that implies is best expressed by one of his poems:

Friendship
No wonder we're happy just to meet,
As the spirit moves us, on and off;
An easy rapport of nothing to prove
As we unwind, stretch in the light of
Each other's sun.

Freundschaft
Kein Wunder, dass ein Wiedersehn genügt,
dann und wann, wie der Geist uns führt,
ungezwungen, nichts beweisen müssen,
dieweil wir uns entspannen, ausstrecken,
Jeder in des andern Sonnenlicht.

Each other's sun.
Little wonder we're content to meet
reicht, Once in a while, just as it suits.
Such concurrence never frets or doubts;
We've shot our long wedge-shaped roots
To the water plane.

No wonder a fluid runs from root
To root, a conduit of eau de vie,
An underground, our liquid conspiracy
The cherishings and waterings of intimacy
For a feast or drought.

Jeder in des andern Sonnenlicht.
Kein Wunder, dass ein Wiedersehn uns
ab und zu, gerade wie es passt.
Einklang ohne Bange, ohne Zweifel.
Wir haben unsere Würzelkeile
tief ins Grundwasser getrieben.

Kein Wunder, dass Wasser von Wurzel
zu Wurzel fließt, Ader aus *eau de vie*,
unterirdischer, flüssiger Pakt,
Vertrautheit, getränkt und gehegt
Für Dürre und Fest.

Titles of poems from which lines are quoted, in the order in which they occur:

1) *Courtesy*
2) *Friendship*
3) *Hostel*
4) *How?*
5) *Lunchtime in a London Café*
6) *Friendship* (full text)

15 | Micheal O'Siadhail: A Poet of Feeling

Maurice Harmon

In the 'Introduction' to *Poems 1975-1995*, Micheal O'Siadhail writes, 'I suppose I have been attempting, at each stage of my fifty odd years, both to cope with my own temperament and to search for meaning against the backdrop of a world rearranging and repairing itself.' The backdrop, as he sees it, includes the 'excesses of Modernity' and two world wars. The idea that the poet in the twentieth century has to search for meaning is shared by many modern writers, as is the feeling that the world is in a state of instability – 'rearranging and repairing itself'.[1] Nor is it generally felt that the process has concluded in a more orderly world. The old systems of belief, in religion and politics, were undermined and have not been replaced. The massive wars of the century determined the feeling of disorder with the additional reason for anxiety in the knowledge that the violence and destruction were the products of human minds.

Thomas Kinsella has observed that the 'most sensitive individuals have been shaken loose from society into disorder ... Everywhere in modern writing the stress is on personal versions of the world ... The detailed exploration of private miseries is an expedition into the interior to find out what may guide us in the future.'[2] While similarly aware of the loss of certainties, Micheal O'Siadhail did not make the exploration into 'private miseries' the main focus of his search for order. He has a restless, flickering intelligence that considers the engagement between the individual and experience, both external and internal. When he, in turn, investigates the major example of moral evil in his time, he studies the Holocaust.

In the previous generation, thinking about novelists who emerged in the 1920s, Seán O'Faoláin remarked on the prevalence in their lives of estrangement and dislocation. With the disappearance from fiction of the conceptual Hero and his opposite, the Villain, there emerged the anti-Hero who had to discover personal codes of behaviour. The Hero had represented the socially approved norms. With his disappearance the individual was, in Kinsella's words, 'shaken loose from society' and forced to find his own values.[3]

Some writers, like W.B. Yeats, pursued systems of belief in the past, some, like Thomas Kinsella, sought order within the psyche. Many turned to mythology. O'Siadhail's attachment to Irish culture provided for a time a set of values that gave him a sense of belonging, and his first three collections of poems were written in Irish. Instead of finding order in an external system of beliefs, he finds it within the experience of love. Essentially, however, his heart is a lonely hunter ranging widely in European thought, finding comfort in love, and devoted to poetry. In the final analysis poetry has been his consistent passion.

The 1950s, he recalled, were a good time to be young and free. Childhood had been middle-class and settled. Being educated at Clongowes Wood College prolonged the feeling of security. In the 1960s, when he was a student at Trinity College, there was, he recalls in a mixture of amusement and regret, 'a huge surge of freedom as we broke the taboos and, socialists all, lived our Bohemian student life'.4 There was talk of existentialism, of Sartre and Camus, and the ideas of Marx, Nietzsche, and Freud were in the air. 'We were all angry young men and women and read those paperbacks about sociology and psychology, and we felt we knew what lay behind everything.'5

Bliss was it to be alive in the liberating 1960s when ideas inspired confidence and the world was at their feet, but young men leave university and discover the 'ordinariness' of existence. In the 1970s, 'Many glimpsed the abyss and peered over its edge.' O'Siadhail does not define the abyss, nor say if he descended into it, but he goes on to indicate a process of recovery in which the world 'seemed sweet and new'. It is a mark of the direction his life would take that he avoided the existential void and felt secure. There were 'tiny glimpses of infinity' and he 'gave into the world of wonder' which, although it has eluded him ever since, he has continued to seek. So, he concludes, 'a universe that might have been narrowed became now an endless jazz improvisation'.6 To live by improvisation carries its own emotional and technical challenges. He has been a devotee of Madam Jazz ever since.

When Micheal O'Siadhail began to publish poetry in the 1970s, the revival of Irish literature that had begun in the 1950s, much of it associated with the Dolmen Press, was well underway. The poets of that time – Richard Murphy, Thomas Kinsella, and John Montague – had published significant work with the result that the tradition of Irish poetry, which had gained definition and status in the work of W.B. Yeats and been reshaped in the next generation by Austin Clarke, Patrick Kavanagh, Louis MacNeice, and others, received fresh momentum. It was characteristic of this World War II generation of writers that they found models outside of Ireland as well as within. From the evidence of the epigraphs in his eleven collections, it is clear that O'Siadhail also avoided insularity and looked abroad.

A postmodernist, he is a traditionalist both in form and in subject matter. He uses well-established forms – couplet, triplet, quatrain, and sonnet. The issues that permeate his work, those of love, death, time, and mutability, are found throughout English literature, and elsewhere. Questions of nationalism, of Irish political and social issues, or of Catholicism do not preoccupy him. Born and raised in Dublin, he is not drawn to the land nor does he try to connect his work with a particular locality. Even Dublin is not a primary concern.

His first three collections, *The Leap Year* (1978), *Rungs of Time* (1980), and *Belonging* (1982), published in Irish, were then translated by himself into English. The first presents a persona who is content to celebrate the natural world. The second reflects the stresses and strains of life. The third contains poems of vigorous self-examination and includes the determined

> I'm coming to grips
> with a world. I hunger for life.7

In the fourth collection, *Springnight* (1983), O'Siadhail comes into his own. Although he still celebrates, he is aware of time's remorseless beat; although he delights in the rhythms of an African-American, he remembers the chains that once shackled his feet; although he keeps a sleepless vigil until the appearance of dawn, he notes the 'wonderful terror, terrifying wonder of waiting'. The jazz rhythms of the man 'In a New York Shoe-Shop' are significant.

> Unbargained for,
> a handsome inky coloured man catching
> the snappy syncopation, jazzes across the floor
>
> to proof-dance a pair of cream loafers.
> Beaming, he bobs and foot-taps; pleased
> with his purchase, he jives a short magnificat. (48)

The occasional lyrics of this collection are marked by a playful use of language. The poet delights in the possibilities of language and will share his pleasure. He has given his heart up to the play and at times the work is self-consciously artful. Madam Jazz sometimes leads him a merry dance in which technique exceeds substance.

The Image Wheel (1985) also has occasional poems – about Grafton Street, a London café, a juggler. 'For My Friends' has a disciplined mesh of words:

> Crossed, matted fibres long inwrought,
> Friendships prove the fabric of a common story,
> The web which takes the strain of every thought,
> Shares the fray or stain, joys in our glory.
> Interwoven, at last I dare to move without misgiving;
> I touch the invisible, love this gauze of living. (77)

'Autumn Report', however, is overdone. 'Absence' is personal. Left on his own, he cannot settle down; his mind

> hovers
> Uneasily ...

he wanders through the town conscious of lovers as they pass. Without her, he is lost:

> Without you, my love, too many thoughts unspoken,
> Words are babble, a sacred thread is broken. (81)

O'Siadhail is a poet of feeling and it may be that his best work, most humane and deeply-felt, deals with ordinary, quotidian experience – situations, relationships, thoughts, feelings – that accord with the experience of many people. At the centre is a man of feeling who responds prolifically to the immediate and objectively registers what it is like to be human.

That sense of the ordinary runs throughout The Chosen Garden (1990) which recreates his years as a boarder at Clongowes and his memories of what it was like to enter bohemia thereafter. In these poems he is content to record such matters as his adjustment to school, the preoccupations of its self-contained world, teachers, rugby, and a setback when he fell from favour. Being away creates an unbridgeable gap with home. He recognizes what has happened when his parents visit.

> I had left for good – son and émigré.
> Four months' days ticked off a calendar,
> at last I'd return a displaced guest
> uneasy with neighbours, missing school-friends,
> my eye proportioned to halls and arches
> and home diminished as a doll's house. (90)

One of O'Siadhail's deepest discoveries was Irish language and culture. 'Visionary', a poem in the first person, bears witness to the attractions of the Aran Islands. It is both a love song and an elegy, a falling in love with a place that is dwindling. It is the familiar theme, sounded years before in William Carleton's lament for what had been lost in the Clogher valley; it is a melody heard in Douglas Hyde's anthologies of a vanishing culture; in Seán O'Faoláin's awakening to the landscape of West Cork; in John Montague's reflections on shards of a lost culture; in Thomas Kinsella's anthologizing of Irish literature. O'Siadhail tries to understand the attraction.

> What was it then, what commanded such ardour?
> A scattering of lonely islands, a few gnarled
> seaboard townlands, underworld of a language frail
> as patches of snow hiding in the shadows of a garden.
>
> But the dwindling were so living. In this wonderland
> of might-have-been I fell for the rhythm, the undertone
> of my father's speech, built a golden dream.
> (As you dreamt that land was falling asunder). (109)

It may, he thinks, have been a romantic dream, a wish for a paradise on earth. Like the third son in the old story, he did not shun the *caillech*. 'Visionary' is one of his best poems, the feeling of love and loss intertwined.

Another aspect of O'Siadhail's emotional life appears in 'Dark', which deals with depression. It acknowledges both the positive – 'there was a will, there was a way' and the negative – 'there's a will but no way'; but he is not a man for half-measures. He fears 'the half measure of greyness'.

> I choose the dark (or does the dark
> choose me?) I want to fall,
> open a chasm black and deep. (110)

As he plunges defiantly 'into an anarchy of gloom', he hopes to find some light, 'creation' as well as 'chaos'.

> But dark is dark: saddle of nothing
> riding black hogs to the abyss.
> Travel velvet spaces of despair;
> terror, like a dredge, is scooping
> out a void for love's surrender. (110)

He prefers the black, the experience of 'nothing', 'despair', and 'terror', the definite rather than the indefinite, the challenge of the absolute.

The persistent theme of poems about family in *The Middle Voice* (1992) is attentiveness to his wife:

> Your lavish sunlight
> wakes and stretches these Van Winkle limbs ... (126)

He is one of the few Irish poets who write openly and frequently about love. John Montague is another. O'Siadhail's approach, while less sensual, has its own appreciation of physical objects, its ornamentation within the sonnet's strict form.

> Idle with pleasure, I let my misty gaze
> find its slow way through the subdued
> light to where the contour of a porcelain vase,
> busy in silent meditation, alludes to you.
> Along the dressing table a ceramic bazaar
> Of creams, moistures, lotions, ointments,
> an exotic row of shapely pots and jars
> stoppers the scents and vapours of a presence.
> Your spirit travels in such lovely earthenware,
> at ease in its clay, a vessel well turned,
> cajoling the mind down from a castle in the air
> back to the sweeter givenness of your world.
> Still, like a wooer on his first sightseeing,
> I relish the emblems, your haberdashery of being. (122)

The poem is emblematic; its extravagant language reminds us that O'Siadhail's models include Elizabethan and Jacobean poets.

He believes in the importance of trust in relationships. *A Fragile City* (1995) considers the desire of every human for caring; it is prefaced by a line about community from Epictetus, 'This world of ours is one city.' The subject, as he notes, is relevant to Northern Ireland where sectarianism has broken trust within the two communities of Catholics and Protestants, but it has a wider application. Ultimately, trust is a moral issue affecting public and private life.

Even the title of this collection draws attention to brittleness. As though to offset fragility, the poems are carefully structured and adhere to a strict metrical form. The first section, for example, is made up of sonnets, many of which record meetings and farewells. O'Siadhail has the capacity to measure, respect, and absorb the faces of others.

> Those eyes that welcomed
> Without reserve. Open-faced ... (166)

It is a gift of seeing and of trust that has found expression earlier, particularly in the attentiveness of love poems; it is a perception of hidden quality in which he respects the individual as in 'Quartet': 'A shining between faces, a listening inward and open' (168).

The compassion embraces all who suffer. The recurrent question in 'Outsider' is 'Where did last night's Christ lie down?' (180) That point of view enables the poet to appreciate relationships:

> Here are my roots. I feast on faces.
> Boundless laughter. A radiance of friends. ('Delight', 224)

These make up his 'fragile city'.

> This complicity
> Of faces, companions, breadbreakers.
> You and you and you. My fragile city. ('Courtesy', 226)

The passing of time has been one of his concerns from the beginning. In *Our Double Time* (1998), he reflects that our perception of time in the present may be affected by our memory of time in the past and that when these two awarenesses coalesce we have the experience of double time. He remembers despair – 'Endless and narrow caverns of satin dark'[8] – and the nightmare of love lost. He has been in an Intensive Care unit. Released, he perceives the world in 'Twofold' with freshened senses.

> Has a world ever been so carefree, so debonair,
> That morning you fetched me from Intensive Care?

Lavish with feeling, he is able to express delight in an uninhibited manner. 'Twofold' pursues its theme of relief and renewal, enjoying the intensity of pleasure. His awareness, he believes, calling attention to the poem's own form, 'vibrates like a twofold rhyme' and he wants to live 'in double time' (24).

In 'Dread', he is in his fiftieth year; he can imagine growing 'old and dour', but is reinvigorated by memories. 'All the more I live in double time'.

> More than anything I think I dread
> The set jawbone of grim resignation.
> Nothing to expect. Nothing to discover.
> The sullen greyness of the living dead.
>
> I go when I go. Let me go a lover. (27)

His spirit is affected by the immanence of decline, but he finds the strength to be positive. 'Yearning light shines through my broken being' ('Ageing', 41).

In another mood, in the poem 'Whatever Else', he asks to be told when his time has come and for forgiveness if he shrinks 'In dread, rage, refuse or despair'. This is the 'darkest leap of trust'; he may baulk at the brink. The poem articulates his fear.

> Remind me of images that in their shortfall gave
> Some inkling of what remains beyond me:
> How energies of a particle re-feature as a wave
>
> Or how our music of being, though made in time,
> Keeps on resolving beyond its silence,
> Architecture of flux, both transient and sublime.

Tell me while there's still the time to mend
Breaches or even ask for pardon.
Whatever else please for my sake don't pretend.

Just tell me gently. Then, love me to the end. (45)

The poem is focused on what lies beyond, in the final silence, where echoes may still sound, where something may be resolved. In danger of sentimentality, it takes the risk, admitting weakness, while asking in trust for honesty.

O'Siadhail is direct about death, imagining himself in the area of transition between life and death.

A good leaving. This moment I try to rehearse,
But will it come the way I've least expected?
Unfulfilled desires, dreams I needed to nurse
Left undone? Regrets? Energies misdirected?
For all the beauty of what's brittle and finite
I'm loathe to go. So heal what can be healed.
Beyond that, kindly don't spin out my fight.
However well-meant, I think I'd want to yield. ('Three Wishes', 47)

He is poised in double time, between attachment to life and a readiness to go through to the other side. He knows about the death experience of those who seem to have entered that bourne from which no traveller returns, yet do.

The concept of double time is a binding motif. Like Patrick Kavanagh, who celebrated a Franciscan openness to nature when he came out of hospital, O'Siadhail returns to his moment of release. In 'The Hospital', Kavanagh declared 'nothing whatever is by love debarred'[9] and proceeded to give examples. In 'Canal Bank Walk', he embraced the plenitude of the natural world.

O unworn world enrapture me, encapture me in a web
Of fabulous grass and eternal voices by a beech,
Feed the gaping need of my senses ... (224)

O'Siadhail focuses intensely on the subject. Despite the apparent aloneness and introspective pattern of his life, he continues to speak of love and connection and in the end is satisfied to have been a voice. Out of its complex considerations of death's happening, the title poem of the collection ends on a note of triumph.

From now every single moment our double time.
Not that I've grown blasé or no longer care,
More a deeper listening to music's densities.
No matter how or when, no matter where,
The feel of a line sung with consummate ease.
I love and am loved. All my tinyness rejoices
That I'll have been a voice among your voices. (126)

Many of the poets who preceded O'Siadhail wrote historical meditations. Richard Murphy wrote *The Battle of Aughrim* in which he used the battle to study the origins of his own family; Thomas Kinsella wrote 'Nightwalker' in which he reflected on events and conditions that had shaped him; and John Montague wrote *The Rough Field*, an investigation of political, social, and cultural issues that affected his family in Northern Ireland. Given his imaginative engagement with suffering and death, as well as his concern with trust, it may not be surprising that Micheal O'Siadhail should write *The Gossamer Wall. Poems in Witness to the Holocaust* (2002). It is a daunting task, the subject so overwhelming in scale that it is difficult to relate to it. There is, O'Siadhail declares,

> ... no Richter scale of tragedy.
> How to measure suffering?

'Behind each agony a name, a voice, a face'.[10] 'The black sun shines'. It is, he says, a 'Quantum leap in some darker mystery of evil' ('Entrance', 25). It requires considerable preparatory reading to make him sufficiently familiar with the subject and to be able to respond with the appropriate feeling. Indeed, Part I, 'Landscapes', deals with the problem of scale, both of event and emotion, reacting to the immensity of the eruption of hatred and violence. Metaphors are drawn from natural cataclysm. Historical contexts provide a measurable background and remind us that the violence had historical roots. O'Siadhail's purpose is to ensure that we will not forget the appalling disruptions that marked the mid-twentieth century. It is difficult in the face of such vast suffering to tone down the language, to reduce the litany of woe.

> It's best another generation remembers
> Never to forget it could happen now.
> No, not so much to rake the embers
>
> But to recall how something not faced
> Goes underground and then reappears
> To haunt us. ('Numbers', 12)

The will works the imagination hard.

> Factories, trains and railroads now gearing up,
> Machinery of oiled governance in a modern state;
> Grindings and cogs of greasy calculation
>
> And the one strain singled out for elimination.
> This breed apart. A whole apparatus of hate
> Bent on wiping a people from Europe's face. ('Signatures', 22)

In places a staccato rhetoric jabs the catalogue of pain into place. The voice is relentless, the evidence grows.

There is an Old Testament quality to O'Siadhail's voice and manner as he responds to calamity, points backward to earlier events that presage what was to come, and drives home the message that the Holocaust must never be forgotten. He bears witness to horror for a moral purpose and brings his intelligence, will, imagination, and poetic skills to bear upon the subject: 'Beware, beware a beast that slumbers' (12), echoing the Yeatsian image of the great beast slouching towards Bethlehem to symbolize the barbarism that came to birth in the twentieth century.

In Part II, 'Descent', O'Siadhail focuses on the small and sinister ways in which the town of Northeim succumbed to the forces of Nazism, then goes on to outline the descent of one battalion into evil. It is the humane element in all of this that keeps the poem from bombast. O'Siadhail constantly provides the little human details, the individual instances of suffering or of evil deeds. In Part III, 'Figures', he returns to the problem for the poet. The opening poem, 'Summons', sounds a warning in italicized phrases: *'Meditate that this came about'*. *'Try to see!'* and *'...try to look, to try to see'*, because 'A muted dead demand their debt of memory' (63). The poem spreads before us like an extensive tapestry. We move along its portrayals, its common thread of suffering, its colour-tone of compassion, its details of routine, the Germanic efficiency, and the madness of punishment. It is a moving attempt at remembrance, bleakly and sometimes bluntly described.

> They untangle, lug, stack and kindle the dead.
> Chosen on the platform for brawn, broken in
> Hell for leather, men clubbed and goaded
> As still among the bodies they recognise kin.
> Shirkers are shot. Others harden to endure
> As stokers of hell, well-fed privileged caste
> High on their pickings. A three-month tour
> Of duty before they in turn are gassed. ('Ravens', 72)

The poet is the voice of conscience, the informed witness who animates horror and pity so that we may not forget. Some dance in the face of death, others confide in diaries. They leave a spoor. Gradually, in alleviation, the poem affirms that life goes on. 'Dissonant cries of silence refuse to quiesce' ('Waking', 118). Those who have gone behind the gossamer wall will not be quiet. It has been argued, as O'Siadhail knows, that after Auschwitz any poem is 'obscene'. He accepts that risk and transcends it. He salutes the inevitability of new growth. 'A black sun only shines out of a vacuum' ('Never', 120). The poem is 'a narrative struggling to understand' ('Soon', 123). It is almost a relief when, in his next collection, he returns from this descent into the darkness.

In *Love Life* (2005), O'Siadhail invokes the sensuous *Song of Solomon* as he examines his love for his wife Bríd.

> My skin wants to glow,
> All of my being glistens.
> Divine shining through.
> *Your lips like a crimson thread,*
> *Your mouth is lovely ...*
> *You're all beautiful, my love.*
> Honeyed obsession
> Of unreasonable love.
> Pleased, being pleased,
> I caress this amplitude,
> Eternal roundness.
> Voluptuous golden ring.
> Sap and juices sing
> Eden's long song in the veins.

> Spirit into flesh.
> The flesh into the spirit.[11]

It is rhapsodic, and poems that follow immediately continue in this vein.

> Milk and honey spice and wine
> I'm your lover. You are mine. ('For Real', 14)

'Shulammite, Laura, Beatrice, Bríd' ('Candle', 15). The poems throb with these outpourings, the style overcharged and playful.

> Coy, bold, knowing, insolent, outré
> Madam, goddess, nymph, vamp, flirt;
> Play each woman you know how to play. ('Play', 32)

In the second section the temperature is lowered as O'Siadhail, in quieter mode, describes domestic life, the ordinary conditions in which love has to survive. For better or worse, they 'intersperse' their 'strands'. The metaphor of sailing helps to bring coherence to the poems. In 'Plunge', the language of ships and seafaring is employed to convey the idea of their journey through life – 'Our ark of covenant still steered by variation' (38) – and in 'Reckoning' their

> plotted course
> That didn't count sudden squalls or detour. (39)

O'Siadhail is at ease with these terms, allows the language to convey what he wants to say, without drawing attention to the connection. Indirectly we realize what is implied and this contrasts with the more over-the-top style of the first section. He also develops the metaphor of the house in which they settle. The tendency to celebrate and to be ecstatic sits uneasily with the accents of ordinary living.

> House-proud excitement of hosts
> Blue napkins folded
> And tall glasses anxious.
> To bring extra chairs,
> To fix our table placings,
> We check kitchen timings,
> Guessing the first to arrive. ('Guests', 46)

Although the poems are directed towards the beloved, the poet himself, his squalls of desire and anxiety, are also expressed. Some poems are directed inward, confessing his dependence on her, his delight and admiration, but also the force that sends him in pursuit of other interests.

> As the restless boat of my nature changed tack
> Shifted so suddenly onto a different course,
>
> Me almost overboard, you dragging me back. ('IOU', 68)

She is his 'mistress mariner' (68), keeping him on a steady course. He has had to learn the 'double vision' – to see her and her roles as well as himself and his interests. 'And, yes, yes', he acknowledges in 'No-man's-land', 'things will fade, things will change'. He has learned 'To love what is and not what might have been' (80), to know restraint, acceptance, and recognition of the 'Slow repetition of sober days' ('Ceremony', 81). There is a tension between his natural exuberance and the need to batten down and live the life that has been given. He finds it hard to give in. He is the restless voyager, the adventurer in search of new horizons. The chameleon complexity that he identifies in her is to some degree his own. At the same time he is tenderly responsive because of her being the victim of Parkinson's disease. She suffers 'The brain's vagaries'. This is another 'shift' in love's 'long process' ('Parkinson's', 87). So he attends her. 'Any breeze shivers' in her limbs. In this crisis he is steadfast. 'A face is beautiful once a face is loved' (88). He ends as he began with echoes from the sublime *Song of Solomon*: '*My sister, my bride ... I come to your garden*' (116).

O'Siadhail arrives at a particular time in the history of Irish poetry, after the emergence of a distinctive generation in Murphy, Kinsella, and Montague, and before the emergence of poets like Seamus Heaney, Derek Mahon, and Paul Muldoon, whose confident handling of material and technical skill helped to establish the continuity and independence of Irish poetry in the second half of the twentieth century. By then the tradition was defined. They were not overshadowed by W.B. Yeats as the Austin Clarke-Louis MacNeice generation had been. When they looked about for models and wanted to feel connected with tradition, there was a line of poets going back through the century. The habit of responding to literary developments and events outside of Ireland was well established. O'Siadhail shares their confidence and self-reliance, but his work is detached from the main stream of Irish poetry. While in many respects he resembles Austin Clarke – for his response to particular incidents, for his linguistic energy – he does not deal with the issue of the Catholic conscience, social injustice, or the panoply of myth, legend, history, and topography that marked Clarke's career. Even in relation to Patrick Kavanagh he is different, since he is not preoccupied with rural life. While he is still developing as a poet, his career shows him to be mainly independent of other poets. A traditionalist in the use of language, in form and subject matter, he has pursued his own interests and preoccupations. Giving up two careers in order to devote himself to the writing of poetry, Micheal O'Siadhail now has a large oeuvre and, at this stage, it may be suggested that a *Selected Poems* would give us a sharper understanding of his poetry.

16 | *Globe*

Daniel W. Hardy

Introduction

Nauset Beach, Cape Cod, Massachusetts, near the site of the first Transatlantic telegraphic cable: daily reports of new conflict between Israel and the Hezbollah movement said to be supported by Syria and Iran, with many hundreds of rocket and air attacks on Lebanon and Israel, of more and more dead and wounded in Iraq, and of another tsunami in Java, but none of this very visible here; the seas and tides of life are much as they were. Streams of people arrive in Japanese- or German-made sports utility vehicles for a day out at the beach. Never for long out of contact by cell-phone (mobile), they are more and more poly-ethnic but few are black. They live *in their worlds*, concerned only about what is immediate to them: family and friends, surf, water temperature, sun, sandcastles and summer novels, and how to develop a tan. In the sunshine, play and laughter, relationships are easy, no danger and no anger or enmity; at most, tempers flare when something does not work, like a recalcitrant folding chair. Although all the variables – cosmos, earth, biology, humanity, history, geography, commerce, and demography – are hidden in the complex reality of their *worlds*, the beach-sitters are neither aware of how all these factors converge as they do, nor of *a globe* at all. Formative factors and future possibilities are invisible or forgotten, too complex, interwoven, and contingent to bear thinking about.

In a top-floor room in a Dublin town, a poet-seer takes a wider and deeper view: he sees and expresses the fluid connections within and between these 'worlds', and their significance, as others do not. On the evidence of this book, his primary concern is with the *context* in which we now live: this is not unlike the mathematician's questions, 'what is the space in which we live?' and 'what is the shape of this space?' Unlike a mathematician, however, he seeks to identify the main factors formative for life in the world today. In other words, how does the *globe* as it is now affect the *worlds* in which different peoples live their lives?

In the four sections of *Globe*, he looks, first at factors involved in the multi-faceted re-texturing of worlds through time; then at some who have stood astride history and shaped it; after that at the wounded memories of Africa, Europe, Palestine, the United States South, Japan, and Ireland; and finally at the complex 'blur' of ever-increasing change in which the possibilities of renewal must – and can – be found. What is most remarkable in his poems, perhaps, is not only their realism but also their wrestling with the meaning of the situation in which we live. They show a sure grasp of the deeper aspects and movements of particular things and contexts – as distinct from speaking of them in fixed, general, and departicularizing terms – and an ordering of their connections at different levels. Of course there is some selectivity at work; he concentrates on the human face and possibilities of today's 'globe'. Nonetheless, it is both because of his 'earthing' ('grounding' Americans would call it) in particular realities and because of the range of his awareness that the poet can see how they are internally related in manifold ways, and the implications for the world itself and those within it.

Akin to this is an extraordinary quarrying of language – in all its variety and use – as itself a key to other realities. Shifting as it is –

> slidings,
> Differences of use and tone,
> Subtle plays of emphasis ...
>
> As one strong verb shifts
> Type
> To settle down in another groove
>
> Which bit by bit starts a pattern
> That just may or may not take ('Shift')

– language shows the same characteristics as reality itself, and partners the grasping of moving connections. Words here are much more than standardized labels – like 'stable', 'complex', and 'changing' – for features of reality: they reveal the dense and changing connections which make the extensity of life in the world what it is, and carry the consolations and anxieties people now feel. As we will see, O'Siadhail's wordings are so carefully wrought that it is nearly impossible to restate his poems without reverting to his language.

A major issue in this book is O'Siadhail's continuous wrestling with history. How does it need to be seen? With delicate awareness of a long-standing debate in historical interpretation, he identifies the perspective needed for his task. This is the 'Middle Distance' which allows the observer

> neither a loom too close to view,
> Or a shape so vague as not to matter ... ('Perspective')

one avoiding the reductionism of detached overviews by which we avoid the more confusing 'encounters in our daily mess' while also avoiding the permissiveness of over-detailed 'labyrinths of remembrance'. What is especially remarkable about this is that O'Siadhail, in holding a balance between generalization and particularity, also *temporalizes* the question, so that the 'middle distance' is the 'middle of a cosmic dance' in which are averaged the fullest range 'from the Big Bang's scatter' to

> the swing
> Of atoms [of] a femto[1]-world. ('Perspective')

The exclusively spatial notion of perspective normal to the 'middle distance' is transformed into a *spatio-temporal one*, and historical interpretation is itself temporalized. And one of the major suggestions he makes is that the globe is, as I would say, a 'turbulent spatio-temporality'. It resembles the view found in T.S. Eliot's *Four Quartets*, in 'Burnt Norton'.

Such finely-tuned ways of tracing the *globe* in the *world*, the more widely formative factors in the immediate and particular and their relations, probe the very things that lie invisibly within the lives of those on that beach, for whom – though often hidden from them – the dimensions of global life cross in mutual implication. Micheal O'Siadhail keeps pressing to find the meaning to be discovered there and expressed in poetry: here there is nothing discrete, simple, or final except complex movement where words are as shifting and permeable as what they express. This is nothing less than a re-description of emergent awareness of the *globe* in widely varying *worlds*, in different voices. (One of the most intriguing questions is what voice is being used.) At the least, it is indicative, but at key points this conceals interrogative, subjunctive, and occasionally optative moods. It is remarkable, thought-provoking in the deepest ways, and ultimately unforgettable, leaving us with the prospect of having (if the speeding of time permits!)

> All time to understand
> Infinite blues of *what ifs*,
> Breaks and tragic riffs
> As traditions wander into other spaces
> Zigzagging and boundary crossing
> In clustered face-to-faces
> Commonplace and grand,
> Sweet nuisances of our being
>
> On song and off-beam,
> Hanging loose, hanging tough,
> Offbeat, off the cuff,
> Made, broken and remade in love,
> Lived-in boneshaking pizzazz
> Of interwoven polyphony above
> An understated theme.
> The only end of jazz is jazz. ('Only End')

Seeing Farther by Seeing Better: Wider Contact by Speaking More Profoundly

In touching on some of the remarkable intentions and characteristics of these poems, however, we are already too close to an over-generalized account of Micheal O'Siadhail's book, one which is not altogether compatible with what it is. And we should not linger too long in such an account. Before turning more directly to the poems themselves, however, there are a few other things which repay attention.

How can Micheal O'Siadhail see and express so much more than the Nauset beach-sitters? What leads him to see so much of the *globe* in their *worlds*, where they – whose worldly horizons seem at first less limited – do not? The capacity to see more comes from discovering and 'wording' the denser spatio-temporal configurations which appear unrecognized in different 'worlds' – their spatio-temporal 'intensities' as I call them – as if to say 'see *better* and you will see *farther*', or 'speak more profoundly and you will "jazz" with more people'. It is not that these goals can be achieved simply and finally, by ascertaining an invariant order of things and stating it clearly and finally, as philosophers have often tried to do. His 'seeing better' sees more deeply into the particularities comprising the world's extensity, precisely by probing them to uncover the ways in which they are densely and dynamically related within and beyond themselves, for they and their relations concentrate the ways the *globe* is in the *world*. His 'communicating better' *words* new patterns, in due course to be superseded by others, 'making way for something new'. And both are the means by which

> we ... accumulate a past ...
> A sense of what's steadfast
> And still
> ... feel the sway and pull of growth. ('Shift')

What is found always allows other new configurations, which can also yield farther sight. The particular configurations and patterns he finds help sensitize him – and us – to others, so that we see things to which we were formerly blind.

To what end Micheal O'Siadhail pursues these pathways is a most interesting question: do the configurations found here, each leading to others, open the way to 'purer' conceptions, and the farthest sight? The achievement of *Globe* is closely related to this important question. As a whole, does the book provide *clusters*, or a *series*, of importantly connected insights, or *more*? That question remains with us throughout the book, from first poem to last, from the 'swing' of newness as 'a gene [is juggled] from within a phrase' (*'Given'*), to the

> Infinite blues of *what ifs*,
> Breaks and tragic riffs ...
>
> Made, broken and remade in love,
> Lived in boneshaking pizzazz ... [where]
> The only end of jazz is jazz. ('Only End')

Perhaps the implication is that the true lesson to be learned about human life is that chancing 'non-stop becoming, to flourish in transit' is less 'chancy' and 'dream-driven' than 'an understated theme', the great possibility of achieving harmony in complexity through love. If so, the book proves to have its own trajectory, the movement from sheer newness to fulfilment: an extraordinary lesson!

From what standpoint does O'Siadhail proceed to 'see better' and help us to do so? The poems which comprise this book are the evidence and expression of one who *engages* – Fermi-like – with the globe from within, whether within the 'worlds' of other people are more directly himself, not from Olympian heights (or dismissively) but very closely, sensitively and intelligently – unafraid of the puzzles embedded in them, both in their multiple aspects and in their impact on other realities. These are the poems of one searching from within worlds in which people live for whatever 'globe' is hidden there. All, I find, stimulate extraordinary insights in one patient enough to wrestle with them, where even the choices of word, phrase, or versification may provoke new awareness. As we have seen, our position is not to arrive in the end at *final understanding* of the 'globe', but to contemplate the history of possibilities and disappointments,

> Infinite blues of *what ifs*,
> Breaks and tragic riffs ...

and – while 'Hanging loose, hanging tough' – to be 'Made, broken and remade in love'. The 'answer' is not so much understanding as self-transcending moral activity, the 'understated theme' of love.

What kind of pathway is followed? The purpose of the book is not trivial, but to help us engage with the *globe* in our *worlds*. Much of what makes this book so distinctive are the manifold ways of contemporary life in which Micheal O'Siadhail traces the generativity, patterns, dangers, possibilities, and sociality which mark human 'worlds'. Instances of these ways are so expressed as to uncover the features of the 'globe' which now can be seen by those with the eyes to see. For example, the 'givens' he finds in their 'worlds' are kinds of stability within and from which people find security, but they are not fixed and free of chaos, and are better seen as 'footprints' in the new, transitory, complex, preparatory, and fragile, where

> Sometimes ground vanishes under our feet
> As tidal waves of change sweep in so fast
> Over sand too shifting now for any retreat.
>
> But neither fogys nor spirit-rappers of a past,
> All thumbs, slowly we text our mobile tidings
> Copping on to Gr8 & c u @ 3.
>
> The only rule of thumb to learn new things
> As our middle voice tips towards passivity
> Allowing another generation show us how
>
> To program memories and delete what's old
> Or out-of-date as making way we bow
> With grace to let another crowd take hold. ('Footprint')

It is the same with the 'ends' he later finds. Jazz, therefore, is the metaphor most suitable to the realities he finds as givens and at the end: 'the only end of jazz is jazz'.

The way toward 'better' conceptions and expressions of the globe is just that, *a way*. Some years ago, a philosopher suggested that the ideal of true simplicity, the final goal of philosophy, is reached when there is minimal need for 'extra information',[2] in other words when one need no longer invoke relatedness to other things. Micheal O'Siadhail's vision is not so much this kind of simplicity, however, but more and more refined *configurations of relationships* in the world. The configurations most true to the globe will not be 'pure' intensities where relations are minimized, but those in which there is a 'humbler in-betweenness of non-stop becoming' in which relations of love are 'made, broken and remade'.

The special value of the book lies in the poems themselves, however, not in such general conclusions, and to those we now turn. The architecture of the book – and the sequence of the sections and poems – is important for the statement it makes. We must therefore attempt both to narrate its sequence, and – because O'Siadhail's argument is so closely bound up with the ways in which he expresses himself – present the poems themselves. Sadly, limitations of space make selection necessary: all of the poems deserve closer analysis than we can give them.

Shadow-Marks: Traces of Elementals

In beginning to read this book, it is well to remember that human beings have not always been aware of 'a globe' as the context in which they live. The world was understood and described otherwise, in terms of its being or fixed points of its history, especially as created, redeemed, and perfected in the eternal purposes of its divine Author. Nowadays, however, even if there is some memory of what it was to have firm bearings, there is much more disillusionment with them:

> In all our moods and changes some groundplot,
> Some sense of what was to give us bearings,
> A recorder tuning in to where we were;
> Even in such doubting days when we're aware
> How grand flight plans so often clip the wings
> Of underlings to justify the have and have-not.
>
> Cold comfort in the cosy no-man's-land
> Of huffing theorists busy trying to climb
> Out of history, seeing everywhere deceits,
> The half-aware cheatings of previous elites
> Or reaching back to chide another time
> Where long ago is a city built on sand
>
> Of disillusion at ideas so fallen from grace
> Once they knew explained the line and sweep
> Of certain progress, stage by stage ascent
> Of man and so their fingers burnt they're bent
> On undermining everything, determined to keep
> Cutting off our nose to spite our face. ('Touch-down')

Memory itself needs to be renewed by recontextualizing it, by reference to what (or who) has been forgotten or marginalized. Now the marginal and marginal figures – smothered voices, the forgotten dissenters, and the waifs and nomads – are invited back, and complexly resonating elements of the past help us forward.

> Still in curves and echoes of polyphony gone
> Before us, a tune that's both old and fresh
> Among the ties and leaps of complex histories
> Allows the resonance and unforeseen of stories'
> Shifts and vamped progressions that seem to mesh
> Plots wound deep in us and winding on
>
> Into the blue of other flights and offbeat
> Loop the loops to retrieve out of the lurch
> Of fashion things we thought we'd outgrown,

> Out of date jingles on a mobile telephone
> Where we just scroll quickly down to search
> Our main menu's options and thumb *delete*. ('Touch-down')

And *Globe* itself is a sustained meditation on the implications of what has been overlooked, and needed alterations in the understanding of the context within which we now live. These appear when we are aware that our world is wider and more dynamic – 'a globe' – and is defined, not only by the primacy accorded to spatio-temporal conceptions, but also by the factors which shape modern life. Only now, it seems, are we ready to see more fully what these imply. And in order to do that, we need to be prepared to view our context not with the tools only of one discipline or another, but by seeing it through all of them together. Doing that is both the task and achievement of *Globe* and its author.

Micheal O'Siadhail begins with elemental issues expressed in primary terms. The elemental issues are those which – in conventional theology – would be seen as those of creation, but here they are reconstrued by the use of a combination of musical, biological, cosmological, and historical notions. The genesis of things, he says, is in a *gene juggled from within a phrase* from which the 'swing' *of newness* takes wing ('*Given*'). In a number of ways, this is more important than it appears: (1) it implies that newness arises not by the generation of individuals alone, with their relations as subsequent, but the other way around, where relations precede and a particular 'bit' is 'thrown up' ('juggled'). And (2) newness can come surprisingly–

> the planet our earth in space,
> A single offbeat in all that jazz of spheres ...

– and late and small -

> Our human being one second in three years;
> As an atom to the planet. ('Given')

By the nervy choice of the juggler 'to chance it', and even to love the tentativeness and dependence ('a humbler in-betweenness') involved in juggler-like actions of 'non-stop becoming', it is possible to 'flourish in transit', each ball becoming fully itself as it rises from the hand of the juggler into the air and then falls. This is an astonishing affirmation of the generation of the new from a prior relationship, and its contingency on the trajectory of relationships in which it figures, the maps and webs and clusters of movers, always preparing modes of change. *That* is where flourishing occurs.

For us, it is this 'one precious second' of human being, and the dream-driven fragilities of our lineage and shifting landscapes, that constitutes our givenness. All this can be put in more ordinary terms – the brief spatio-temporality and fragile purposiveness of all that we have and do – but through the use of a mixture of musical, biological, cosmological, dynamically temporal, historical, geographical, moral, and conditional terms, we see far more deeply into the interconnections of our existence.

Moving then to the cultural, O'Siadhail surveys the 'slippage' of language and meaning, by which shifts may start a new pattern, only to break and give way to something new. That, it appears, is how a past builds up,

> So we slowly accumulate a past
> In stirring of grammar's overspill
> Which seems to allow us both
> A sense of what's steadfast
> And still
> To feel the sway and pull of growth
>
> Unless some sudden unforeseen
> Upheaval or leap brings so swift
> A change our whole context
> Alters, a switch of scene,
> A rift
> Between one era and the next. ('Shift')

So what philosophers call 'paradigm shifts' occur, bringing wholly different contexts, each displacing the previous to such a degree that we are immersed in new spatio-temporal frames of reference: 'Globe unmapped, globe we make.' And a new juggler's ball is thrown into the air that recontextualizes all the rest.

One of the marks of modern life is the collapse of distance through what is too easily called the 'communication revolution'. Where 200 years ago, moving away meant heartache and no return – so vividly seen in narratives and paintings of 'Emigrants' – the coming of mobile telephones ('cell phones') has brought moment-by-moment co-presence

> Across all busy skies the prodded phone.
> *Nihau!* thumbs a sojourner in China Town.
>
> Each node of belonging homed by satellite
> Travels the dark fibres of a breakfast update.

But this familiar practice also brings significant changes in our spatio-temporality and the sharing of our histories.

> Lenses of time and space now telescope
> And the long reels of a plot are speeding up
>
> As lineaments of so many histories cross
> A blurred zigzag between a 'them' and 'us'.
>
> Our line of country shifts and reconfigures.
> We are the world. The face of the earth is ours. ('Mobile')

By now our identity has shifted from nation- to world-dweller, even taking possession of the world.

One of Micheal O'Siadhail's earliest books was *The Chosen Garden*. From the point of view of the few poems we have looked at, however, that seems 'a time when our lives stayed still', before the first satellite initiated a new form of the old game – which originated as a way of fending off the plague – 'ring a ring a rosie'.

Was it make believe of childhood
That made the garden chosen seem
A time when our lives stayed still

Before the half-remembered thrill
At how a Russian sputnik hurtled
Ring a ring a rosie around an earth. ('Sputnik')

I first recall seeing the sputnik hurtling through the night sky while I was standing with some friends in their garden in the late 1950s. And *we did not* know either that this was a new 'girth' – a demonstration of the objectivity of the 'we' – for a divided planet *or* that it signalled the ending of divisions ('walls fall down') and the need to tend not only 'this fragile raft in space' but also every person in every place, whole or hungry.

The 'raft in space' has proved more fragile than any of us – especially in a West convinced that all natural events are law-like and can be controlled by human beings – could have anticipated. The enormity of the disaster produced by the cracking of the floor of the Indian Ocean is described by dwelling on the graphics of Japanese characters:

Tsu: water and a brush in hand
To sign a sweep of sea, a stretch
Of deep for safe crossing, a haven.

Nami: liquid and a flaying hand
To symbolise a wave, as if to sketch
An ocean peeling off its skin.

Together a billowing towards land,
A tidal wave gathering its fetch
To deliver a long roll of misfortune.

The frightful image, reminiscent of the worst pre-modern punishment by which people were executed by being flayed alive, of a wave as a *flaying hand peeling off the skin of the ocean* destroying the safety of harbours, leaves the sea itself safer.

Safer at sea:
In shallows the swells heighten,
Irony
Of a harbour now danger's haven.

But the cosmic implications are greater and more enduring; the cosmos itself sweeps like the sea, tossing human beings as 'humble riders' on a 'trembling globe', crying out – to whom?

Earthlings our toss
And turn frail in the sweep
Of a cosmos,
Humble riders on a moody spaceship,

A trembling globe.
Some hundred and eighty thousand.

Like Job
We cry out what is our end? ('Tsunami')

It is important to remember this cry, because the last poem of the book responds to it.

The section ends with a poem ('Traces') facing the ultimate post-modern question: in 'an ocean only ever the sum of its drops', 'all that we can' may never survive the 'chops and changes'. And yet, history conspires – through 'strands given [and] lines we splice or tie', 'some looping in the least expected strand' – to allow people to tie knots even when the world is not ready to understand.

> The lucky may even get their timing right,
> Knotting a moment's perfect knot and yet
> Others, years ignored, may walk the light
> Long enough to see their mend in the net.

And history comes through small things.

> For most nothing momentous or too high-flown,
> Just some trace laid down, our mark made
> In the give and take of lives, a loan of a loan
> Passed on as mention of our names will fade.
> It's mainly fallen angels with our clayed feet
> And yet moments in stories no one has told,
> Split seconds of our double time, a pleat
> In a cloth of histories that takes so long to unfold.
> A promise kept, something done for someone
> As rumours of decency gone to ground for years
> Re-emerge, the way suddenly in a niece's son
> A gene that ducked and weaved then reappears;
> Gestures of love on streets of a fragile city,
> Memory inscribed in action, a scratch on eternity. ('Traces')

It is by such traces passed on, 'split seconds of our double time', that 'genes'– like those genes juggled from within a phrase to give wing to newness mentioned earlier – reappear as

> Gestures of love on streets of a fragile city,
> Memory inscribed in action, a scratch on eternity.

That is the way history is both made and renewed.

Knot-Tying: Heroes, Heroines and Doers

The dynamics of history with which O'Siadhail was so often concerned in his earlier books reaches a new stage of refinement in *Globe*. As we have already seen, both history and historical interpretation are now temporalized. They are also exemplified as such in a number of people whom O'Siadhail regards as key figures, 'pleats' 'in a cloth of histories that takes so long to unfold'. Although the choice seems arbitrary at first, those chosen are similar by virtue of their perspective and their passionate involvement in what concerns them, the two together combining in the *integrity* visible in them.[3] It seems to me that it is their integrity – both historically informed and also involved in the shaping of life – that O'Siadhail admires, possibly because they are prototypical for his own historical reason and moral passion. Some of the characteristics are these: 'watch[ing] so far ahead', 'burn-out and burning through', pondering and reminding us of 'our broken fellowship and slipping civilisation' ('The Burning Bush').

In that sense, the people to whom O'Siadhail gives sustained attention in the second section of *Globe* exemplify aspects of his own vocation as poet-seer. And his poems, discerning the interaction between their lives and their enduring contribution, provide clues to what he finds most important both personally and for the world. They are a fascinating group: Gregor Mendels (botanist), Emmanuel Levinas (philosopher), Patrick Kavanagh (poet), William Shakespeare (poet), Jean Vanier (founder of L'Arche communities), Sigrid Unset (novelist), Nelson Mandela (former President of South Africa), Mohandas Gandhi (liberator of India), Bartolomé de Las Casas (Dominican missionary), and Máirtín Ó Cadhain (Irish writer). Here we can touch only on some of them.

Like most of the others, Bruder Gregor Mendel was a marginal figure, his fame

> a fragile gene
> Another forty years beyond your garden.

He understood

> how genes play,
> a mulish hide and seek

where one may be hidden 'to flare anew across a later generation' ('Fame'). Emmanuel Levinas, student of Heidegger and Talmud,

> between the double helix
> of heritage, good gene and true,
> between Rabbi and Plato always
> Jews and Greeks

transformed the position of the self in modern philosophy, reconstituting it by reference to the 'infinite command' in the face of the other into an 'inviting self', inviting – the stranger/outsider – in, for 'I am the one thou shalt not kill!' ('Après Vous Monsieur!') Patrick Kavanagh, 'an awkward customer at best' faced 'a world of failure', yet – whether by genetic code or mystic tendency – immortalizes what he finds through love and praise:

> Behind, before, beyond its time
> A star still rises. ('Lodestar')

Another inner motif of O'Siadhail's is how an obscure person can still serve as an important mediator of historical significance. William Shakespeare is such a person,

> so long engraved in us,
> we both speak your mind and do not know
> what story shaped an extravagant unerring spirit.

His characters, however, particularized yet universal in their import, provide the 'mirrors' by which we find who *we* are, and what our role is:

> No one and everyone as each role stares
> into the eye and prospect of his soul.
> An acorn's ambitious recipe of genes
> well sunned and rained unfolds an oak,
> nature and nurture scheme with such a will
> to soak and breathe all our foibled lives.

It is especially significant that this became pivotal between old and new worlds in so many ways.

> Such timing well-graced actor to arrive
> and enter at this creaking hinge of history
> to strut a glittering stage as Europe wakes
> out of a sleepy middle-age to retrace
> profaner youth, such flair to tread
> the boards in this giant-world of feverish states,
> hotbed of new voyages, emissaries and spies,
> so barefaced and fancy-free at one
> fell swoop to shape and hammer a language,
> daring all that Bacon's Latin couldn't dare.
> Things dance attendance on fortune's knave,
> a talent bursting through as a moment readies,
> flawless match of chromosome and chance,
> set, props, backdrop every detail
> of a plot conspires to cue the lead in
> as Burbage lugged his father's lumber to frame
> The Globe. As luck would have it the finest
> London troupe and a will to hold the mirror up
> to what we do, not what we should do,
> to tell the story and let it tell itself. ('Cue')

The irony is that Shakespeare was: 'Greatest mirror, most hidden holder up.'

Even in great Shakespearean dramas, the marginality of the other is muted. Jean Vanier found his compassion awakened by the most marginal in society, the handicapped, those 'crying *I am who I am*' – protesting that they bear the fullest identity of the Lord – 'in some muddled sequence of a gene'. Vanier founded the worldwide L'Arche communities for the handicapped. What was so important about them? O'Siadhail quotes the Old Testament saying which was also applied to Jesus: 'The stone that the builders rejected has become the chief cornerstone.' (Ps. 118:22) Now, those who might today be aborted are 'a refused slab [that] becomes the corner-stone'. 'To wash the feet of servants of my Lord' becomes the joy of life, and puts everything else in new perspective ('Admiral of Arks').

Amongst the literary figures in this group, also rooted in ancient sagas, Sigrid Unset is stubbornly possessed by writing of 'what's worldly and real', and worries – like every realist –

that 'I must make art but haven't lived enough'. Such

> A burning bush of temperament needs
> To be everything

and out of the passions of her sad and happy life come two historical novels, *Kristin Lavransdatter* and *Olav Audunssøn*. In them issues of interpretation, human being, and relations prove to be crucial for history itself:

> How in a tangle of isms and fragmentation
> to find an angle of vision where
> love knows no rules and breaks them all
> not in a free-fall of lone egos
> but a knot in a greater story that throws
> its light both back and forward to catch
> the infinite in flight? ('The Burning Bush')

In the central figures of these two books, it seems, is the epitome of those who non-egotistically refashion history, whose passions bring them to 'wind back to stare forward' and thus 'knot' and thereby 'catch the infinite in flight'.

The next two figures are political ones, but the concern here is with their personal qualities of steadfastness, moral courage, and prophecy. Formed as stone by long indignities, Nelson Mandela transcended them and shed all narrow identities – 'clan, tribe and stock' – 'to become his names for all people' and 'win but never humiliate', and become 'father to a country', indeed of Africa ('I've Crossed Famous Rivers'). Gandhi too – 'both guru and bargainer' – was a puzzling combination of 'pure soul and cunning clay', prepared to 'wait my hour' and 'purify just one soul for the sake of all', to bring all together. He knew

> To love truth in one glint of a stone,
> ... live and let live in a fractured gleam. ('A Fractured Gleam')

All of these people knew hardship, and what it was to bear the 'burden of being outside and within', which is especially costly as the

> Burden of being both outside and within:
> To count the cost
> Because you've walked beyond,
> To know the loss because you grew
> Inside and feel so double-crossed
> By your own who still can't respond
> To your dream. Has the weave begun to thin
> Unable to renew?

And yet they

> Burrow[ed] deeper [than their own loss] to embrace a whole
> Planet. ('Unbroken')

That perhaps is the lesson all of these people taught us, and the one with which O'Siadhail is most concerned.

Wounded Memory: Tragedies

Although the poems up to this point were centred mostly on individuals and the hope they bring, the focus now changes to the dynamics of social historical tragedies across the face of the earth. Bushmen in South Africa, like wanderers elsewhere (New Guinea and SE Asia are mentioned), are at ease with cosmos and history, and

> Big in their trance as dreaming upwards they adore …
>
> Stars and Bushmen reconcile
> Their oneness in this dance they weave …

'Drift' or 'rift' between them are healed 'in a hell-for-leatherness of dance'. But all the virtues they exemplify – the delicacy of their regard for the earth, the 'life-thread' of lines passed between them, 'nothing owned', their constant moving on, their life in 'praise names of our God' – are now lost and their footprints blown away ('Bushmen').

One step away from them is the varied and elemental life of the small *shtetls* of Eastern Europe, with their itinerant Jewish musicians (klezmer), dreaming of Palestine but still – after 2000 years – together and at odds with the surrounding *Goyim*. Sensing challenge, some

> cross to grim Lower East Side sweat
> shops beyond the Hudson

their lifetime study of Midrash 'argu[ing] the toss of progress with endless fever'. Back in Eastern Europe, after the holocaust, even when Jewish grave stones are used for paving and whetsones, they and

> A scatter of Jewish words remain – the gone within,
> A trace of woven *us* and *them*. The *goy* and Jew.
> 'Richer but they too had their poor ones, *oy*, they did.
> But one becomes used to people. I feel their absence'.
>
> They are only truly dead who've been forgotten.
> 'Yes,' agrees another, 'I grew up on this street
> As I walk here I recall exactly who lived where:
> Shapiros, Gottliebs, Goldwasser, Tykocki and in
> The next house that man, what was his name, the one
>
> 'Who did business with my Papa?' Once thick and thin
> Of side-by-sideness slowly fades. The Gemora knew
> To kill a human is to kill a whole world, to cheat
> Them of all their children's children unbegotten.
> A questioning prayer in the long anguish of a *shofar*.
> Master of the Universe, why? O what have you done?

Even in such tragedy – 'to kill a human is to kill a whole world' – and apparent forgetfulness by the very One who promised always to be with them, the traces of their presence remain ('Blizzard').

Ironically, 'Palestine' begins with the old Roman saying, *'Let him who desires peace prepare for war,'* which appears to authorize any strategy which promises security. But can opposition – the polarization of two parties – ever preserve peace? That question seems to underlie this whole poem: the isolation of an Arab substate stimulates 'Glow-eyed martyrs [to] dodge to freight a bomb':

> Each cold revenge of eye for eye for eye
> And so this grieving turn and turn about.
>
> The *saheed* wafted straight to paradise,
> Sweet juices drunk to fête the newly sainted
>
> But cameras watch the tell-tale swollen eyes
> Of mothers wailing over their lonely dead.
>
> This endless blindfold ring of anger vent.
> Abraham's children pitch their mourning tent.

This seems to be an allusion to today's 'tent of meeting' (in Scriptural Reasoning) in which by studying their Scriptures together Jews, Christians, and Muslims seek reconciliation by suspending the exclusivity of their claims. Here, however, O'Siadhail presents it negatively by reference to I Kings 3.16-27: every tent where Jew and Muslim are unreconciled, the justice of Solomon – determining to settle the dispute between two 'mothers' by dividing the child in half – brings the true mother to sacrifice her motherhood to save her child. The implication is that Israel as true mother will cry out on behalf of the Palestinian – 'light alone can lead you to the light' – and reconcile all the tribes of Abraham.

> Poet Aharon Shabtai like Amos dresser of the sycamore tree
> Cries out *my lips mutter: Palestine! Do not die on me!*
>
> *A creature born of our people's love will burst forth into the blue.*
> *Listen, his heart is beating through mine – I'm a Palestinian Jew.*
>
> *Whirlwind,* earthquake, then, fire. But even in the end you find
> The stiller smaller voice. At last Elijah is learning to unwind.
>
> O Abraham, could you not bear the fire-worshipper a single night?
> As mystic Rumi's *cavernous shadows need the light to play*
>
> *And light alone can lead you to the light,* so too, so too
> *Each soul will know what it has done and what it has failed to do.*
>
> The evening dove's olive leaf and the chatter under the palm.
> *Abraham, Ishmael, Isaac, Jacob and the tribes. Shalom! Salaam!* ('Palestine')

O'Siadhail's litany of tragic histories continues as he narrates the history of the blacks in America, the Armenian genocide (forgotten because upstaged by 'Hitler's upscaled *Vorbild*'), the dropping of the atomic bomb on Hiroshima, the extinction of the Ainu in and beyond Japan, and the steady loss of Irish identity and language since Elizabethan times. In every case, the human and cultural costs are incalculable.

Angels of Change: Transcendence?

The challenge with which this final section deals is enormous: how in this cosmos/world, with such tragic histories, yet with a history of surprising possibilities of the new, can there be transformation, a gene juggled 'From within a phrase [so that] Newness takes wing' in the words of the first poem in the book. And as the beginning quotation from Emily Dickinson shows, we are to look in the spaces of ordinary life if we are to find Heaven and the Angels. Expectancy is the keynote, but it occurs within a world now even more complex, and much speeded up, with still more problems in the wake:

> Giddy world of shuffle and hotchpotch
> Criss-cross planet of easy mix and match.
>
> Keyboards tap a galaxy of satellites
> And monies shift in nervous kilobytes
>
> Across a grand bazaar of cyberspace.
> Migrants roam our busy market-place.
>
> Noise and anguish of an age. Free-range.
> Free-wheeling. Nothing endures but change.
>
> Given a globe where borders leak and flow
> A violin pleads beside a sitar and *koto*
>
> As nightly starving Sudanese now stare
> Out of the tube. And no hiding unaware
>
> Or folding out again an old cocoon.
> No turning back. We've reached the moon.
>
> Adam, atom-splitter, rider in space.
> Is this our earth's frail and wispy face? ('Overview')

This is a narrative of the present, of the globe as we have it now. And, if we have learned from all we have seen earlier in the book, the identities of everything change, but now to such an extent that the cocoon of life on earth is torn, and mother-earth herself suffers and weeps. What tragedy this is! And we make it more so, hesitating and teetering on the brink of chaos before venturing forward, unwilling – despite the abundance of information 'in case' – to look forward. Yet within all this, something new may be happening.

Boundless world of hidden loops and re-loops,
A noiseless trace
Of complex feedback and feedforward hoops.

Is something in the making, something new?
Another place
Over and under our boundaries, a reaching through

And linking up both in and beyond regimes,
Fuzzy embrace
Of overlapping maps, our mesh of dreams. ('Mesh')

'Fuzzy' here very likely refers to fuzzy logic, a branch of set theory where 'fuzzy truth' represents membership in vaguely defined sets. 'Fuzzy embrace' is an uncertain combination of possibilities, not the likelihood of some event or condition. The

noiseless trace
Of complex feedback and feedforward hoops

with all their unseen historical loops, is nothing less than our new context, one in which the new may be happening.

As we are reminded by a poem about the past misreadings which so seriously led all Europe astray, there are no clear maps. But correcting these and their consequences allows us to find there what may move us forward:

Searching a silken clew to the maze,
We retrace steps to mend our ways.
Something old is harking onwards. ('Mending')

We now have to reckon, however, with new threats. In the first place, there is a 'new upping of pace', a sliding of certainty which accompanies the new openness and negotiability of a world driven by information technology, and we have no 'somewhere to stand' if we are to move the world. In the second, the world is now dominated by a

One-eyed market giant
Driven by haggle and deal
Straddling a whole sphere,

Plateau or atoll,
Desert or jungle basin,
Our earth's four corners.

High-speed, space-shrinking,
One sprawling, planet-girdling
Game of here-there-ness.

Foods or goods or tools,
All chains of commodities,
Our tastes and desires.

Mergers or movements
Of labour, takeover bids,
All the tricks of trade.

Hungry pliant giant,
Bringer of all invention,
Heeder of what works.

Lattice of silk routes.
Worldwide pitch. Grand casino.
Globe of all play all. ('Giant')

But it is this unchecked, success-driven and unaccountable 'circus' which spawns the terrorist:

Rock stars, nomad managers, tycoons;
under four hundred billionaires
belting half our planet's wealth.

Somewhere in slums or refuge camps,
in ramshackle sweat shops or shanty
with fists of stone and clenched teeth

a Gilgamesh grown angry in his youth
seals his heart to fell the cedar
and slay the all-preying ogre.

How now to yoke the avid beast,
a tamed Humbaba broken in
to see what one-eyed giants can't see? ('Seeing')

If there is any remedy, it lies in giving new sight to the giant, in mythology the Humbaba who simultaneously personifies the 'river of the dead' and guards the home of the gods. And the only way is to loop back to 'an older track' of sharing and debt-relief.

Less a ring than another looping back,
Relearning to cross again an older track.

In nooks of harvest fields the forgotten sheaf,
Each seventh year's share-out and debt relief

Bent on offsetting our market's *quid pro quo*:
A tithe to Levite, sojourner, fatherless, widow.

An overflow shared, our balance re-tipped.
Can we forget the starving years of Egypt? ('Loop')

This is a matter of recalling the haunting image of 'Abel's child [who] now starves before our eyes' ('Update') and learning accountability. As we do, small actions will have great effects. Whatever we do will follow the so-called 'Butterfly effect' of chaos theory, in which

Beyond fluke or the end of fate's weary tether
Sweet chaos transcends and breaks old spells
As somewhere under the folds of summer sky
A flapped red admiral shifts a planet's weather.
Again everything matters to everything else;
Vision gathers in the span of one butterfly. ('Butterfly')

Learning our place as 'players all in our jazz of things' will bring:

Bluesy scales of how we cope.
Neither returning or losing the way,
All vision in rhythms of how it is.

Each-in-otherness, ad hocery of hope
Keeping all our difference in play,
Quarrelsome sessions of beloved noise. ('Shuffle')

The implication is that we learn the richness of difference and new ways to 'play' our differences and otherness, 'all vision in rhythms of how it is'. Of course there are casualties, and they will overemphasize their value, and protest, but some of history is 'stillborn milk'.

In a fashion reminiscent of Randall Collins,[4] there is social logic in the rhythm:

Huddles of players face to face that change
A rhythm's logic, curve our psychic range
To sift and fuse and rearrange progressions
That shape the mood of an age, jam sessions
Over time and the teacher-to-pupil baton:
Socrates, Plato, Aristotle on and on
Or chez Café Guernois Degas, Manet,
Cézanne and Pissarro busy arguing their way
Around their darker masters. Switched modes,
Nests and seedbeds, genealogies of nodes
As Satchmo Armstrong once played with King
Oliver and Jelly Roll. In musics of doing.
Yesterday's not today or now tomorrow's way
Which of course is never simply to say
That though there's no one way there's no
Yardstick and yesterday we sometimes know
Was better or not as good, just as tomorrow
May hoop either way to cobble joy or sorrow...
While everything is now local, together we make a
Polyphony of phrase, each open-hearted probe,
Clusters of goodwill in swap-shops of a globe;
Where music aims the music holds within.
The jazz is as the jazz has never been. ('Clusters')

Many things may follow from this logic. For one thing, this 'open-hearted probe' has much in common with the so-called primitive societies viewed earlier, and supplants societies of domination ('a dominant bringing a dominant peace'): there is

a remembered undertone,
A quivering earthy line of soul
Crying in all diminished chords.
Our globe still trembles on its pole. ('Tremolo')

For another, it makes it possible, even after so much torture and suffering, to forgive. Still again, a new civility follows

As slowly we relearn each other's worth,
Difference and sameness incommensurable ('Skeins')

(a reference to the collision of paradigms mentioned earlier). And a fragile city – restricted in O'Siadhail's previous book to society – now weaves the planet together.

Instead of pounding each other into submission and 'suspicious minds that never unwound',

S'assemble – all over flock together,
Skeins of hope, gleich und gleich ...
Like to like, kind calls fellow -

Rui wa tomo o yobu in Tokyo.
Around our globe a netted Reich,
Of random trust, cross-ties of civility,

Farflung jumbles of non-violent voices
Argue our intertwining choices
To weave one planet's fragile city. ('Skeins')

For a strategy, therefore, we will have

Comity of good will,
Delicate growth that thrives
On thriving and yet always so bound

Up with states and their staked out
Limits, a brokerage between
Determined hit-and-runners
Who still think their bombs can pound

An earth to submission and the too naïve
So easily taken for a ride
By every thug and trafficker,
All the more hard-bitten on the rebound.

Our brittle city of Trojan horses,
Hijacked battering rams,
Poison on the market shelf,
Gas canisters in the underground

Or the underminers within the psyche,
Unmasked unmaskers of power's

Bleak and stalking beast,
Suspicious minds that never unwound.

Give us a policy? At least a strategy?
The slow hatchings of peace,
Our stumbled unfinishedness
Dealing with everything just as it's found,

A trust in openness, the barer daring
Of players out on a limb;
No iron curtain here,
Fragile theatre of worlds in the round. ('Strategy')

In the opulence of the world in which we then live, everything of value continues

the way white light contains all waves
and a sound wakes its every partial
or from one cell any limb unfolds.

There within it is the

Deepest river, least its noise
in worlds kept by core keepers
where stiller waters still run deep. ('Bridges')

There in that deep, deep 'tune womb' our stories part or combine, there is such a fine 'line between what's open and shut'. While some enjoy the power of 'know[ing] always what's true

Some new
Delight in playing face to face
Grace notes
For a line that steadies as it floats,
Without a theory or a base,

Shared space
Holding what we hold and not to fear
Those bars
Where our history clashes or jars
And in lines unsymmetrical to the ear

Still hear
Deep reasonings of a different lore.
No map
Of any middle ground or overlap
Yet listening as never before -

No more –
Just hunched jazzmen so engrossed
In each
Other's chance outleap and reach
Of friendship at its utmost.

> No host
> And no one owns the chorus or break.
> Guests all
> At Madam Jazz's beck and call.
> For nothing but the music's sake. ('Session')

This is a remarkable vision of an unmapped 'listening as never before', fully attentive to the dynamics of each other in maximal friendship. In this trio of unlimited mutual dynamics, full attentiveness, and the dynamics of reality itself, it is 'for nothing but the music's sake'. It reaches far beyond the lesser possibilities when these are separated. It reminds me of what it is to love the world and each other for God's sake, but in O'Siadhail's poem the stress is on the dynamics of each.

This extraordinary exuberance shows the fecundity of the 'given Globe',

> Off-chance jazz forever bringing
> More being into being
> Out of history's tangled knots and loops
> Spirituals and flophouse bands
> In hymns and charismatic whoops,
> In night-clubs' vibe and strobe,
> *Nothing buts* now *everything ands.*

We have to relearn the way beyond the perfectionisms of thought and law, and to learn spontaneity as the way to understand.

> Our mind can pulse to intransigent
> Musics of once broken to play
> Beyond perfect techniques
> The livelong midrash of a moment.

> Given a globe of profusion,
> We players are no legislators
> More like mediators,
> Who extemporising seem to up the ante
> To find the nit and grit that has
> A universal image for a Dante,
> An aim without conclusion
> To play mein host to Madam Jazz

> Playing without end.
> Growling, wailing, singing Madam
> In anguish and joys we jam.

Amidst the total history of possibilities, of brokenness, tragedy and losing plot and social direction, our life is to be

> Made, broken and remade in love,
> Lived-in boneshaking pizzazz
> Of interwoven polyphony above

An understated theme.
The only end of jazz is jazz. ('Only End')

No facile optimism this, it is an amazing vision of how – in its new dress – our globe is to be knit together again. That is the great achievement of Micheal O'Siadhail's *Globe*.

Endnotes

1 | Life, Work, and Reception

[1] As regards the evidence for his life I am indebted mainly to oral material gathered from O'Siadhail himself, his wife, various friends, and others who have known him in different contexts. In addition there is my personal knowledge of him since we first met in 1966 in Trinity College Dublin. For all except three of the years of friendship since then we have lived in different countries, but I have followed his life and writings closely. This chapter therefore does not pretend to be a 'neutral' account. My own ideal for it is, on a very small scale, to reach towards something of the quality of the biography of Dietrich Bonhoeffer by Eberhard Bethge, which manages to combine scholarly reliability on Bonhoeffer's life and perceptive appreciation of his work with insight born of friendship.

[2] Pronounced MEE-HAWL O'SHEEL.

[3] For his own prose account of Clongowes see 'Leitmotiv: A Brief Memoir' in *The Clongownian* (1994).

[4] *Dáithí Ó hUaithne: Cuimhní Cairde*, eds Proinsias Mac Aonghusa and Tomás de Bhaldraithe (Baile Átha Cliath: An Clóchomhar Tta, 1994).

[5] Epigraphs begin to appear in *The Chosen Garden* and usually give helpful clues to the section they introduce, as well as together representing a good proportion of the authors most influential on O'Siadhail.

[6] Including embedded sonnets, the count is: *Springnight*, 2; *The Image Wheel*, 4; *The Chosen Garden*, 16; *The Middle Voice*, 3; *A Fragile City*, 14; *Our Double Time*, 29; *The Gossamer Wall: Poems in Witness to the Holocaust*, 16; *Love Life*, 20; *Globe*, 6.

[7] I myself saw one such encounter at the Oxford conference 'Remembering for the Future 2000', a gathering of historians, artists, and survivors of genocide, when he was approached after his reading by a survivor who had been deeply moved by the poems.

[8] For a discussion of this with reference to both O'Siadhail and the Book of Job see David F. Ford, *Christian Wisdom: Desiring God and Learning in Love* (Cambridge: Cambridge University Press, 2007), Chapters 3-4.

[9] *In Dublin* (December-January 1978).

[10] *In Dublin* (August 1980).

[11] *Sunday Press* (24 June 1984).

[12] *Irish Literary Supplement* (1983).

13 *The Irish Times* (27 April 1985).

14 *Sunday Independent* (24 February 1991).

15 *The Sunday Tribune* (25 November 1990).

16 *Irish Literary Supplement* (Spring 1993).

17 *Galway Advertiser* (26 November 1992).

18 *Sunday Independent* (3 December 1995).

19 *The Irish Times* (28 October 1995). The latter verdict is hard to credit given the attention to form and metre throughout. I have passed over some similar examples in other reviews, though a special case is James J. McAuley's criticism of poems 'clogged with Latinate cognitives' (*sic*) in which, of the five examples given, two are in fact Anglo-Saxon (Review of *Poems 1975-1995* in *The Irish Times*, (8 January 2000)).

20 See Bibliography – though since there must be many reviews that I have failed to track down, the numbers may be greater for any of the collections.

21 Michael O'Neill in his perceptive review in *London Magazine* (October/November 1998).

22 *The Irish Times* (16 May 1998).

23 *Times Literary Supplement* (8 January 1999).

24 *Jewish Currents* (March-April 2005).

25 *Times Literary Supplement* (15 August 2003).

26 *Irish Catholic* (24 October 2002).

27 *Harvard Review* 26 (2003).

28 *The Irish Book Review* 1.2 (Autumn 2005). Eugene O'Brien is head of the Department of English Language and literature at Mary Immaculate College, Limerick.

29 My judgement here differs from that of Maurice Harmon in his essay below.

30 Kavanagh did have a period when satire dominated, but he came through it.

31 A thirteen-line 'sonnet'!

32 *Patrick Kavanagh. Collected Poems* (London: Martin Brian & O'Keeffe, 1972).

33 Patrick Kavanagh, *Self-Portrait* (Dublin: The Dolmen Press, 1964), 24-5.

34 Kavanagh, *Self-Portrait*, 27.

35 Robert Bly's translation of the seventh sonnet from *Die Sonette an Orpheus* (1923) :
Rühmen, das ists! Ein zum Rühmen Bestellter,
ging er hervor wie das Erz aus des Steins
Schweigen. Sein Herz, o vergängliche Kelter
Eines den Menschen unendlichen Weins.
- *Selected Poems of Reiner Maria Rilke* (New York: Harper and Row, 1981).

2 | A New Voice in the City

1 Mícheál Ó Siadhail, *An Bhliain Bhisigh* (Dublin: An Clóchomhar Tta, 1978). He published two further collections of poetry in Irish: *Runga* (Dublin: An Clóchomhar Tta, 1980) and *Cumann* (Dublin: An Clóchomhar Tta, 1982). Cf. Seán Ó Cearnaigh, *Scríbhneoirí na Gaeilge 1945-1995* (Dublin: Comhar Teoranta, 1995): 218-19.

2 Mícheál Ó Siadhail, *Téarmaí tógála agus tís as Inis Meáin* (Dublin: Dublin Institute for Advanced Studies, 1978).

3 Micheal O'Siadhail, *Poems 1975-1995* (Newcastle upon Tyne: Bloodaxe Books, 1999): 13.

4 Ibid., 13.

[5] Ibid., 13.

[6] Ibid., 13

[7] Ibid., 14.

[8] In the poem 'In memoriam Máirtín Ó Cadhain', O'Siadhail speaks of Ó Cadhain as an 'outsider untamed and untamable, scorner of prudence, blind and wide-eyed, a hurt innocence striking out on every side': *The Chosen Garden* (Dublin: Dedalus Press, 1990): 42. For David Greene see Micheal O'Siadhail, 'Athair de mo chuid' in *Dáithí Ó hUaithne cuimhní cairde*, eds Proinsias Mac Aonghusa and Tomás de Bhaldraithe (Dublin: An Clóchomhar Tta, 1994): 31-7; Proinsias Mac Cana, 'David Greene (1915-1981)', *Ériu* 34 (1983): 1-10. For E.G. Quin see Proinsias Mac Cana, 'Ernest Gordon Quin (1910-1986)', *Ériu* 38 (1987): 1-3.

[9] Mícheál Ó Siadhail and Arndt Wigger, *Córas fuaimeanna na Gaeilge: na canúintí agus an caighdeán* (Dublin: Dublin Institute for Advanced Studies, 1975).

[10] *Poems 1975-1995*, 13-14.

[11] *The Chosen Garden*, 42.

[12] 'Don bhean álainn aoibhinn/ A bhronn ar Mhícheál pinsean bliana/ Le suí ar bhinse i bhFaiche Stiabhna/ Mo mhíle buíochas': *An Bhliain*, 7.

[13] Ibid., 15.

[14] Ibid., 18.

[15] *Poems 1975-1995*, 14.

[16] The unique question of O'Siadhail as translator of his own work from Irish to English awaits investigation. His seminal influence on Irish cultural policy in relation to literary translation is addressed in Marc Caball, 'ILE: translating Ireland to the world', *Éire-Ireland* 35 (Spring/Summer 2000): 112-21.

[17] *An Bhliain*, 19.

[18] *Poems 1975-1995*, 20.

[19] *An Bhliain*, 19.

[20] *Poems 1975-1995*, 20.

[21] *Téarmaí*, 1.

[22] *An Bhliain*, 25.

[23] *Poems 1975-1995*, 20.

[24] Dorothy Walker, *Modern art in Ireland* (Dublin: Lilliput Press, 1997): 68, 143.

[25] *An Bhliain*, 25.

[26] *Poems 1975-1995*, 20.

[27] *An Bhliain*, 22.

[28] *An Bhliain*, 15.

[29] *An Bhliain*, 32. O'Siadhail's reworking of the second verse runs as follows: 'As if determined to pose for months in the nude, to allow the low sun warm their leafless blood': *Poems 1975-1995*, 24.

[30] *An Bhliain*, 32.

[31] *Poems 1975-1995*, 24.

[32] *An Bhliain*, 32.

[33] *Poems 1975-1995*, 24.

[34] *An Bhliain*, 16.

[35] *Poems 1975-1995*, 22.

[36] *An Bhliain*, 16.

[37] *Poems 1975-1995*, 22.

38 For the source of O'Siadhail's allusion to the monk and the Vikings see James Carney, *Medieval Irish lyrics*, no. 10 (Dublin: Dolmen Press, 1967): 22-3.

39 For an introduction to early Irish poetry see *Early Irish lyrics eight to twelfth century*, ed. Gerard Murphy (Oxford: Clarendon Press, 1956); *Early Irish poetry*, ed. James Carney (Cork: Mercier Press, 1967); Carney, *Medieval Irish lyrics*.

40 Mícheál Ó Siadhail, *Springnight* (Dublin: Bluett and Company Ltd, 1983): 16.

41 Murphy, *Early Irish lyrics*, 4-5, 172. Gerard Murphy's translation of the entire quatrain is as follows: 'A hedge of trees overlooks me: a blackbird's lay sings to me (an announcement which I shall not conceal); above my lined book the birds' chanting sings to me'.

42 *An Bhliain*, 30. In St Matthew's Gospel, it is recounted how the wise men when they had listened to Herod 'departed; and, lo, the star, which they saw in the east, went before them, till it came and stood over where the young child was. When they saw the star, they rejoiced with exceeding great joy'. Matthew 2: 9-10.

43 Pádraig Ua Duinnín, in his *Foclóir Gaedhilge agus Béarla* (Dublin: Irish Texts Society, 1927), also translates *lúdrach* as a 'hinge, pivot'.

44 *Téarmaí*, 27.

45 *An Bhliain*, 24.

46 *Poems 1975-1995*, 21.

47 *An Bhliain*, 24.

48 *Poems 1975-1995*, 21.

49 *Téarmaí*, 13.

50 *An Bhliain*, 24.

51 *Poems 1975-1995*, 21.

52 *Téarmaí*, 48.

53 Ibid., xiii.

54 Ibid., x.

55 *Comhar* (Márta, 1979): 19, 22.

56 'Tá leanúnachas agus céimniú nádúrtha ó dhán go dán sa chnuasach seo agus é ag léiriú na téise atá aige, is é sin chomh fada is a thuigim é: nach bhfuil rún na beatha aige ná ag duine ar bith eile b'fhéidir; nach cóir a bheith ag súil go mbeadh agus gur chóir an tairbhe is mó agus go deimhin an taitneamh is mó is féidir linn a bhaint as an bhfeiceáil a fhaighimid': *Comhar*, 19.

3 | A Life of Love, a Love of Life: O'Siadhail's Love Poetry

1 All page references are to *Love Life* (Newcastle: Bloodaxe, 2005), unless otherwise indicated.

2 See Carol Ann Duffy's much acclaimed *Rapture* (London: Picador , 2005).

3 Helen O'Shea, 'Interview with Seamus Heaney', *Quadrant* 25 (1981): 12-17, cited in Kerry McSweeney, 'Literary Allusion and the Poetry of Seamus Heaney', *Style* 33 (Spring 1999): 130-43.

4 Thomas Hardy, Ted Hughes, and Douglas Dunn wrote significant cycles of poems to their wives, but these were written after their wives were dead.

5 *Poems 1975-1995* (Newcastle: Bloodaxe, 1999), 124.

8 | The Poetry of Musical Perception

[1] 'Rubato', *Our Double Time* (Newcastle upon Tyne: Bloodaxe Books, 1998): 61.

[2] 'Quartet', *A Fragile City* (1995) in *Poems 1975-1995* (Newcastle upon Tyne: Bloodaxe Books, 1999): 168, ll. 1-4.

[3] Ibid., ll. 5-8

[4] Ibid., ll. 13-14.

[5] 'Quartet' (Beethoven's String Quartet No. 12, Opus 127), *Our Double Time*, 114-15.

[6] 'Late Beethoven Quartet', *Springnight* (1983) in *Poems 1975-1995*, 62.

[7] 'Folksong', *The Chosen Garden* (1990) in Poems 1975-1995, 104.

[8] Ibid., ll. 18-19.

[9] Ibid., l.1.

[10] 'Rowan', *Our Double Time*, 81.

[11] 'Our Double Time', *Our Double Time*, 126.

[12] 'Springnight', Springnight in Poems 1975-1995, 50.

[13] 'Easter', *Springnight* in *Poems 1975-1995*, 54.

[14] 'An East Wind', *Belonging* (1982) in *Poems 1975-1995*, 43.

[15] 'St Stephen's Green', *Our Double Time*, 123

[16] 'Streetscene', *Springnight* in *Poems 1975-1995*, 51.

[17] 'Morning on Grafton Street', *The Image Wheel* (1985) in *Poems 1975-1995*, 66.

[18] 'Underworld', *The Chosen Garden* in *Poems 1975-1995*, 113-14.

[19] 'Perspectives', *The Chosen Garden* in *Poems 1975-1995*, 132-33.

[20] 'Embrace', A Fragile City in Poems 1975-1995, 188.

[21] 'Arrival', *The Chosen Garden* in *Poems 1975-1995*, 139.

[22] 'Train Journey', *The Chosen Garden* in *Poems 1975-1995*, 129-30.

[23] 'Dread', *Our Double Time*, 27.

[24] 'Passivity', *Our Double Time*, 28.

[25] 'Light', *Our Double Time*, 89.

[26] 'Vertigo', *Our Double Time*, 102.

[27] 'In Crosslight Now', *Our Double Time*, 94.

[28] 'Madam', *Our Double Time*, 93.

[29] See, for example, *Globe* (Northumberland: Bloodaxe Books, 2007): 'Only End' and 'Session' where she is directly invoked; but also 'Behind', 'Clusters', 'Shuffle', 'Ad Lib', 'Doggone Blues', 'Tension', and 'Given'.

[30] 'Cosmos', *The Middle Voice* (1992) in *Poems 1975-1995*, 154.

[31] 'Apprentice', *Our Double Time*, 75.

[32] 'Aubade', *Springnight* in *Poems 1975-1995*, 48.

[33] Ibid.

[34] 'Invocation', *The Image Wheel* in *Poems 1975-1995*, 66.

[35] 'Summerfest', *The Middle Voice* in *Poems 1975-1995*, 159.

[36] 'Blues', *The Image Wheel* in *Poems 1975-1995*, 79.

[37] 'Dance', *A Fragile City* in *Poems 1975-1995*, 227.

[38] Ibid., 229.

[39] 'Matins for You', *Our Double Time*, 107.

[40] 'Uncertain', *Our Double Time*, 99.

[41] 'Clarinet', *Our Double Time*, 95.

[42] 'That in the End', *Our Double Time*, 96.

[43] 'Underwritten', *Our Double Time*, 98.

[44] 'Overflow', *Our Double Time*, 105.

[45] The complete poem is cited in paragraph two of this article.

[46] 'Elegy for a singer', *Springnight* in *Poems 1975-1995*, 62.

[47] 'Train Journey', *The Chosen Garden* in *Poems 1975-1995*, 129-30.

[48] 'Music', *A Fragile City* in *Poems 1975-1995*, 210.

[49] 'Perspectives', *The Chosen Garden* in *Poems 1975-1995*, 132.

[50] 'Handing-On', *Our Double Time*, 119.

[51] 'In a New York Shoe Shop', *Springnight* in *Poems 1975-1995*, 48.

[52] 'Long Song', *Love Life* (Northumberland: Bloodaxe Books, 2005), 13.

[53] 'Concertina', *Love Life*, 22.

[54] 'House', *Love Life*, 60.

[55] 'Voyage', *Love Life*, 39.

[56] 'Ceremony', *Love Life*, 81.

[57] 'Tandem', *Love Life*, 77.

[58] 'Selves', *Love Life*, 83.

[59] 'Overflow', *Our Double Time*, 105.

[60] 'Duration, *Love Life*, 97.

[61] 'Caprice', *Love Life*, 95-96.

[62] 'Anniversary', *Love Life*, 100.

[63] 'Question', *Love Life*, 109.

[64] 'Quartet', *A Fragile City* in *Poems 1975-1995*, 168.

[65] 'Homage', *The Image Wheel* in *Poems 1975-1995*, 73.

[66] 'Psalm in the Night', *Belonging* in *Poems 1975-1995*, 413.

[67] 'In the End', *A Fragile City* in *Poems 1975-1995*, 193.

[68] 'Whatever Else', *Our Double Time*, 45.

[69] 'Our Double Time', *Our Double Time*', 126.

[70] Clarinet', *Our Double Time*, 95.

[71] 'Signals', *The Gossamer Wall* (Northumberland: Bloodaxe Books, 2002), 26.

[72] 'Forebodings', *The Gossamer Wall*, 15.

[73] 'Measures', *The Gossamer Wall*, 55.

[74] 'Culmination', *The Gossamer Wall*, 60.

[75] 'Summons', *The Gossamer Wall*, 63.

[76] Ensemble', *The Gossamer Wall*, 71.

[77] 'Dust-veil', *The Gossamer Wall*, 108.

[78] 'Glimpses', *The Gossamer Wall*, 117.

[79] Ibid., stanza three.

[80] 'Faces', *The Gossamer Wall*, 122.

[81] *The Naked Flame*, Aylish Kerrigan (mezzo), Seóirse Bodley (piano) (Echo Classics Digital, 1996).

[82] *The Earlsfort Suite*: first performed on 17 September 2000, National Concert Hall, Earlsfort Terrace, Dublin, Bernadette Greevy (mezzo) and RTE Concert Orchestra conducted by Proinnsias O'Duinn.

[83] 'Interrogation', *Our Double Time*, 16, l.14.

10 | Close Reading/s

[1] Charles Williams, *He Came Down from Heaven* (Grand Rapids, MI: Eerdmans, 1984): 7.

[2] Micheal O'Siadhail, *Poems 1975-1995* (Newcastle upon Tyne: Bloodaxe Books, 1992/99): 14.

[3] Ibid., 15.

[4] As O'Siadhail has commented in a private conversation (Cambridge, 24 January 2003): 'good poetry is not an argument but an invitation ... into a world of images, into a worldview'; 'a poet does take responsibility, but in an *interrogative mood*' (my emphasis).

[5] He is, accordingly, the patron saint of poets (having also once rescued the bardic order from extinction) and of bookbinders; but, ironically, also the patron saint of plagiarists and computer pirates. This latter affinity arose from the account, or possibly legend, of his having surreptitiously, and illegally, copied the priest Finnian's edition of the Psalter, an act of which he was subsequently exposed, and for which, after being forced to return his copy, Columba was exiled to Iona, Scotland. He is most famously portrayed riding at the helm of a small boat to Iona with the twelve monks who accompanied him, a figure also earning him the title of patron saint of floods. Taken together, one can see the significance of his presence in O'Siadhail's poem. Columba is the very embodiment of a sea-voyager (even his grandmother's maiden name, Mac-naue, is translated in English 'son of a ship'), and of an artist-traveller.

[6] Micheal O'Siadhail has himself used this vocabulary to describe the overall structure and intended effect of the collection (in a seminar discussion at Cambridge on 23 January 2003).

[7] In a letter of 1 April 2003, the author explained the intention of his 'flat style' as an attempt to convey the 'banality of evil'.

[8] By this phrase I mean those ways in which literary form itself may convey an ethical stance, which returns ethical reflection and moral prompting. For demonstrations of this method of formal analysis, see, e.g., Martha Nussbaum, *Love's Knowledge: Essays on Philosophy and Literature* (New York: Oxford University Press, 1987), and Stanley Cavell, *Disowning Knowledge in Six Plays of Shakespeare* (Cambridge: Cambridge University Press, 1987).

[9] O'Siadhail advanced this point in the seminar discussion at Cambridge (23 January 2003). His statement in full was: 'Poetry has a special way to cut through history with images', and like all art it 'can help us to remember' by adding 'a different dimension to our remembrance'.

[10] The line *'Meditate that this came about'* comes from Primo Levi's poetic epigraph to *Survival in Auschwitz*. O'Siadhail's addition of 'Imagine' suggests his own project as well as the means by which we with him must seek to traverse the distance that separates us from Levi's own. The plea 'to try to look, try to see' comes from Charlotte Delbo's *Aucun de nous ne reviendra* (*None of Us Will Return*).

[11] An allusion pointed out to me by David Ford. References to this poem are taken from *Lyrical Ballads* (London: Penguin Books, Poetry First Editions, 1999).

[12] Lawrence Langer, *The Holocaust and the Literary Imagination* (New Haven, CT: Yale Univ. Press, third printing 1977): 20-1. In a similar vein, in his book *Holocaust Testimonies: The Ruins of Memory* (New Haven, CT: Yale Univ. Press, 1991), Langer adopts an attitude of suspicion towards any effort to address the experiences of Holocaust victims (including their *own* interpretation) with 'bracing pieties like "redeeming" and "salvation"'. He argues, 'Such accolades do not honor the painful complexities of the victims' narratives ...' (2; cf. xi).

11 | *The Gossamer Wall:* Poetry as Testimony and History

[1] (Bloomington: Indiana University Press, 2003).

[2] Robert Franciosi, '"Detailing the Facts": Charles Reznikoff's Response to the Holocaust', *Contemporary Literature* 29.2 (Summer 1988).

[3] Levi's own harrowing Holocaust poetry, which was both autobiographical and full of literary allusions, was published under the title *Collected Poems* (London: Faber & Faber, 1988).

[4] (London: Continuum, 1996).

[5] Seamus Heaney, 'Crediting Poetry', Nobel Lecture, 7 December 1995, http://nobelprize.org/literature/laureates/1995/heaney-lecture.html.

[6] See William Heyen, 'Riddle', first published in *Erika: Poems of the Holocaust* (St. Louis [MO]: Time Being Press, 1991).

[7] Nelly Sachs was awarded the Nobel Prize for Literature jointly with Israeli novelist Shmuel Yosef (SY) Agnon in 1966.

[8] 'Poet, Essayist Anthony Hecht Dies at 81', *The Washington Post*, 21 October 2004.

[9] (Selma [IN]: The Barnwood Press, 2003).

[10] Janet Sutherland, 'Reznikoff and His Sources', in *Charles Reznikoff: Man and Poet*, ed. Milton Hindus (Orono [ME]: The National Poetry Foundation, 1984): 297-307.

[11] Dan Featherston, 'Poetic Representation: Reznikoff's Holocaust and Rothenberg's "Khurbn"', *Response: A Contemporary Jewish Review*, 68 (Fall 1997-Winter 1998), republished at http://epc.buffalo.edu/authors/reznikoff/danfeatherston.html.

[12] Paul Auster, 'The Decisive Moment', in *The Art of Hunger: Essays, Prefaces, Interviews* (New York: Penguin, 2001): 35-53.

[13] Sarah Kafatou in *Harvard Review*, Issue 26, http://hcl.harvard.edu/harvardreview/26/contents.html.

[14] Robin Shepherd, 'In Europe, an Unhealthy Fixation on Israel', *The Washington Post*, 30 January 2005.

[15] Baron's most important work was the monumental 27-volume *A Social and Religious History of the Jews*, written between 1952–83, and still incomplete at the time of his death in 1989.

[16] Leon Wieseltier, *Kaddish* (New York: Alfred A. Knopf, 1998).

[17] See Mendelssohn's 1782 Preface to Marcus Herz's translation of Manaseh Ben Israel's *Vindiciae Judaeorum*.

[18] For three excellent studies on *The Protocols* and the anti-Jewish hatred and violence they have cultivated and perpetuated see Norman Cohn, *Warrant for Genocide: The Myth of the Jewish World Conspiracy and the Protocols of the Elders of Zion* (London: Serif, 1996); Stephen Eric Bronner, *A Rumour About the Jews: Reflections on Antisemitism and the Protocols of the Elders of Zion* (New York: St. Martin's Press, 2001); Hadassa Ben-Itto, *The Lie That Wouldn't Die: The Protocols of the Elders of Zion* (London: Vallentine Mitchell, 2005)

[19] George Steiner, In Bluebeard's Castle: Some Notes towards the Redefinition of Culture (New Haven: Yale University Press, 1971).

[20] Irving Howe, *A Margin of Hope: An Intellectual Autobiography* (London: Secker & Warburg, 1982): 277.

[21] Zarah Warhaftig, 'The Jewish State: The Next Fifty Years', *Azure* 6 (Winter 5759/1999): 215.

12 | *The Gossamer Wall:* 'We Can't Sing Dumb'

[1] Georges Bernanos, *The Diary of a Country Priest*, trans. Pamela Morris (New York: Carroll & Graf, 1983): 41.

[2] Micheal O'Siadhail, 'Crosslight', *Essentials of Christian Community*, eds David F. Ford and Dennis L. Stamps (Edinburgh: T & T Clark Ltd, 1996): 55-6.

[3] Micheal O'Siadhail, *The Gossamer Wall: Poems in Witness to the Holocaust* (St. Louis: Time Being Press, 2002): 120; references to this work are hereafter in the text: (*GW*, page).

[4] Micheal O'Siadhail, 'Covenants of Trust: The Citizen Poet', *Éire – Ireland* (Fall 1994): 11. See also Micheal O'Siadhail, 'Poetry and Society', *Poetry Ireland Review* 33 (Winter 1991): 3.

[5] Poetry reading at University of Mary Washington (then Mary Washington College), 9 October, 2002.

[6] The noun is present in the verb. In 'Threads' (a significant image) is the line: 'As cold claws and ices deep in the marrow' (*GW*, 69). Both 'claws' and 'ices' are verbs and nouns. See p.149 and n.31.

[7] This concern returns in conclusion. See p. 155.

[8] This symmetry is signalled quantitatively by decline into the centre and increase on the other side: 'Landscapes' – 12 poems, 19 pages; 'Descent' (*Northeim*) – 9 poems, 13 pages; 'Descent' (*Battalion 101*) – 8 poems, 12 pages; 'Figures' – 14 poems, 14 pages; 'Refusals' (*Spoors*) – 8 poems, 10 pages; 'Refusals' (*Le Chambon*) – 10 poems, 12 pages; 'Prisoners of Hope' – 14 poems, 18 pages.

[9] Such internal rhyming may also be called 'interlaced', 'crossed', and 'leonine' (where the last syllable of a line rhymes with a syllable in mid-line). I owe some of this terminology to Distinguished Professor of English (Mary Washington) Richard E. Hansen.

[10] Pliny, *Letters*, I, trans. William Melmoth, rev. W.M.L. Hutchinson (Cambridge, Massachusetts: Harvard University Press, 1961): Book VI, xvi, 479, 481 (The Loeb Classical Library). I thank my colleague, Professor of Classics Liane Houghtalin, for this reference. I am grateful to David Ford for the following reference and for many helpful suggestions. Ford's close reading of a draft contributed significantly to – and significantly altered – this essay. Paul Celan's *Todesfuge* ('Death Fugue') further informs this imagery: 'Black milk of daybreak we drink you at night / we drink you at noon death is a master from Germany ...' (*Schwarze Milch der Frühe wir trinken dich nachts / wir trinken dich mittags der Tod ist ein Meister aus Deutschland ...*'), cf. *Paul Celan: Poems, A Bilingual Edition*, trans. Michael Hamburger (New York: Persea Books, 1980): 52-3. See *GW*, 89, 114 ('Black milk, black snow, black sun, black bloom ...'). The final poem of *The Gossamer Wall* includes the line, 'Your golden hair, Margarete, your ashen hair ...' (*GW*, 124) from 'Death Fugue': '*dein goldenes Haar Margarete / dein aschenes Haar ...*' (Celan, 52). Is there also a hint of Abraham Sutzkever's 'Stalks' – 'o the sun that gathers back its light ...'? – cf. *A. Sutzkever: Selected Poetry and Prose*, trans. Barbara and Benjamin Harshav (Berkeley: University of California Press, 1991): 174. Note the quotation from Sutzkever at the head of 'Refusals' (*GW*, 77). And what of 'Orange trees have leaves as black as ravens; / The damp sun hasn't fed their narrowness. / That blackness is a sign of health ...' – Abraham Sutzkever, 'From "Spiritual Soil"' in *A Treasury of Yiddish Poetry*, eds Irving Howe and Eliezer Greenberg (New York: Holt, Rinehard and Windston, 1969): 356 (hereafter in text: *SS*, page).

[11] See pp.146f. and n.24.

[12] In working with the poems, I came to place a note sign by lines which obviously or not so obviously referred or alluded to music. My text resembles a musical score.

[13] In his 'Acknowledgements', O'Siadhail gives an account of important works – and persons – contributing variously to *The Gossamer Wall* (*GW*, 127-8).

[14] J. Hillis Miller, 'Literature and Religion', *Religion and Modern Literature: Essays in Theory and Criticism*, eds G.B. Tennyson and Edward E. Ericson, Jr. (Grand Rapids, Michigan: William B. Eerdmans Publishing Company, 1975), 39-40. Miller also employs the image of 'concentric circles':

a poem's '... relations to its surroundings radiate outward like concentric circles from a stone dropped in water ...' (40). In his essay, Miller follows his outline of the circles.

[15] Micheal O'Siadhail, *Hail! Madam Jazz: New & Selected Poems* (Newcastle upon Tyne: Bloodaxe Books Ltd., 1992): 18; hereafter in text (*HMJ*, page). See also Micheal O'Siadhail, *Poems 1975-1995: Hail! Madam Jazz, A Fragile City* (Newcastle upon Tyne: Bloodaxe Books Ltd, 1999): 24; hereafter in text (*P*, page).

[16] See p.150.

[17] Micheal O'Siadhail, *Springnight* (Dublin: Bluett and Company limited, 1983): 7; hereafter in text (*SN*, page).

[18] Micheal O'Siadhail, *The Image Wheel* (Dublin: Bluett and Company Limited, 1985): 27; hereafter in text (*IW*, page).

[19] Micheal O'Siadhail, *The Chosen Garden* (Dublin: The Dedalus Press, 1990): 49; hereafter in text (*CG*, page).

[20] Micheal O'Siadhail, *A Fragile City* (Newcastle upon Tyne: Bloodaxe Books Ltd., 1995): 32; hereafter in text (*FC*, page).

[21] Micheal O'Siadhail, *Our Double Time* (Newcastle upon Tyne: Bloodaxe Books Ltd., 1998): 28; hereafter in text (*ODT*, page).

[22] See p.155 and 'Entrance', 1 (*GW*, 23).

[23] See David F. Ford, *The Shape of Living: Spiritual Directions for Everyday Life* (Grand Rapids [MI]: Baker Books, 1997). This work is a fecund, intense, and sensitive consideration of our lives in terms of 'multiple overwhelmings', utilizing several sources but two in particular: '... there are two sources that will be drawn on continually, interwoven as the ground bass of the book. One is the Bible ... . The other is the poetry of Micheal O'Siadhail ...' (16). The Bible and O'Siadhail! The vocabulary of O'Siadhail's poetry is appropriated as concentric circles both reach out and receive focus. Among much else, this book is a discerning introduction to the concentric circles of O'Siadhail's poetry.

[24] Bergen-Belsen, Babylon, Versailles, Jutland, Somme, Verdun, Oder, Vista, Bug, Baltic, Black Sea, Leine, Ruhme, Skibbereen, Grosse Isle, Munich, Berlin, Bad Weisee, Hamburg, Wisla, Sobibór, Treblinka, Belzek, Lublin, Józefów, Bremen, Minsk, Norway, Serokomla, Buna, Monowitz, Auschwitz, Birkenau, Amsterdam, Sosnowiec, Dabrowa Tarnowska, Kelme, Warsaw, Vilna, Lvov, Jersey, Dachau, Bialystok, Le Chambon-sur-Lignon, Nantes, Lignon River, Le Mazet, Paris, Le Puy, Silesia, Lyon, Montpéllier, Uist, Shetland, Ireland, Danube, Nile, Nineveh, Blechhammer, Palmnicken, London, Chelmo, Nowy Targ, Kielce, Lódz, Tenochtitlán, Hekla, Riga, Kovno, Salonica, Praha, Iscariot, Isaiah, Pilate, Aaron, Elihu, Cain, Mordecai, Haman, Esther, Yahweh, Herod, Jeremiah, Babel, Atlas, Titus, Argus, Elijah, Newton, Leibniz, Nietzsche, Montaigne, Marx, Macbeth, Heine, Sophocles, Sancho Panza, Bolsheviks, Napoleon, Orthodox Slavs, Catholic Poles, Lutheran *Volksdeutsch*, Chazot, Rothschild, Wilhelm, Rommel, Shylock, Etty Hillesum, Grandmother Schicklgruber, Gerlich, Röhm, Fräulein Schröder, Der Führer, Heydrich, Himmler, Hindenburg, Wilhelm Spannaus, Ernst Girmann, Schulenburg, Ruhmann, Globocnik, Lieutenant Hartwig Gnade (the irony of a name, as O'Siadhail points out: 'Lieutenant / Mercy' [*GW*, 57]), Captain Wohlauf, Hoffmann, Papa Trapp, Steinlauf, Lily, Lulu, Wolf, Bandi, Lorenzo, Scholl, Frank, Elser, Wolski, Ringelblum, Salmonovitch, Blumenfrucht, Rabbi Isaac, Daniel Rabbi, Zalmen Lewental, Olga Lengyel, Carmen, Delbo, Leopold, Albert, Lichtenberg, Anton Schmidt, Primo Levi, Jean Améry, Celan, Dubnov, Sonnenshein, André Trocmé, Kindler, Magda Trocmé, Madame Eyraud, Lévy, Dr Roger Le Forestier, Danielle, Schmehling, Henryk Blaszczyk, Mengele, Anita Lasker, Schumann, Mahler, Szymborska, Laja, Glatstein, Margarete. Names, not numbers, matter: life spilling over – erupting.

[25] The imagery is relentless: 'tremblor', 'epicentre'(*GW*, 12), 'sink further in', 'A depth charge', 'unearthings', 'landscape' (*GW*, 14), 'Rumbles in bowels of myth', 'Eruptions, sulphurous gases', 'angular planes overlapping and awry, / Tragic fault line', 'underground' (*GW*, 15), 'Upheaval',

'cauldron', 'brews in her earth's mantle' (*GW*, 16), 'core', 'seismic', 'Upper crust' (human and natural), 'Belches from its maw', 'old hidden rifts and fissures' (*GW*, 20), 'human fault zone', (*GW*, 21), 'Quakes and eruptions linked in the underearth' (*GW*, 22), 'Convulsions in mother earth, the trembling rock; / Blind forces, a chronology of fault segments', 'Ground swell of history' (human and natural) (*GW*, 23), 'psychic upheaval' (human – natural) (*GW*, 24), 'foreshock', 'seismic' (again) (*GW*, 26), 'Underground' (*GW*, 28), 'Shelves of the earth shunt on different levels ...' (*GW*, 29), etc. Then we have the joining and interweaving of image patterns: volcanic eruption and myth (*GW*, 15), core of resentment (*GW*, 17), humanized volcano, volcanized human – 'Tremblors wait in proud compressions of rock' (*GW*, 17) and the play on 'Upper crust' which the association with 'bourgeoisie' (*GW*, 17) secures.

26 Elie Wiesel writes, 'And yet. Those are my two favorite words, applicable to every situation, be it happy or bleak. The sun is rising? And yet it will set. A night of anguish? And yet it too, will pass' *All Rivers Run to the Sea: Memoirs* (New York: Alfred A. Knopf, 1995): 16 (*Et pourtant*). The final section of the second volume of Wiesel's memoirs, *And the Sea Is Never Full*, is titled 'And Yet' – *And the Sea Is Never Full: Memoirs, 1969–*, trans. Marion Wiesel (New York: Alfred A. Knopf, 1999): 401-10. See Robert McAfee Brown, *Elie Wiesel: Messenger to All Humanity* (Notre Dame: University of Notre Dame Press, 1983): 217 (Chapter 8: '"And Yet, And Yet ...": A Small Measure of Victory (*an unlikely journey*).'

27 This fits with 'Paradise' (*GW*, 114; see p.154f.).

28 Nietzsche is so much more than 'dark-willed'.

29 See 'Longing for any certainty' (*GW*, 17) and '... / to hanker again after the fist of certainty. / Anything for order' (*GW*, 39). A kind of 'order' can be ominous. See David F. Ford and Daniel W. Hardy on order, disorder, and 'non-order' in *Living in Praise: Worshipping and Knowing God* (Grand Rapids [MI]: Baker Academic, 2005 [1984]): 121 – 'Those who lay great stress on order as good like to describe all that is not order as disorder ... . because non-order is indeed a threat to them. Dictators fear laughter and good jokes as much as guns. Non-order thrives in the arts too ...'

30 Again: 'White noise and quivers. Shifts of geology. / What might be salvaged? Hesitance / Of first mendings. Delicate *perhaps* or *maybe* / Tracing detours of repaired advance' (*GW*, 121). These lines are from the poem titled 'Repair'. '[D]etours of repaired advance': how delicate, how fragile.

31 Again, 'a party', 'party-piece', 'Better not to party ...' (*GW*, 42-3), '... that Jew should oven Jew' (*GW*, 72).

32 William Shakespeare, *Pericles, Prince of Tyre*, Act I (Prologue). 'True, a mind gets used to almost anything' (*GW*, 55).

33 Elie Wiesel, *The Gates of the Forest*, trans. Frances Frenaye (New York: Holt, Rinehart and Winston, 1966): preceding 1.

34 Elie Wiesel, *Night*, trans. Stella Rodway (New York: Hill and Wang, 1960): 23; see Ellen S. Fine, *Legacy of Night: The Literary Universe of Elie Wiesel* (Albany: State University of New York Press, 1982): 14.

35 In 'Faces' are girls again: '... A named few. / Did they hold hands the moment they knew?' (*GW*, 122).

36 Pompeii comes to the death camps. Its victims and the camps' victims have volcanic fate in common.

37 Theatrical imagery returns in 'Elite' (*GW*, 73).

38 Unmistakably we are in the world of Micheal O'Siadhail.

39 Anne Michaels, *Fugitive Pieces* (New York: Vintage Books, 1998): 31.

40 Lecture, University of Mary Washington (then Mary Washington College), 4 October, 2000.

41 Rachet: 'a hinged catch, or pawl, arranged so as to engage with a toothed wheel or bar whose teeth slope in one direction, thus imparting forward movement and preventing backward movement', *Webster's New Twentieth Century Dictionary of the English Language*, 2nd ed. (Cleveland: The World Publishing Company, 1970): 1495.

[42] Wiesel can entertain the possibility that God is ashamed. In *The Accident*, Eliezer reflects, 'Whoever sees God must die. It is written in the Bible. I had never quite understood that: why should God be allied with death? Why should He want to kill a man who succeeded in seeing Him? Now everything became clear. God was ashamed. God likes to sleep with twelve-year-old girls. And He doesn't want us to know. Whoever sees it or guesses it must die so as not to divulge the secret. Death is only the guard who protects God, the doorkeeper of the immense brothel that we call the universe' – Elie Wiesel, *The Accident* (*Le Jour*), trans. Anne Borchardt (New York: Hill and Wang, 1962): 92-3. With reference to Nicholas Wolterstorff, David Ford tenders a dramatically different interpretation: '[Wolterstorff] ... rethinks why it might be that we cannot see God's face and live: The sorrow in that face would be too much for us' (*The Shape of Living*, 173).

[43] 'So, Christians live in the world, but they are not of the world' from 'The Letter to Diognetus' in *Christian Ethics: Sources of the Living Tradition*, eds Waldo Beach and H. Richard Niebuhr (New York: The Ronald Press Company, 1973): 69. See also 'The So-called Letter to Diognetus' in *Early Christian Fathers*, ed. Cyril C. Richardson (New York: Collier Books, Macmillan Publishing Company, 1970): 218 ('... Christians dwell in the world, but do not belong to the world').

[44] 'Two Sacred Paths / Christianity & Islam: A Call for Understanding', Washington National Cathedral, Washington, D.C., 7 November, 1998.

[45] I owe this identification to David Ford.

[46] '*The sea is sea*.' [Absence of the definite article is a more powerful celebration of things which are what they are.]

[47] This is a bold line – if eternity is infinite, endless, no halving is allowed; and why should God's time – eternity, timelessness – be 'restless,' implicating temporality (note the upper case 'G') – or why should it not be?

[48] Are these related and jarringly anticipatory words: '*But how should I sing unless I burn?*' (CG, 83)?

[49] C. S. Lewis, *An Experiment in Criticism* (Cambridge: Cambridge University Press, 1969): 4.

[50] Fyodor Dostoevsky, *The Brothers Karamazov*, trans. Constance Garnett, rev. Avrahm Yarmolinsky (The Heritage Press: New York, 1949): 79-80.

[51] Ford and Hardy, *Living in Praise*, 179.

13 | A European Poet

[1] This is odd because Edna Longley, Frank Ormsby and the well-known poets of Northern Ireland who uphold this tradition are not journalists. Consistently with his position, Kinsella underplays Northern poetry in his choices and highlights the tradition of poetry in Irish. Michael Hartnett's 'Farewell to English' closes Kinsella's book, emphasizing just how carefully constructed his position is.

[2] Nobuaki Tochigi, 'Micheal O'Siadhail: A Brief Introduction', in *Gendaishitechoo* (1999), 176-81 (in Japanese).

[3] Shigeo Shimizu, 'Micheal O'Siadhail: Urban Poet', in *Yeats Studies* (1998), 94-102 (in Japanese).

[4] Audrey O'Toole Pfeil, 'Das Leben ist im Fluß – Der Dichter Micheal O'Siadhail', *Irland Journal* (March 1997).

[5] Michael O' Siadhail, 'The Poet as Citizen', *Poetry Ireland Review* 30 (Autumn/Winter 1990): 72.

[6] Emmanuel Levinas, *Totality and Infinity*, 79.

[7] The relationship between American and Irish poets has, arguably, always been an easier one to sustain, given the open and generous interest towards Irish letters demonstrated by American writers, an interest which has, traditionally, been reciprocal and upheld through universities on both sides of the Atlantic.

[8] Derek Mahon *Journalism* (Gallery Press, 1996): 168.

[9] Michael O' Siadhail, 'Poetry and Society', *Poetry Ireland Review* 33 (Winter 1991): 2.

[10] Anna Karennin, Effi Briest, and Madam Bovary, arguably paving the way for the Norwegian Nobel prize-winning novelist Sigrid Undsen.

[11] The paralysis endures in the form of the ongoing Arab-Israeli tension, between Muslim and Jew, and Muslim and Christian. The formidable cultures of the Jew and the Arab still confront homelessness, imprisonment, and – in psychoanalytical terms – an 'absent' historical parent.

[12] Stein Mehren, 'Sirens in December', *Fire & Ice: Nine Poets from Scandinavia and the North*, ed. Gordon Walmsley (Salmon Publishing, 2004).

[13] Martin Gilbert, *The Holocaust, A History of the Jews of Europe during the Second World War* (New York: Holt, Rinehard & Wilson, 1985).

[14] Jaan Kaplinski, 'Ice and Heather, Notes of a migrant', *Everything Brings Everything Back* (Bloodaxe Books, 2004).

15 | Poet of Feeling

[1] Micheal O'Siadhail, *Poems 1975-1995* (Newcastle upon Tyne: Bloodaxe Books, 1999): 13.

[2] Quoted in Maurice Harmon, *The Poetry of Thomas Kinsella* (Dublin: Wolfhound Press, 1974): 11.

[3] See Maurice Harmon, *A Critical Introduction to Seán O'Faoláin* (Notre Dame and London: University of Notre Dame Press, 1966): 168 and *passim*.

[4] Micheal O'Siadhail, 'Introduction', *Poems 1975-1995*, 13.

[5] Ibid.

[6] Ibid., 14.

[7] Micheal O'Siadhail, 'Ghetto', in *Poems 1975-1995*, 46. Poems from *The Leap Year* (1978), *Rungs of Time* (1980), *Belonging* (1982), *Springnight* (1983), *The Image Wheel* (1985), *The Chosen Garden* (1990), *The Middle Voice* (1992), and *A Fragile City* (1993) are collected in *Poems 1975-1995* and cited from that text.

[8] Micheal O'Siadhail, 'Surrender', *Our Double Time* (Newcastle upon Tyne: Bloodaxe Books, 1998): 21. Subsequent references are given in the text

[9] Patrick Kavanagh, *Collected Poems*, ed. Antoinette Quinn (London: Allan Lane, 2004): 217. Subsequent references are given in the text.

[10] Micheal O'Siadhail, *The Gossamer Wall. Poems in Witness to the Holocaust* (Highgreen, Tarset, Northumberland: Bloodaxe Books, 2002): 22. Subsequent references are given in the text.

[11] Micheal O'Siadhail, *Love Life* (Highgreen, Tarset, Northumberland: Bloodaxe Books, 2005): 13. Subsequent references are given in the text.

16 | Globe

[1] The femto is a unit of measurement denoting a factor of 10^{-15}.

[2] Elliot Sober, *Simplicity* (Oxford: Oxford University Press, 1975).

[3] For S.T. Coleridge, 'reason' and 'passion' combine in the integrity of a person.

[4] In *The Sociology of Philosophies: A Global Theory of Intellectual Change* (Cambridge: Belknap Press, 1998).

17 | Bibliography

Publications

– Poetry Books

An Bhliain Bhisigh (The Leap Year) (Dublin: An Clóchomhar, 1978).
*Runga (*Rungs of Time) (Dublin: An Clóchomhar, 1980).
Cumann (Belonging) (Dublin: An Clóchomhar, 1982).
Springnight (Dublin: Bluett, 1983).
The Image Wheel (Dublin: Bluett, 1985).
The Chosen Garden (Dublin: Dedalus, 1990).
Hail! Madam Jazz: New and Selected Poems including a new collection
    The Middle Voice (Newcastle upon Tyne: Bloodaxe, 1992).
A Fragile City (Newcastle upon Tyne: Bloodaxe, 1995).
Our Double Time (Newcastle upon Tyne: Bloodaxe, 1998).
Poems 1975-1995 (Newcastle upon Tyne: Bloodaxe, 1999).
The Gossamer Wall (Tarset: Bloodaxe, 2002).
Love Life (Tarset: Bloodaxe, 2005).
Globe (Tarset: Bloodaxe, 2007).

– Published and Uncollected Poems

'The Enchanted Horse' in *Thistledown: Poems for Unicef*, ed. John F. Deane (Dublin: Dedalus, 1990).
'Evensong' in *Robert Greacen: A Tribute at the Age of Seventy*, ed. Rory Brennan (Dublin: Poetry Ireland, 1990).
'Earlsfort Suite' (part of) in *The National Concert Hall: A History*, Patricia Butler and Pat O'Kelly (Dublin: Wolfhound Press, 2000).
'Birthday Call' in *Something Beginning with P*, ed. Seamus Cashman (Dublin: O'Brien Press, 2005).

– Commissions for Music

1987 *The Naked Flame*, poem suite (music: Seóirse Bodley)
    RTÉ commission for performance and broadcasting.

1993 *Summerfest*, poem suite (music: Colman Pearce)
    RTÉ commission for performance and broadcasting.
2000 *Earlsfort Suite*, three poems (music: Seóirse Bodley)
    commissioned for Irish Government Department of Arts, The Gaeltacht,
    Heritage and The Islands as part of the Millennium *Frozen Music* celebration.
2002 *Dublin Spring*, poem suite (music: James Wilson)
    commissioned for performance.

– Books in Translation

Madamu Jazu Yookoso (*Hail! Madam Jazz*), Selected Poems of Micheal O'Siadhail,
    Vol. 1, translated to Japanese by Shigeo Shimizu, Shichigatsu Doo (Tokyo: July House, 1999).
Bokutachi No Niju no Toki (*Our Double Time*), Selected Poems of Micheal O'Siadhail, Vol. 2,
    translated to Japanese by Shigeo Shimizu, Shichigatsu Doo (Tokyo: July House, 2001).
Aus Heiterem Himmel, Selected Poems of Micheal O'Siadhail, translated to German by Audrey and
    Walter Pfeil (Eisingen: Heiderhoff Verlag, 2001).

– Literary Essays

'Poet as Citizen', *Poetry Ireland Review* 30 (Winter/Summer 1990): 71-4.
'Poetry and Society', *Poetry Ireland Review* 33 (Winter 1991): 2-10.
'Covenants of Trust : The Citizen Poet', *Éire-Ireland* (Fall Fómhar 1994): 7-21.
'Broken Silence' (Orbis, 1997).
'Wise in Words: Art and Spirituality', *Crux* 33.4 (December, 1997).
'*Middlemarch*: A Novel for Our Times', in *Céide* 1.4 (1998).

– Academic Books

Córas Fuaimeanna na Gaeilge (The Irish Sound System) with Arndt Wigger (Dublin: Dublin Institute
    for Advanced Studies, 1975), 190 pp.
Téarmaí Tógála agus Tís as Inis Meáin (Building and Domestic Terms from Inis Meáin) (Dublin:
    Dublin Institute for Advanced Studies, 1978), 78 pp.
Learning Irish (Dublin: Dublin Institute for Advanced Studies, 1980), with New Printing (New Haven
    [CT] and London: Yale University Press, 1988) and 2nd ed. (New Haven [CT] and London: Yale
    University Press, 1995), 309 pp.; German Translation *Lehrbuch in der irischen Sprache*, translated
    by Arndt Wigger (Hamburg: H. Buske Verlag, 1985); Welsh Translation *Dyscu Gwyddeleg*,
    translated by Ian Hughes (Aberystwyth: Prifysgol Cymru, 1998).
Modern Irish (Cambridge: Cambridge University Press, 1989), with Paperback Edition (1990), 369 pp.

– Academic Articles

'Abairtí Freagartha agus Míreanna Freagartha sa Nua-Ghaeilge' (Response Sentences and Response
    Particles in Modern Irish), *Ériu* 24 (1973): 134-59.
'Liosta Focal faoi Thógáil Tí as Inis Meáin' (Building Vocabulary from Inis Meáin), *Éigse: A Journal of
    Irish Studies* 16 (1975-1976): 75-95.
'Roinnt Athrúintí Suntasacha i gCanúint Chonallach' (Some Remarkable Developments in a Donegal
    Dialect), *Ériu* 30 (1979): 142-7.
'Diabhal (deamhan 7rl.) mar Dheis Chomhréire sa nGaeilge' (Devil etc. as a syntactic device in Modern
    Irish), *Ériu* 31 (1980): 46-58.
'Cardinal Numbers in Modern Irish', *Ériu* 33 (1982): 99-107.

'The Erosion of the Copula in Modern Irish Dialects',*Celtica* 15 (1983): 117-27.
'A Note on Gender and Pronoun Substitution in Modern Irish Dialects', *Ériu* 35 (1984): 173-7.
'Agus (is) /And: A Shared Syntactic Feature', *Celtica* 16 (1984): 125-37.
'Irish labhaois, labhaoiseach', Celtica 17 (1985): 158.
'Some Modern Irish Loanwords describing people', *Celtica* 17 (1986): 53-6.

Selected Commentary and Critical Studies of O'Siadhail's Work

Denver, Gearóid, 'Filíocht Mhíchíl Uí Shiadhail' (The Poetry of Micheal O'Siadhail), in *Comhar*, 1984.
Schricker, Gale C., 'From Yeats's "Great Wheel" to O'Siadhail's "The Image Wheel"', *Learning the Trade: Essays on W.B. Yeats & Contemporary Poetry*, ed. Deborah Fleming (West Cornwall [CT]: Locusthill Press, 1993).
Swiontkowski Schricker, Gale C., 'Rondo to Jazz: The Poetry of Micheal O'Siadhail' in *Éire/Ireland* (Fall 1994).
Nolan, Lorraine, 'The Poetry of Micheal O'Siadhail', MA Thesis, University College Dublin, 1994.
Ford, David F., *The Shape Of Living* (London: Harper Collins, 1997).
Pfeil, Audrey O'Toole, 'Das Leben ist im Fluß – Der Dichter Micheal O'Siadhail' in *Irland Journal* (March 1997).
Shimizu, Shigeo, 'Micheal O'Siadhail: Urban Poet' in *Yeats Studies* (The Bulletin of the Yeats Society of Japan), in Japanese.
Tochigi, Nobuaki, 'Micheal O'Siadhail: A Brief Introduction' in *Gendaishitechou* 42, 10, 99, 176-181, (1999), in Japanese.
Adams, Jennifer, 'Can How We Remember Shape What We Become? Micheal O'Siadhail's *The Gossamer Wall: Poems in Witness to the Holocaust* in dialogue with Emil L. Fachenheim', MPhil Dissertation, St. Catherine's College, University of Cambridge, 2003.
Mahan, David C., 'Poetry as Public Theology: Poetic Witness in the Work of Charles Williams, Micheal O'Siadhail, and Geoffrey Hill', PhD thesis, University of Cambridge, 2005.
Rust, Richard Dilworth, 'Micheal O'Siadhail, Irish Poet for the World', in *The Irish Literary Supplement* 26.1 (Fall 2006).

Reviews and Interviews

'An Bhliain Bhisigh'
'The Leap Year'
Review by Brendan Kennelly in *In Dublin* 67, 22 December 1977 – 11 January 1978.
Review by Tomás Mac Síomóin in *Inniu*, 16 February 1978.
Review by Máirtín Ó Direáin in *Comhar*, March 1979.

'Runga'
'Rings of Time'
Review by Pádraig Mac Éamainn in *Inniu*, 29 January 1980.
Review by Máire Mhac an tSaoi in *In Dublin*, 8 – 12 August 1980.
Review by Douglas Sealy in *Hibernia*, 28 August 1980.
Review by Declan Kiberd in *Irish University Review*, Spring 1982.
Review by Douglas Sealy in *Books Ireland*.

'Cumann'
'Belonging'
Review by Douglas Sealy in *Books Ireland*, April 1983.

'*Springnight*'
Review by Conor Kelly in *In Dublin*, 25 March – 7 April 1983.
Review by Heather Ingman in *Trinity College Gazette*, 14 April 1983.
Review by Adrian Kenny in *The Sunday Press*, 22 May 1983.
Review by Robert Greacen in *Books Ireland* May 1983.
Review by Sean Lucy in *The Irish Press*, 27 June 1983.
Review by Brendan Kennelly in *The Sunday Independent*, 1983.
Review by Augustine Martin in *Irish Literary Supplement* 1983.
Review by Michael O'Neill in *TLS*, 11 May 1984.
Article by Frank Delaney in *The Listener*, 21 June 1984.
Review by Frank Delaney in *The Sunday Press*, 24 June 1984.

'*The Image Wheel*'
Review by Conor Kelly in *Magill*, 7 March 1985.
Review in *In Dublin*, 21 March 1985.
Review by Brian Lynch in *Sunday Press*, 7 April 1985.
Review by Augustine Martin in *The Irish Times*, Saturday 27ᵗ April 1985.
Review by John F. Deane in *Books Ireland*, July/August 1985.
Review by Peter van de Kamp in *Irish Literary Supplement*, Fall 1985.
Interview by Michael Murphy in *The Irish Times*, Friday 8 March 1985.

'*The Chosen Garden*'
Review by Fred Johnston in *The Irish Times*, Saturday 2 February 1991.
Review by Gale C. Schricker in *Irish Literary Supplement*, Spring 1991.
Review by Fred Johnston in *Books Ireland*, Summer 1991.
Review by Kathleen Bernard in *James Joyce Literary Supplement*, Fall 1992.
Interview by Sean Dunne in *The Cork Examiner*, 23ᵗNovember 1990.
Interview by Ciaran Carty in *The Sunday Tribune*, 25 November 1990.
Interview by Francine Cunningham in *The Irish Times*, 29 November 1990.

'*Hail Madam Jazz*'
Review by Hugh McFadden in *The Irish Press*, Friday 6 November 1992.
Review by Conor Kelly in *The Sunday Tribune*, 29 November 1992.
Review by Michael Smith in *The Irish Times*, Saturday 2 January 1993.
Review by Sean O'Brien in *The Sunday Times*, 17 January 1993.
Review by Victor Luftig in *Irish Literary Supplement*, Spring 1993.
Review by Máirín Martin in *Books Ireland*, September 1993.
Review by Lawrence Sail in *Stand Magazine*, Winter 1993/1994.
Review by JAW in *Academic Library Book Review*, December 1994.
Review by Fred Johnston in *Poetry Ireland Review*.
Interview by Katie Donovan in *The Irish Times*, Wednesday 21 October 1992.
Interview by Barbara McKeon in *The Irish Press*, Thursday 22 October 1992.
Interview by John O'Mahony in *The Irish Post*, 14 November 1992.
Interview by Jeff O'Connell in *The Galway Advertiser*, 26 November 1992.
Interview by Patricia Deevy in *The Sunday Independent*, 20 December 1992.

'*A Fragile City*'
Review by Pat Boran in *The Sunday Tribune*, 1 October 1995.
Review by Brian Lynch in *The Irish Times*, Saturday 28 October 1995.
Interview by Ciaran Carty in *The Sunday Tribune*, 24 September 1995.
Interview by Madeleine Keane in *The Sunday Independent*, 1 October 1995.
Interview by Andrew Lynch in *Trinity News*, 26 October 1995.

Interview by Jo Ind in *The Birmingham Post*, Friday 3 November 1995.

'Poems 1975-1995'
Review by James J. McAuley in *The Irish Times*, Saturday 8 January 2000.
Review by Roselle Angwin in *Orbis*, Spring/Summer 2000.
Review by Conor Kelly in *Poetry Review*, Winter 2001/2002.

'Our Double Time'
Review by Eibhlís Ní Dhuibhne Almqvist in *The Sunday Tribune*, 19 April 1998.
Review by Emer O'Kelly in *The Sunday Independent*, 29 April 1998.
Review by Owen Kelly in *The Irish News*, 4 May 1998.
Review by Rory Brennan in *The Irish Independent*, 16 May 1998.
Review by Caitriona O'Reilly in *The Irish Times*, 18 May 1998.
Review by Mike Shields in *Orbis*, Spring/Summer 1998.
Review by Alan Brownjohn in *The Sunday Times*, June 1998.
Review by Thomas O'Grady in *Poetry Ireland Review* 59, Summer 1998.
Review by Tom Durham in *The David Jones Journal*, Summer 1998.
Review by Paul Donnelly in *Poetry Quarterly Review*, Summer/Autumn 1998
Review by Colin Walter in *The School Librarian*, 3 September 1998.
Review by A. M. Allchin in *Church Times*, 11 September 1998.
Review by Fred Johnston in *Books Ireland*, October 1998.
Review by Michael O'Neill in *London Magazine*, October/November 1998.
Review by Brian C. Brown in *New Hibernia Review*, Winter 1998.
Review by Kevan Johnson in *Times Literary Supplement*, 8 January 1999.
Interview by Kitty Holland in *The Sunday Tribune*, Sunday 19 April 1998.
Interview by Katie Donovan in *The Irish Times*, Tuesday 28 April 1998.

'The Gossamer Wall'
Review by George Szirtes in *The Irish Times*, Saturday 21 September 2002.
Review by David McLoughlin in *The Irish Catholic*, Thursday 24 October 2002.
Review by A. M. Allchin in *David Jones Journal*, 2002.
Review by Daniel Weissbort in *The Jewish Chronicle*, 14 February 2003.
Review by Fred Johnston in *Books Ireland*, May 2003.
Review by Michael Kinsella in *The Times Literary Supplement*, 15 August 2003.
Review by Liz Cashdan in *Jewish Renaissance*, Winter 2003.
Review by Sarah Kafatou in *Harvard Review* 26, 2004.
Review by Shalom Goldman in *Jewish Currents*, March/April 2005.
Interview by Ciaran Carty in *The Sunday Tribune*, 22 September 2002.
Interview by Patsy McGarry in *The Irish Times*, 23 September 2002.
Interview by Declan McCormack in *The Sunday Independent*, 27 October 2002.

'Love Life'
Review by Fiona Sampson in *The Irish Times*, 28 October 2005.
Review by Sarah Crown in *The Guardian*, 29 October 2005.
Review by Eugene O'Brien in *The Irish Book Review*, Autumn 2005.
Review by Peter Costello in *The Irish Catholic*, Thursday 24 November 2005.
Review by Martyn Halsall in *Church Times*, 2 June 2006.
Interview by Ciaran Carty in *The Sunday Tribune*, 11 September 2005.
Interview by Rosita Roland in *The Irish Times*, 24 September 2005.
Interview by Emily Hourican in *The Irish Sunday Independent*, 9 October 2005.

Other Interviews
Interview by James Liddy and Janet Eagleston Dunleavy in *Cream City Review* 10.2 (1986).

Index

A

N

O

O'SIADHAIL, MICHEAL

Poems